D1606723

# THE
# Investor's Desktop Portfolio Planner

# THE
# Investor's Desktop Portfolio Planner

*By* **GEOFFREY HIRT**
**STAN BLOCK**
**FRED JURY**

**PROBUS PUBLISHING COMPANY**          **Chicago, Illinois**

This publication is designed to provide accurate and authoritative information in regard to the subject matter covered. It is sold with the understanding that the publisher is not engaged in rendering legal, accounting or other professional service. If legal advice or other expert assistance is required, the services of a competent professional person should be sought.

FROM A DECLARATION OF PRINCIPLES JOINTLY ADOPTED BY A COMMITTEE OF THE AMERICAN BAR ASSOCIATION AND A COMMITTEE OF PUBLISHERS.

**Library of Congress Cataloging in Publication Data Available**

**ISBN 0-917253-33-7**

Printed in the United States of America

1  2  3  4  5  6  7  8  9  0

# Dedication

Dedicated with love in memory of my mother, Ilene Mae Jury, and to my father, Earl Wilbur Jury, for his steadfast support.    *—Fred Jury*

To Mary Ann and Mary    *—Stan Block*

To My Dorsh Road Friends    *—Geoff Hirt*

# Acknowledgments

A special thanks for the research assistance and contributions provided by each of the following friends and associates:

> Pat Gudsnuk, Fox Capital Corporation
> Jack Hagood, Paine Webber Inc.
> Phil Pendergraft, Minton Schmid Securities
> Betty Ganser Rubin, John Nuveen & Co.
> Jay Tice, Minton Schmid Securities

Tim and Beth, Rob Katzman, Greg and Cynthia Post, Joe Mayo, Allan Nutkiewicz, Susan Deering, Bob and Amy Olsen, Rex Brockman, Bob Swanson, Dave Hambright, Paul Vinton, Phil and Susan Nemni, and especially Pat.

It is impossible to properly recognize the dedicated effort of Denise Nelius in manuscript preparation of this book. To you Denise, our sincere thanks.

# Contents

# PART 1

# Overview of Investment Types and Portfolio Management

# CHAPTER 1

# Introduction

A middle-aged couple invested $5,000 in a high-tech computer company in 1977. Eight years later, the stock was worth $122,000.

A noted investment advisor told his readers to sell all their stock holdings . . . three months later, the most vigorous bull market in Wall Street history began . . .

A story in *The Wall Street Journal* described a well-educated executive who invested $100,000 in a zero-coupon U.S. bond mutual fund, thinking it was a low-risk money market mutual fund. Six months later the fund was worth $68,000, and he sued his broker.

After reading the sales literature, an investor decides to put $2,000 of IRA money into a municipal bond fund—obviously confused by the tax exempt status of these bonds. . . .

A conservative investor is led to believe that an oil and gas partnership is a very safe investment—fortunately, his partnership found oil and paid off handsomely. . . .

Uncommon situations? Not at all. Stories like these are repeated over and over again. Our experience over the years with people and investments has shown that too many investors have the uncanny ability to select the wrong investments, at the wrong time, and for the wrong reasons. Sometimes the decision turns out favorably, but not often. Even a positive rate of return does not mean that an investment has performed as well as others of equal or less risk.

Are most investors naive? Are investors being sold products by unscrupulous agents and brokers? Typically, the answer to both questions is no. What, then, is the source for much of the confusion surrounding many investment decisions?

If today's investors were able to stand back and view the evolution of the financial markets over the last 15 years, they would see an industry that has introduced new products at an unprecedented rate. No longer are stocks, bonds, government securities, and whole life insurance the only choices available to investors. Zero-coupon bonds, options on stocks and stock indexes, financial futures, universal life insurance, and much more compete for an investor's attention and resources.

Today's investors are swamped by investment choices. New products and aggressive marketing, combined with slick advertising pieces, bombard investors. Each product promises to be just what the investor needs.

With all the product "hype," how does the investor go about making choices? The first step, clearly, is a rational understanding of the products/ investments themselves. Good investment decisions are made because investors have accurate and specific information about their investment choices. The ability to compare and contrast investment choices is what this book is all about.

Secondly, investors must realize that while the characteristics of individual investments stay relatively the same through time, the needs of people change dramatically over time. The investments that made sense at age 25 do not necessarily make sense for a 35-year-old couple with three children. What may be appropriate for young professionals today probably would not fit the needs of the same people when they retire.

Finally, investors must begin to think of their assets as a portfolio of investments. Supposedly, only wealthy investors have so-called "portfolios." In fact, any combination of assets—real estate, savings accounts, IRAs, and securities—is a portfolio in the true sense. A rational approach to investing recognizes that every investment choice must be made in light of all other investments already in place within a portfolio.

In Chapters 2 and 3 we discuss portfolio management and the trade-offs between risk and return. Model portfolios appear in Chapters 4 through 8. These portfolios have been constructed for a young married couple with two incomes, a single professional, a young family with three children, a middle-aged couple with an empty nest, and a retiring couple. Each model portfolio covers issues of portfolio management, such as the need for current income, liquidity, stability of principal, capital growth, educational funding, life insurance, hedging against inflation, retirement income, speculative gains, and tax reduction. The model portfolios are by no means all inclusive, but they provide guidelines that can help investors select investments that fit their individual needs.

The chapters on specific investments comprise the rest of the book. They provide the kind of information that will help investors select investments appropriate for their portfolio goals and risk level. To facilitate a rational selection and matching process, investors will need to know basic information on each investment—liquidity, tax treatment, transaction costs, and risk characteristics.

Each type of investment is covered in a separate chapter using a standardized format so investments can be compared easily. After going through the first three chapters, the reader can select chapters in any order desired, much like an encyclopedia. The investments are grouped into three general risk classes—low, moderate, and high.

Each chapter in Part 3 has 12 distinct sections. The first section provides a basic description of the investment, while the second and third sections are succinct presentations of the asset's basic strengths and weaknesses. Usually after reading the first three sections on any investment, the reader can tell if the investment is appropriate for his or her individual needs. If so, the rest of the chapter will provide a more complete examination of the investment.

The following outline is used for each investment.

1. **Description**
   A description of each investment or product is given at the beginning of each chapter. Some investments, such as Treasury bills, have a one-paragraph description, while others, such as real estate income partnerships, have several pages of description and include examples of return calculations.

2. **Strengths**
   Each investment has at least one positive point. In this section, the major strengths are presented as clearly and briefly as possible.

3. **Weaknesses**
   Each investment has at least one weakness. The major weaknesses are outlined here.

4. **Unique Features**
   This section fully describes the investment's other features besides strengths and weaknesses. Subtle characteristics of the investment that the investor should know are presented here.

5. **Tax Consequences**
   Almost all investments have some tax ramifications. Since tax laws can change yearly, all investors should check the individual tax implications with a qualified professional at the time they buy or sell an investment. The particular tax treatment in effect when this book was published is included for each type of investment. Since the capital gain/loss provision of the Internal Revenue Code is similar for many capital assets, parts of this section have similar features for several investment types in the same risk category. Additionally, many investments—municipal bonds, mutual funds, real estate and oil-drilling

partnerships, futures, zero coupon bonds, annuities—have special tax
provisions that appear in this section.

6. **Where and How to Buy**

   Not all investments are bought through stock brokers. Some investments that may be available through a no-load mutual fund are not
   available through a full-service retail broker. Other products, such as
   insurance and annuities, may be best purchased through insurance
   agents rather than brokers. Often there are several places to buy the
   same investment, but investors only know of the primary purchase
   locale. This section describes the various places and methods for
   purchasing the investment.

7. **How to Sell**

   The main topic of this section is the liquidity of a particular security.
   Liquidity concerns two questions. How long will it take to sell the
   investment? Can it be sold at a fair price? Some investments, while
   easily bought, may not be liquidated nearly as easily—they are *not
   liquid*.

8. **Transaction Costs**

   Most investments have a cost of buying and selling. In some cases,
   such as money market mutual funds, there is no cost; in real estate
   partnerships, the total costs of placement may run up to 20 percent of
   the invested capital. Some investments can be purchased through special channels more cheaply than others. While many investments appear to be costly, the lack of competition for the product or the unique
   features of the product make the cost worthwhile. This, however, is
   not always the case, and the investor should read this section to judge
   the impact of commissions and placement fees on his or her total
   return.

9. **Portfolio Fit**

   By the time the reader reviews this section for an investment, he or
   she will be somewhat familiar with the characteristics and risk associated with the investment. Many investors will already know if the
   individual investment will fit their portfolio goals, but some sugges-
   tions are given about the appropriateness for different portfolio goals.

10. **Sources of Additional Information**

    Most often this section includes an address for the reader to use in
    obtaining further information about the investment. Sometimes the
    resource is a professional investment service or a periodical that regu-
    larly features articles or standard data that can help investors select
    securities. Product pamphlets about the investment often are available

where the investment trades. The Federal Reserve banks and the Securities and Exchange Commission can provide useful information about some types of investments.

11. **Comments**

Information appears here that pertains to features of the investment other than those covered in earlier sections. We present words of caution about some investments or explain commonly misunderstood features of the investment.

12. **Investment Profile**

The last section of each investment chapter is actually a table, or investment profile, of the particular type of investment. The profile form, shown in Exhibit 1-1, is the same for all vehicles, with the specific features of the vehicle checked off. Basic risk characteristics—liquidity, safety of principal, stability of principal, reinvestment protection, capital growth, cash income, growth of income, inflation hedging, and tax advantages—are summarized in the matrix format.

This summary is keyed to the investor's understanding of the material presented in the chapter and ranks each investment on a scale graded excellent, good, average, poor, and none. Occasionally, an investment has different risk characteristics, depending on the length of time the investor may hold the investment. For example, common stocks have been a very good inflation hedge over the long run, outperforming the consumer price index by over 6 percent. On the other hand, when inflation increases in the short term, common stocks often decline as interest rates rise in response to the increased inflation. If a dichotomy occurs in an investment's performance over time, the investment profile is marked with an "LT" for its long-term characteristics and an "ST" for its short-term characteristics. In the example of common stocks shown here in the profile, common stocks are shown to be good long-term inflation hedges and poor short-term inflation hedges. The investment profile helps investors determine whether a particular investment matches their individual portfolio goals and willingness to accept risk. The investment profile is presented here, but Chapter 2 presents a complete description of each investment characteristic.

**Exhibit 1-1.　Sample Investment Profile Matrix**

**INVESTMENT PROFILE**

| INVESTMENT CHARACTERISTICS | Excellent | Good | Average | Poor | None |
|---|---|---|---|---|---|
| Liquidity | _____ | _____ | _____ | _____ | _____ |
| Safety of Principal | _____ | _____ | _____ | _____ | _____ |
| Price Stability | _____ | _____ | _____ | _____ | _____ |
| Reinvestment Protection | _____ | _____ | _____ | _____ | _____ |
| Growth of Capital | _____ | _____ | _____ | _____ | _____ |
| Cash Income | _____ | _____ | _____ | _____ | _____ |
| Growth of Income | _____ | _____ | _____ | _____ | _____ |
| Inflation Hedge | _____ | _____ | _____ | _____ | _____ |
| Tax Advantaged | _____ | _____ | _____ | _____ | _____ |

**Liquidity**—the ability to quickly realize cash from the sale at fair market value

**Safety of Principal**—the principal is safe from bankruptcy or default

**Price Stability**—the market value of the asset does not change in value

**Reinvestment Protection**—protection against reinvesting cash flow at lower rates as interest rates decline

**Growth of Capital**—the original investment increases over time to create capital gains

**Cash Income**—the cash income relative to treasury bills returns

**Growth of Income**—the ability of the cash income stream to increase over time

**Inflation Hedge**—the ability of total return (cash income plus capital gains) to keep pace with inflation over time

**Tax Advantaged**—the ability to reduce or defer current federal income taxes

# CHAPTER 2

# Choosing Goals and Selecting Investments by Risk Tolerance

The basic goal of investing should be to maximize aftertax return for a given level of risk. Investors should assess two factors before they begin to decide how to reach this goal. First, they must assess the potential income characteristics of available investments. Then they must assess the risk characteristics of each investment type they select for their portfolio.

Too often investors have an unrealistic view of what they can earn in the market. Possibly this is because the popular news media tends to focus on stocks, gold, commodities, and other investments when they are doing extremely well. The man on street hears that "gold is up 20 percent in the last month," that "common stocks of small companies have more than doubled over the last two years," and that "on an initial investment of $25,000 John Q. Pits made $3 million speculating in futures contracts during 1985." While stories like these are likely to catch the attention of most investors, these stories are certainly not indicative of the long-run experience for each of these types of investments. Since most markets tend to move up and down over time, the average returns are much less than the "advertised" return during roaring markets. Most people realize that they are not smart enough or lucky enough to be invested in the biggest winner at all times.

9

#### Table 2-1. Compounded annual rates of return*

|  | 15 years (ranking) | | 10 years (ranking) | | 5 years (ranking) | | 1 year (ranking) | |
|---|---|---|---|---|---|---|---|---|
| Oil | 20.4% | (1) | 10.1% | (4) | 14.8% | (2) | 0.0% | (8) |
| Coins | 17.3 | (2) | 21.4 | (1) | 11.3 | (5) | 7.4 | (3) |
| Gold | 16.3 | (3) | 9.5 | (6) | 7.4 | (8) | −4.0 | (12) |
| U.S. stamps | 16.1 | (4) | 17.1 | (2) | 9.8 | (6) | −4.0 | (13) |
| Chinese ceramics | 13.7 | (5) | 5.9 | (14) | 15.7 | (1) | 3.0 | (6) |
| Silver | 11.7 | (6) | 7.2 | (12) | 2.4 | (13) | −25.2 | (15) |
| Diamonds | 10.4 | (7) | 9.8 | (5) | 6.1 | (9) | 0.0 | (7) |
| Farmland | 9.6 | (8) | 9.4 | (7) | 3.3 | (12) | −0.7 | (9) |
| Treasury bills | 9.0 | (9) | 10.1 | (3) | 12.7 | (4) | 9.4 | (2) |
| Old masters | 8.5 | (10) | 9.1 | (8) | 1.5 | (14) | 14.3 | (1) |
| Housing | 8.5 | (11) | 8.6 | (10) | 5.8 | (10) | 5.5 | (4) |
| Consumer price index | 7.2 | (12) | 7.9 | (11) | 7.9 | (7) | 4.6 | (5) |
| Bonds | 5.7 | (13) | 6.3 | (13) | 4.6 | (11) | −7.2 | (14) |
| Stocks | 5.3 | (14) | 9.0 | (9) | 13.5 | (3) | −1.2 | (10) |
| Foreign exchange | 3.0 | (15) | 0.9 | (15) | −4.9 | (15) | −3.0 | (11) |

* Values computed through June 1, 1984.
*Source:* Salomon Brothers Inc. Reproduced with permission.

Salomon Brothers publishes a table of returns on many different investments that covers their performance over 1, 5, 10, and 15 years. While all these investments are not covered in this book, Table 2-1 illustrates the vagaries of the market. Last year's winner will not necessarily be in first place next year.

The trap into which many investors fall is buying last year's winners. Each investment is impacted by economic variables in a somewhat different way. While some financial assets, such as stocks and bonds, react favorably to a decline in the inflation and interest rates, real estate and precious metals most often do not. In an environment with rising interest rates, Treasury bills and short-term securities will provide investors with an increasing return, but long-term assets, such as corporate bonds, will lose market value. Investors should not blindly buy last year's top investment vehicle without understanding economic conditions and how that particular investment will be influenced by future economic variables such as interest rates and inflation.

What should investors know about an investment before buying it?

The investment profile at the back of each chapter in Parts 3 through 5 identifies nine characteristics that are important in selecting or comparing investments. Each characteristic is discussed separately in the following sections.

## LIQUIDITY

*Liquidity* is measured by the ability of the investor to convert an investment into cash within a relatively short period of time and receive the fair market value of the asset. Many definitions of liquidity ignore the concept of fair market value. The highest degree of liquidity exists for very short-term assets, such as Treasury bills and money market funds, which can be liquidated in minutes at prices very close to the market. Many financial assets provide a high degree of liquidity—actively traded stocks and bonds usually can be sold within minutes at close to the last price. This usually is not the case for real estate. Almost everyone has seen a house or piece of commercial real estate sit on the market for months. These assets might be sold quickly at "bargain" prices, but certainly not at their fair market value.

Liquidity can also be measured indirectly by the transaction costs or commissions involved in the transfer of ownership. The lower the costs of buying and selling, the more likely that the asset has high liquidity. In many cases the lack of immediate liquidity can be justified if there are unusual opportunities for gain. An investment in a real estate or an oil-drilling partnership may provide sufficient return to more than compensate for the added transaction costs.

Investors should carefully assess their own situation to determine their need for liquidity. If invested funds will be used to make the next house payment or to pay for a summer vacation, then immediate liquidity is essential, and short-term financial assets are preferable. If funds can be tied up for long periods of time, investors can evaluate bargain-buying opportunities of an unusual nature.

## SAFETY OF PRINCIPAL

*Safety of principal* involves the risk of default or bankruptcy of the issuer of the investment. If an investment can be guaranteed to return all principal at maturity, then it is safe. Safety will be highest in U.S. government securities; insured deposits held at financial institutions; mutual funds invested in U.S. securities; many municipal securities; and strong, financially healthy corporations. There are rating services, such as Standard & Poor's Corporation and Moody's Investor's Service, that rate both corporate and municipal securities. Standard & Poor's gives the highest quality (lowest risk) companies a rating of AAA, and then reduces the scale to AA, A, BBB, BB, B, and so on. Securities rated B or less fall into the junk bond category and are considered speculative.

Investors who wish to assume low risks probably will confine a large portion of their portfolio to short-term debt instruments in which the party responsible for payment is the government or a major bank or corporation. Some conservative investors may choose to invest in a money market fund. More aggressive investors may look toward longer-term debt instruments and common stock. Real assets, such as gold, silver, oil, and real estate, may also be included in the aggressive portfolio, but these assets do not guarantee much safety of principal.

## PRICE STABILITY

An asset with the highest price stability has little or no fluctuation in market value. Short-term instruments, such as Treasury bills, savings accounts, and money market funds, are examples of the highest category for stability of principal. As a general rule, the longer the maturity of an asset, the greater the price fluctuation. Additionally, the less safe the principal, the more price fluctuates. Financial assets (common stock) and real assets (gold, silver, artwork) have no guaranteed principal value at some future point in time and therefore exhibit high price volatility.

Interest rate changes are one of the most important variables affecting the price stability of long-term assets. Long-term bonds are especially affected by what is called the *interest rate risk*. This risk arises because bond prices and interest rates are inversely related. As interest rates (yields) rise, bond prices fall. Prices of longer-term bonds generate bigger price changes than prices of shorter-term bonds. Table 2-2 demonstrates how changing interest rates impact bond prices.

Not only does Table 2-2 show that interest rates and bond prices are inversely related, but that short-term securities are less sensitive to inter-

Table 2-2.   **Movements in interest rates and resultant changes in market prices of bonds (12 percent coupon rate bonds)**

| Yield change (percent) | Maturity in years (percent change) | | | | |
|---|---|---|---|---|---|
| | *1* | *5* | *10* | *20* | *30* |
| +3 | −2.69 | −10.30 | −15.29 | −18.89 | −19.74 |
| +2 | −1.81 | −7.02 | −10.59 | −13.33 | −14.04 |
| +1 | −.91 | −3.57 | −5.01 | −7.08 | −7.52 |
| −1 | +.92 | +3.77 | +5.98 | +8.02 | +8.72 |
| −2 | +1.86 | +7.72 | +12.46 | +17.16 | +18.93 |
| −3 | +2.81 | +11.87 | +19.51 | +27.60 | +30.96 |

est rate changes than long-term securities. Careful analysis of Table 2-2 would also reveal several other important relationships. Bond prices are more sensitive to decreases in interest rates than increases. Also, in response to a change in interest rates, bond prices change at a decreasing rate as the maturity gets longer.

The *interest rate risk* demonstrated in the table refers to the relationship of interest rates and yields. For example, investors who purchase long-term bonds hope that interest rates will decline, causing bond prices to increase. Obviously, as rates fall, the investor would want to be invested in long-term bonds to lock in the current, higher interest rates. The opposite is also true: if investors expect interest rates to rise, they invest in short-term securities or those that perform well during inflation, to minimize the interest rate risk of being locked into low rates as interest rates rise. While this might not be considered part of the risk, the problem with interest rate risk is predicting interest rate movements correctly.

Depending on the type of investment, other factors can cause unstable prices. When investors change their attitudes about risk in a particular market, prices fluctuate. When investors in general are willing to take more risk, prices rise. If the willingness and ability to accept risk decreases, prices will decline. Investors' uncertainty over economic or corporate health usually causes these risk adjustments. The more uncertain the market, the less risk investors as a group will want to accept. Since short-term assets have less uncertainty than long-term assets, they will have the most price stability. Inflation is another variable that creates changing market values; this will be discussed in a separate section.

## REINVESTMENT PROTECTION

The *reinvestment risk* arises when an investor must reinvest cash flow at lower rates than the yield on the original investment. This is perhaps the most overlooked and least understood risk among all investors. Many people simply buy those assets that provide the highest current rate of return and never even think about the consequences of reinvesting the periodic cash flows from their investments at a different rate of return.

Most investments provide cash income monthly, quarterly, semiannually, or annually; investors must decide at these times what to do with the income. If the income is not used for living expenses, investors must find new places to invest it. If currently available investments do not earn an equal or higher rate of return than the previous investment, the return on the total portfolio declines. This risk is most prevalent when interest rates are declining. During the early 1980s, when bond yields were 16 to 17 percent, investors in bonds earned record high rates. This was also true at this time for Treasury bills, money market funds, certificates of deposit, and many other assets. However, as interest rates declined beginning in 1982, all income from bonds was reinvested at lower rates. Very short-term assets (such as Treasury bills) matured, and the principal had to be reinvested (rolled over) at much lower rates.

While it is very difficult to protect investments from this risk, some assets are better than others at maintaining high yields in times of declining interest rates. For example, the advent of zero-coupon bonds during this high interest rate period was a result of their ability to eliminate the reinvestment risk—no cash needed to be reinvested during the life of the bond. Long-term assets provided much better protection against reinvestment risk, because the high yield on the original investment was maintained even though current cash income was invested at lower rates.

Short-term securities provide the least amount of protection against reinvestment risk. How many people bought bank certificates of deposit with four-year maturities to yield 14.5 percent during 1981? When they matured in 1985, rates on four-year certificates were closer to 8 percent. A $100,000 investment would generate $8,000 per year instead of $14,500. For people living on investment income, this risk can be devastating.

## GROWTH OF CAPITAL

To build long-term wealth, usually investors benefit most if they select assets that increase in value over time. Growth of capital is usually associated with common stocks; convertible bonds; real estate investments; and real assets, such as collectibles and precious metals. In general, short-term securities (such as debt instruments) do not provide the opportunity for growth of capital. Long-term debt purchased at its face value and held to maturity also provides no growth potential. However, long-term bonds can sell at a discount from face value (usually $1,000) if current market interest rates are higher than the bond's coupon rate. Investors purchase these bonds at a price below face value and eventually enjoy a growth in value to the face value ($1,000).

Growth of capital should be considered as an investment goal for long-term purposes, such as retirement or building a college education fund for children. Investments that provide growth of capital usually have less price stability and more risk than other investments. For this reason, investors should not select growth oriented assets if the investors may have to liquidate them on short notice. Long-term investments in such assets are best made when the investor can choose when to sell.

## CASH INCOME

Surprising as it may seem at first, not all investments provide regular cash income. Generally, the goal of high cash income and high capital growth do not go hand in hand. Investors usually have to choose between the two. For some investments, such as certificates of deposit, cash income provides the total return. For other investments, total return consists of both income and capital gains. Common stocks vary widely in composition of their total return. For example, utility stocks are known for their high cash dividends and low growth rates, while small growth companies usually pay no dividends but generate total return from growth of capital (that is, increasing the worth of the stock) alone.

Many investors believe the "bird in the hand" theory that cash in hand is better than promised growth in the future. Investors who subscribe to this theory are usually unwilling to take much risk and do not have much confidence in an investment's ability to generate promised capital growth. However, even if investors have only long-term investment goals, they probably can benefit from some cash income now. Cash dividends allow a more flexible investment strategy, because they give investors the opportunity to slowly change the makeup of their portfolios over time. Cash income is more important if investors are living off the income. Investors should construct portfolios to generate the appropriate amount of cash and, at the same time, to protect against as many risks as possible. Investors with particularly high income may choose tax advantaged investments that provide no direct cash dividends in the early years, but that shelter the investment's income from taxes—thereby "creating" cash by preserving your income from taxation.

In general, investments that have generated most of their returns from cash dividends have not protected the investor in times of growing inflation. [Cash income of a particular investment on the profile matrix in this book is judged relative to Treasury bill returns.]

## GROWTH OF INCOME

Growth of income is sometimes overlooked in making investment decisions. Investments such as precious metals provide no income at all, and others, such as bonds, pay a contractual rate of interest that does not change over the life of the bond. On the other hand, utility stocks are known for their practice of increasing dividends on an almost annual basis. Investors need to be future oriented in making a choice between stable and growing income. For example, would a 13 percent coupon bond be better than a utility stock paying a 10 percent dividend yield and expecting a 4 percent annual growth in the dividend? Unless investors look four or five years out at their projected portfolio value (including reinvested dividends), they may make the wrong decision. Investing is a game of expectations.

## INFLATION HEDGE

An *inflation hedge* is an investment that allows the investor to earn a rate of return higher than the rate of inflation. The bigger the difference between the investment return and the inflation rate, the better the protection from loss of purchasing power. While many investors benefited from the high levels of inflation between 1973 and 1982, this period was one of the most devastating for many other investors. People who were invested in long-term financial assets suffered large losses in portfolio values as interest rates soared and prices of these investments plummeted. Other investors, who invested in commodities, gold, real assets, and oil earned very high returns.

It has long been argued that the stock market is not a good inflation hedge. Over the long term—30 or 40 years—stocks have done very well compared to the rate of inflation, while Treasury bills have barely held their own. However, in every short-term time period between 1952 and 1985, as the rate of inflation increased from its prior level, stock prices did not keep up with inflation. As the inflation rate abated from its prior level, the stock market rallied. Assets like common stock that have the ability to generate growth of income generally do better in inflationary times than fixed-income securities, but not as well as real assets or short-term investments.

When the rate of inflation is expected to increase, interest rates usually also rise, so the best strategy is to move investments into short-term types, such as Treasury bills and notes. While this strategy is not advisable over the long run, in periods of rising inflation it provides rapidly rising returns and no loss of capital.

## TAX ADVANTAGED INVESTMENTS

A *tax advantaged investment* reduces or defers federal income taxes. This tax advantage arises from the investment's ability to either shelter income through allowable tax deductions or to be exempt from tax on certain types of income. To most investors, tax advantaged investments include real estate, oil drilling, leasing, and various types of partnerships specializing in any of these investments. These investments offer investors depreciation deductions and other expenses that can be subtracted from current income. Other investments also provide tax benefits to the investor. Municipal bond income is exempt from federal taxes. Capital distributions (return of capital) are sometimes paid out as part of the dividend on common stock and are exempt from taxes.

Investors should look for those tax shelters that provide an economically justifiable reason to invest (that is, reasonable return!) and not just tax deductions against ordinary income. The tax laws are extremely complicated, and many sophisticated tax strategies exist. Because of the call for tax reform in the mid-1980s, tax strategies may change with the tax codes. Investors should consult tax professionals before making any tax advantaged investments.

## BUILDING A PORTFOLIO BASED ON PROFILE CHARACTERISTICS

Each investment reflects the previously discussed characteristics in some way. Sometimes an investment has two or three strong characteristics and the rest are negative or neutral. Investors can use the investment profile to help select investments that meet their individual goals.

As an example, an investor has decided that current cash income is his primary investment goal. This narrows his list of investment choices considerably, but he still has to choose secondary goals and the level of risk he's comfortable with for the particular investments. While utility stocks meet his goal of current cash income, they do not have very good price stability. The same is true of long-term bonds, which generate high cash income but are subject to interest rate risk. He might be willing to accept an investment in Treasury notes despite their low return if price risk is a secondary concern to him. If he needs the income alone, and he does not plan to consume the principal, he might hold bonds to maturity, since price risk has no effect on his consumption.

In general, no investor can escape risk entirely. The higher the expected return, the more risk. Trade-offs between investments must be made. Investors should avoid choosing an investment only on its major strength and ignoring its major weaknesses. [If investors want to tailor a strategy to meet investment goals and at the same time feel comfortable with the degree of risk selected, they must understand the trade-offs between investments.] The investment profile is designed to present these trade-offs in a simple, efficient manner. By looking at the relative rankings for the investment characteristics of a particular investment, investors can grasp not only the investment's strengths and weaknesses, but also whether the investment is appropriate for their portfolio and risk tolerance.

Chapter 3 discusses the concepts of risk/return trade-offs and diversification, as well as some guidelines for portfolio management.

# Factors in Portfolio Planning

The first prerequisite for investors constructing a portfolio is to know what their goals are. Too many investors enter the investment arena trying to "make a killing," or "get rich quick." This strategy is motivated more by naive greed than by a careful financial plan; it can ultimately lead to high-risk investing. Some investors can afford to play the game in this fashion, but most, including already wealthy investors, need a financial plan centered around well-understood goals.

## THE INVESTOR'S PERSONALITY

A financial plan helps investors build a portfolio of assets that reflect their goals and personality. Understanding their own personality may be the most important factor in planning a successful investment strategy. Everyone has a unique willingness to work with levels of risks to earn their rewards. Investors are not identical with their neighbors, business associates, or friends, even if they share the same income level, culture, or religious beliefs—nor should they copy each other's investment portfolios.

Investors should ask themselves: How do I accept winning and losing? When I win, do I feel smart and "bet the bank" in an irrational fashion? Investors who take losing extremely hard should invest in more low-risk vehicles to control the probability of losses. Investors who bet the bank can have disastrous results if they push the limits of their risk tolerance. An old Wall Street adage says that the worst thing a new investor can do is to make a killing on his or her first investment. This success creates the misconception that success comes easily in the market. Most successful investors have a healthy respect for the market and know that any investment can go sour, and that the market turns up or down in seconds with no warning. The market swings in gold, oil, coins, common stock, bonds, commodities, and real estate over the last 15 years testify to the fickleness of trends.

Some investors are unable to adhere to a consistent investment strategy. Certain types of investments can help force this discipline on the investor. Other investors cannot tolerate taking high risks with the potential of high returns, yet they envy investors who do so successfully. Each individual must decide the level of risk and types of goals with which he or she will live comfortably. New investors should avoid the temptation to compare themselves with exceptional investors who are written up in the business section of the newspaper! Such exceptional investors may be in the top .5 percent of all investors in their skills—and their luck. There are always big winners in investments; the real issue is how many investors can win big consistently. Research shows that few, if any, investors outperform a market consistently, measured on the basis of risk-adjusted return.

## RISK AND RETURN

The concept of risk is often overlooked when annual returns are presented in the popular press. For example, most annual mutual fund rankings ignore the overall risk of portfolios when they rank the funds. Financial theory holds that the more risk accepted in an investment, the greater the expected returns should be. If an investment manager is generating higher returns that a competitor, it may be a result of taking more risks. All investors should consider risk carefully as they choose investments.

Exhibit 3-1 illustrates the relationship between risk and return for most of the investments and products discussed in Parts 3 through 5 of this book. The risk/return trade-offs are shown relatively, without a numerical scale. These relationships are general, and since several investments are tax advantaged, the marginal tax rate of the investor has a large impact on the after-tax return and relative rank of such investments as municipal securities and tax sheltered partnerships.

The risk or ranking of each investment depicted in Exhibit 3-1 may vary in different economic environments, but the point is that those investments with high risk generally generate high returns with large variations in returns. In other words, those investments capable of generating large returns also can generate large losses. Investors must remember that risk

**Exhibit 3-1.   Risk/return trade-offs for selected investments**

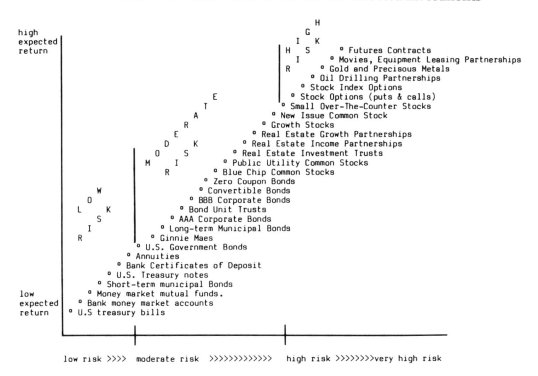

is a double-edged sword—it cuts both ways. While everyone likes the prospect of exceptionally high returns, few investors can afford the potential losses possible with futures contracts, options, and oil-drilling partnerships.

## TIMING THE CYCLES

While it is true that the best way to make a lot of money is to gamble on a long-shot and win, this strategy is also the best way to lose a lot of money. An investment in gold bullion in January of 1979 at $225 an ounce was worth $825 an ounce later that same year. Silver was rising to extremely high prices at the same time that gold soared to more than $800 an ounce. One investor asked advice about purchasing silver bullion at $45 an ounce, and in spite of strong warnings, he purchased 100 ounces—a sizable investment for a person with his assets. Many months later, when silver was

**Table 3-1.  Blue Chip Stock Performance**

| Company | 1982 Low Price | 11/85 Price | Percent Change |
|---|---|---|---|
| Allied Corp. | 19.250 | 46.875 | 143.5 |
| American Can | 25.875 | 65.500 | 153.1 |
| General Electric | 27.500 | 68.750 | 154.6 |
| IBM | 55.625 | 150.00 | 169.7 |
| Merck | 64.000 | 135.375 | 111.5 |
| Owens Illinois | 21.000 | 56.00 | 166.7 |
| United Technologies | 15.625 | 45.50 | 191.2 |
| Westinghouse | 10.875 | 44.75 | 311.5 |
| Woolworth | 15.875 | 60.25 | 279.5 |

in the $20 per ounce price range, the investor was encouraged to take the benefits of a short-term capital loss and repurchase the silver 31 days later if he still wanted to hold silver. He instead sat on his investment, unwilling to admit his mistake; several years later he took a poor long-term loss, selling out at $10 an ounce.

Rising gold and silver prices were accompanied by record inflation rates and much unrest in international financial markets. When inflation fell into the single-digit range and stayed below 4 percent for several years in the 1980s, gold and silver tumbled in value from their highs in the '70s. Gold has always been a "safe" haven for assets in times of war, high inflation, or uncertainty. Investment advisors have made fortunes selling newsletters and advice based on making one right recommendation: "Buy gold." Many advisors have been recommending gold and silver ever since the early 1970s. As for everything else, if advisors keep recommending precious metals long enough, eventually they will be right—the gold bug's time probably will come again.

The old saying "timing is everything," is especially true for investments in cyclical markets. In 1974 and 1975, an investor in the broad stock market would have lost 40 percent of his or her assets in those two years. However, in the four years from 1982 to 1985, many stock investors doubled their money by investing in blue chip common stocks. Some conservative individual issues soared to many times their 1981 values. Table 3-1 compares some blue chip stock prices, their low price in 1982 and their record high prices early in 1986.

How many investors were brave enough to buy in the dismal environment of 1982? Hindsight is 20-20, and many investors could be millionaires today if they could replay those four years.

While the stock market was returning close to 20 percent in 1982, long-term corporate and government bonds generated total returns of over 40 percent because of falling interest rates. These returns were the highest ever, for investments that were thought by many to be safe and provide low returns. Every investment can be an exception to its image—once every 40 or 50 years.

How can investors tell when such an exception will occur? How can they know when bonds will outperform stocks two to one? How can they determine when gold will return to $800 per ounce? Is there a sign when soybeans will sell for more than $10 per bushel again?

Investors cannot continually pick the "right" investment at the right time. Even market professionals have trouble being right more than 50 percent of the time. Unfortunately, too many stories exist about investors who throw disproportionate percentages of their assets into one investment, looking for that pot of gold. Many times the funds are invested after the investment has made most of its climb.

## MARKET RISK VERSUS INDIVIDUAL ASSET RISK

Every asset has some risk, even U.S. Treasury bills, which are sometimes called risk free. Treasury bills are risk free only insofar as the U.S. government is not expected to default on the interest payments or declare bankruptcy. They suffer from the reinvestment risk when interest rates fall (see Chapter 2 for a discussion of reinvestment risk).

No matter what vehicles investors buy, they cannot escape the risk of the market. For example, if investors buy real estate, excess supply of housing may cause vacancies and lower rents, perhaps even causing bankruptcy. If investors buy long-term bonds, rising interest rates can cause the market value of the bonds to decline. Even mutual funds that are professionally managed cannot escape market risk. But with *diversification,* or a portfolio that balances investments with different risks, investors should not have to face the risk associated with only one investment type. Low-quality bonds can default, or companies can go bankrupt. One apartment building can suffer vacancies or low rents. When groups of investments, such as 20 bonds, or 15 apartment buildings, or 15 common stocks are mixed in portfolios, the market risk is still present, but the individual investment's risks are diversified away as the portfolio becomes larger.

## MANAGING RISK THROUGH DIVERSIFICATION

The basic strategy of this book is for investors to hold diversified portfolios of assets that meet their risk profile and investment goals. Even the $5,000 investor can diversify through such investments as mutual funds. As investors' assets increase and incomes rise, greater diversification and more risk are possible. An investor who plans ahead for a five-year time period is better off than one who buys an investment when it seems "hot," only to find that it cools off quickly. The difference in strategy can be likened to the old fable about the tortoise and the hare. The investor who plans ahead to meet certain goals has a strategy; the other investor does not.

If investors cannot *escape* risk, they can certainly *manage* it. There are many avenues in risk management. First, investors can determine how much risk they can financially and emotionally afford. Second, they can manage risks by knowing the types of risks they accept when they purchase the investment—Parts 3 through 5 of this book should help identify these risks. Once the investment risks are apparent, assets can be combined in a portfolio to meet the investors' overall risk/return objectives.

Research reveals that carefully selected portfolios of about 10 to 12 common stocks can eliminate up to 95 percent of the risks associated with a single stock. This diversification primarily leaves the portfolio exposed to the risk of the overall stock market. It stands to reason that a diversified group of assets, such as bonds, stocks, Treasury bills, and real estate, will provide more risk protection than one investment type or a group of vehicles in one investment type.

Although investors with diversified portfolios admit they are not "smart" enough to be right on just one investment, they are in a better position than anyone to be partially invested in an investment with high risk. The question becomes, "How much of my assets will I invest in the stock market, bond market, options, CDs, money market, real estate . . .?" Diversification still allows investors to choose among low-risk, moderate-risk, and high-risk investments for their portfolios. It is a more intelligent way of managing risk than "going for broke" with one investment.

## DYNAMIC COMPOSITION OF PORTFOLIOS

A portfolio is not static; most investments have some degree of liquidity. This allows investors to change the composition of their portfolio if they want to change the risk posture by redeploying their funds into new investments. Portfolios can be altered by liquidation of investments or by reinvestment of dividends, interest, or other income generated from the investments. The portfolio composition can also be altered by periodic additions of new funds. For example, individual retirement accounts (IRAs) allow $2,000 of new money ($4,000 for two-career couples) to be added to a portfolio per year, whether invested a little at a time or in a lump sum. An IRA earning 12 percent annually accumulates $14,590 in five years. If that $14,590 account earns 12 percent cash return, the investor would have $1,750 of income to reinvest, plus the annual $2,000 contribution. This $3,750 would account for 25.1 percent of the portfolio's value. Changing a portfolio's composition does not always have to be achieved through liquidation and reinvestment.

## MODEL PORTFOLIOS

Part 2 includes five chapters that describe model portfolios for five representative types of investors:

Portfolio 1—A single professional with high income.
Portfolio 2—A two-income, college-educated young family without children.
Portfolio 3—A family with three children; the husband is a manager with an above-average income, while the wife works part time.
Portfolio 4—A middle-aged "empty nest" couple whose children are grown and no longer live at home.
Portfolio 5—A couple nearing retirement age; this model also is appropriate for a single person approaching retirement.

While there are certainly many other types of investors, with other needs and goals, many investment firms' clients fall into one of these typical categories of investors. The five model portfolios that appear in Part 2 cover the basic concepts of portfolio planning and provide insights for anyone seriously interested in learning about investment planning. Each portfolio model suggests a strategy to reach a goal appropriate for that type of investor. This strategy is based on an assumed income level, an annual dollar-savings rate, and an investor's level of assumed risk.

Each model portfolio begins with an investor or family profile that includes employment and financial condition. Any anticipated changes in the investor's situation are considered. Then the model lists the present portfolio structure. The Financial Goals Evaluation ranks both current and anticipated goals from the investor's and authors' viewpoint. The goals are then examined in more depth in the Analysis of Investment Goals section. Finally, a restructured portfolio is described that more closely matches the investor's current and future financial goals and needs.

The goals that were defined in Chapter 2 are found on the investment profile: current income, liquidity, growth of capital, safety of principal, and inflation hedge.

## Tax Reduction

The tax reduction goal assumes that investors are in a high enough marginal tax bracket so that it makes sense to lower their federal tax payments through tax advantaged investing. The investment profile for each product will help identify those investments that meet this goal. Several other specific goals appear in the model portfolios—education funding, life insurance, retirement income, and speculative gains. These are not characteristics of specific investments but instead are goals that can be achieved through selection of the appropriate investments.

## Education Funding

Education funding is a specific goal of many families with young children. However, the same strategy used to build up a pool of investments for this purpose could also be used to buy a vacation home or another costly asset.

## Life Insurance

Life insurance is included in the model portfolios because in many cases it is the easiest way to provide financial stability for family members in case of death. This product is discussed in Part 3, which comprises the low-risk types of investments.

## Retirement Income

Planning for retirement is a concern of most investors. Retirement with a guaranteed lifestyle at least as good as that of their working years is an achievable goal for careful investors. This goal is perhaps the ultimate one, after investors address their short-term needs such as education, vacations, real estate down payments, and so on.

## Speculative Gains

Last, the model portfolios examine gains associated with investors who attempt to achieve exceptionally high returns on their investments. These investors attempt to ''make a killing'' or ''get rich quick.''

## How to Use the Model Portfolios

After reviewing the model portfolios, investors should have an idea of which strategies may be appropriate for them. Different investments can be substituted in the portfolios to modify them to meet individual risk tolerances.

Parts 3 through 5 present characteristics of more than 30 potential investments among which to select to construct an individualized, diversified portfolio. The model portfolios serve as a guide in selecting among those products.

# Model Portfolios

# CHAPTER 4

# Model Portfolio for a Single Professional

## CURRENT INFORMATION

| | |
|---|---|
| Marital Status: | Single |
| Employment Status: | Attorney ($200,000) |
| Age: | 34 |
| Residence: | Value $217,000 |
| Mortgage Balance: | $148,000 |
| Dependents: | None |
| Taxable Income: | $158,000 |
| Marginal Tax Bracket: | 49% |
| Annual Amount Saved: | $55,000 |

## EXPECTED CHANGES IN PRESENT SITUATION

This young professional recently became a partner in a major law firm. She does not currently anticipate marriage or a family for the next five years.

Her income should grow at a rate of 8 to 10 percent annually.

Her home is comfortably furnished, and she owns a nice auto and sailboat. Her personal expenses are in line with her income.

## PRESENT PORTFOLIO

| | |
|---|---|
| Certificate of Deposit | $20,000 |
| Money Market Account | 28,000 |
| Common Stock Account | 23,000 |
| Self-Employed Pension Plan | 12,000 |
| Stock Index Options Account | 15,000 |
| Total Investment Assets | $98,000 |

## FINANCIAL GOALS EVALUATION

Investors must "value" several different investment goals by numbering them on a scale from 1 to 10. By assigning a low number (1-3), investors indicate a very low investment priority. By assigning a high number (8-10), they indicate a major priority for the next five-year period.

Investors can use the same number more than once; for example, the number 3 might be used four times. This shows several investment goals have a similar priority for the individual.

| Financial Goal | Value Assigned by Investor | Value Assigned by Authors |
|---|---|---|
| Current Income | 1 | 1 |
| Liquidity | 4 | 3* |
| Safety of Principal | 5 | 5 |
| Capital Growth | 6 | 8* |
| Educational Funding | 1 | 1 |
| Life Insurance Coverage | 2 | 2 |
| Hedge Against Inflation | 9 | 7* |
| Retirement Income | 4 | 4 |
| Speculative Gains | 7 | 5* |
| Tax Reduction | 10 | 8* |

*Represents a change from current goals.

## ANALYSIS OF INVESTMENT GOALS

The highest goals, assigned by the investor, in order are tax reduction, an inflation hedge, and speculative gains.

The young professional has recently been hit with a very large quarterly federal income tax payment. She suddenly realizes that the federal government receives one half of her paycheck. She is not uncommon. The initial tax shock associated with a large increase in earned income can be traumatic. She wants to take a very aggressive posture toward tax reduction.

She also has grown up with inflation as a constant problem. She has seen large inflationary increases in real estate prices. These and other speculative gains have caused her to seek aggressive returns on investment capital.

In addition, she realizes that any short term losses involve only 50 percent of her own money. Uncle Sam pays the other half. Following is the present portfolio and the authors' suggested restructured portfolio.

## RESTRUCTURED PORTFOLIO

| Investment | Present Portfolio | Restructured Portfolio |
|---|---|---|
| Certificate of Deposit | $20,000 | |
| Money Market Account | 28,000 | |
| Common Stock Account | 23,000 | |
| Self-Employed Pension Plan | 2,000 | |
| Stock Index Options Acct | 15,000 | $15,000 |
| Tax Free Money Market Acct. | | 8,000 |
| Municipal Bond Trust | | 20,000 |
| Retirement Plan w/IRA | | 12,000 |
| Real Estate Growth Partnership | | 30,000 |
| Oil and Gas Drilling Partnership | | 13,000 |
| Total Investment Assets | $98,000 | $98,000 |

This portfolio restructuring should eliminate $4,000 of interest income from taxable income by cashing in the certificates of deposit and money market account and switching to a tax free money market fund and other tax advantaged investments.

The municipal bond trusts provide tax free income and can be held as a source of emergency funds. The average maturity can be maintained at 9-11 years. This will prevent any major fluctuations of principal due to changes in interest rates. The expected tax free yield is 7.5 percent, which equals a 15 percent taxable return for this investor.

It is essential that the self-employed pension plan be funded annually for the maximum contribution of $30,000, plus a $2,000 IRA contribution (see the annual funding example). This provides a 100 percent deduction from earned income of the amount invested. The plan can hold a variety of assets. In our example, we assume the plan adopts a family of no load mutual funds to provide a broad variety of investments.

The stock index options account is maintained. Our young professional enjoys the fast pace of stock index options and has had modest success in the past year. Additional commitments to this account will be minimal. The present level of funding allows trading of a large enough number of contracts to save on commission costs and provides for large changes in value frequently.

A commitment to real estate will satisfy the investor's need to hedge inflation and provides additional tax help over a number of years. Over the long run, this investor expects to reinvest any proceeds of the real estate investment back into property.

This high-income professional is a prime candidate for oil- and gas-drilling investments. At the present time, tax considerations are very important to her. The oil and gas partnership provides an immediate tax deduction, and if successful will furnish tax sheltered income in the future. The tax savings generated by the oil and gas will make it possible to contribute the maximum to her retirement plan. Future commitment of funds should be as follows.

## SCHEDULE OF FUTURE COMMITMENTS

| Investment Outlet | 1986 | 1987 | 1988 | 1989 | 1990 | Total |
|---|---|---|---|---|---|---|
| Retirement Plan with IRA (Mutual Funds) | $32,000 | $32,000 | $32,000 | $32,000 | $32,000 | $160,000 |
| Leveraged Equipment Leasing Ptrshp | 5,000 | 5,000 | 5,000 | 5,000 | 5,000 | 25,000 |
| Real Estate Ptrshp | 10,000 | 10,000 | 10,000 | 10,000 | 10,000 | 50,000 |
| Movies, Oil + Gas and other exotics | 8,000 | 8,000 | 8,000 | 8,000 | 8,000 | 40,000 |
| Total Invested by Year | $55,000 | $55,000 | $55,000 | $55,000 | $55,000 | $275,000 |

This investor will use the retirement plan to provide investments in taxable income securities, blue chip and growth stocks, precious metals based investments, and more speculative penny stocks. These vehicles all provide some form of taxable income that certainly is not needed by the investor.

The retirement portfolio will eventually comprise the majority of the assets of this investor. This portfolio must be actively managed (not necessarily traded) to keep up with changing economic circumstances. In the early years, the young attorney may wish to purchase a family of mutual funds to provide portfolio diversification and flexible investment options.

An aggressive tax posture is the reason for the five-year commitment to a leveraged equipment lease. The partnership will provide over a 200 percent writeoff versus invested capital for the next five years. Thereafter, taxable income will be forthcoming for several years if the equipment can be re-leased at attractive rates. In either case, the investor feels she will not be "out of pocket" any real cash due to the big writeoffs.

A regular commitment to real estate partnerships is part of this investor's inflation protection strategy. While using the retirement account to manage stocks, bonds, gold, and so on, the investor will use real estate to add balance to the portfolio and tax deductions for her income tax return.

Movie partnerships, research and development partnerships, additional oil and gas investments, and other exotic investment ideas will provide the potential for speculative gains for our high tax bracket investor. If the economics of the idea are not sound, at least the investor will receive tax deductions. These ideas will vary from one year to the next—some of these ideas tend to follow changes in the tax code.

The bottom line strategy is to use equipment leasing, real estate, and high-risk partnerships to reduce taxes while the investor builds substantial assets in the tax deferred retirement accounts.

## PORTFOLIO STRUCTURE AFTER FIVE YEARS

| Investment | Present Portfolio | Restructured Portfolio | Assets after 5* Years |
|---|---|---|---|
| Certificate of Deposit | $20,000 | | |
| Money Market Account | 28,000 | | |
| Common Stock Account | 23,000 | | |
| Self Employed Pension Plan | 12,000 | | |
| Stock Index Options Acct. | 15,000 | $15,000 | $ 25,000 |
| Tax Free Money Market Acct. | | 8,000 | 10,200 |
| Municipal Bonds | | 20,000 | 28,700 |
| Retirement Plan w/IRA | | 12,000 | 219,500 |
| Real Estate Growth Ptnrshp | | 30,000 | 127,700 |
| Oil and Gas Drilling Ptnrshp | 13,000 | | |
| Leveraged Equipment Lease | | | 2,000 |
| Exotic Investments | | | 20,000 |
| Total | $98,000 | $98,000 | $433,100 |

*These values are based on the restructured portfolio, plus investments over the five years, plus interest, dividends, and capital appreciation. It is assumed that investments were made at the end of each year, although probably they would be made at irregular intervals over the whole year.

Assumptions:    Money Market returns 5%
                Municipal Bonds return 7.5%
                Retirement Plan returns 11%
                Stock Index returns 10%
                Real Estate returns 15%
                Exotics loss
                Equipment Lease n/a

This investor will slowly realize that tax oriented investments must have economic merit. The steady growth of the tax deferred retirement account is impressive and could be slightly higher with especially effective management. Ultimately, this investor may wish to commit some investable earned income and cash flow from other investment assets outside the retirement plan to a larger municipal bond portfolio.

# CHAPTER 5

# Model Portfolio for a Young Two-Career Couple

## CURRENT INFORMATION

| | |
|---|---|
| Marital Status: | Married |
| Employment Status: | Electrical Engineer ($37,000) |
| | Secondary School Teacher ($18,000) |
| Ages: | Late Twenties |
| Residence: | Value $70,000 |
| Mortgage: | $62,000 |
| Dependents: | None |
| Taxable Income: | $42,000 |
| Marginal Tax Bracket: | 33% |
| Annual Amount Saved: | $10,000 |

## EXPECTED CHANGES IN PRESENT SITUATION

This young couple expects to receive a 10 percent increase in the engineer's salary annually for the next five years. A 7 percent salary increase is projected for the secondary school teacher.

They hope to start a family in approximately five years. It is anticipated that a six-month loss of income for the secondary school teacher will result at the time each child is born. Current plans call for three children. The present residence should be adequate for the next 5-10 years.

## PRESENT PORTFOLIO

| | |
|---|---|
| Certificate of Deposit | $10,000 |
| Passbook Savings | 2,000 |
| Options Trading Account | 3,000 |
| Total Investment Assets | $15,000 |

## FINANCIAL GOALS EVALUATION

Investors must ''value'' several different investment goals by numbering them on a scale from 1 to 10. By assigning a low number (1-3), investors indicate a very low investment priority. By assigning a high number (8-10), they indicate a major priority for the next five-year period.

Investors can use the same number more than once; for example, the number 3 might be used four times. This shows several investment goals have a similar priority for the individual.

Most often couples will agree on the relative values. On occasion a difference of opinion arises. Typically, an average of the two values then is used for financial planning.

| Financial Goal | Value Assigned by Investors | Value Assigned by Authors |
|---|---|---|
| Current Income | 2 | 2 |
| Liquidity | 5 | 5 |
| Safety of Principal | 7 | 5* |
| Capital Growth | 8 | 10* |
| Educational Funding | 3 | 0* |
| Life Insurance Coverage | 4 | 2* |
| Hedge Against Inflation | 7 | 8* |
| Retirement Income | 3 | 3 |
| Speculative Gains | 7 | 7 |
| Tax Reduction | 9 | 5* |

*Represents a change from current goals.

## ANALYSIS OF INVESTMENT GOALS

The highest goals, assigned by the couple, in order are tax reduction, capital growth, speculative gains, hedge against inflation, and safety of principal.

This young couple would like to earn an exceptionally high rate of return on their investment portfolio, as evidenced by the high marks for capital growth and speculative gains.

As with most young people, they have a high priority on hedging inflation. This is a result of experiencing high inflation rates ever since they started to live away from their parents' homes. The highest priority (a score of 9) is assigned to tax reduction. Often young couples feel stung by the graduated income federal tax that up until college graduation has worked in their favor.

A marginal tax bracket of 33 percent would not indicate the need for such an aggressive attitude toward tax reduction. While the couple should be tax conscience when making investments, a more valid priority would be growth of capital.

At this juncture the young couple does not have a large portfolio of assets that can be redistributed. The existing portfolio produces taxable interest income and hopefully an occasional gain from options trading. Options trading is very high risk, but in this case may be consistent with the investment objective of speculative gains. Following is the present portfolio and the authors' suggested restructured portfolio.

## RESTRUCTURED PORTFOLIO

| Investment | Present Portfolio | Restructured Portfolio |
|---|---|---|
| Certificate of Deposit | $10,000 | |
| Passbook Savings | 2,000 | |
| Options Trading Account | 3,000 | |
| Money Market Fund | | $ 5,000 |
| Capital Growth Mutual Fund | | 5,000 |
| Real Estate Growth Partnership | | 5,000 |
| Total Investment Assets | $15,000 | $15,000 |

This portfolio restructuring should eliminate $1,000 of taxable interest income by cashing in the certificate of deposit.

In the restructured portfolio, the money market fund will provide a slightly higher yield than a passbook savings account, offer instant liquidity, and serve as an emergency source of funds.

The mutual fund selected should be an aggressive, growth oriented fund. The young couple is looking for growth of capital, not income.

Hopefully, the mutual fund will generate long-term capital gains from the aggressive growth stock portfolio. The tax rate on long-term capital gains is only 14 percent for this couple, as opposed to 33 percent on ordinary income.

The real estate growth partnership will meet multiple goals for this couple. First, real estate will serve as an inflation hedge. Second, growth oriented real estate partnerships normally borrow two-thirds of the total capital invested in real estate. This leverage does not require the personal liability of the couple. The debt obligation exists at the partnership level, with the property serving as collateral. The borrowing of two-thirds of the partnership capital will enhance the rate of return on equity for the investor. This meets the capital growth objective. Third, over a period of four to five years the couple can expect to deduct approximately 100 percent of the amount invested ($5,000) as partnership losses from their taxable income.

Our young couple has two solid paychecks and can afford the risk of the aggressive growth mutual fund and the illiquidity of the real estate growth partnership. The mutual fund also offers liquidity should the young couple's situation change unexpectedly. Future commitment of funds should be as follows.

## SCHEDULE OF FUTURE COMMITMENTS

| Investment Outlet | 1986 | 1987 | 1988 | 1989 | 1990 | Total |
|---|---|---|---|---|---|---|
| Money Market Certificates (6 month) | $ 1,000 | $ 1,000 | $ 5,000 | $ 5,000 | $ 5,000 | $ 2,000 15,000 |
| Aggressive Growth Fund | 4,000* | 4,000* | 5,000* | 5,000* | 5,000* | 23,000 |
| Real Estate Growth Partnership | 5,000 | 5,000 | | | | 10,000 |
| Total Invested By Year | $10,000 | $10,000 | $10,000 | $10,000 | $10,000 | $50,000 |

*$4,000 could be tax sheltered by using an IRA.

As the couple moves closer to starting a family, they will want to avoid additional real estate commitments, because the loss of earned income will automatically lower their tax bracket during the years when the children are born. In addition, they will have built up a reserve of assets to use for family-related expenses in the form of certificates of deposit.

During years three to five, a fairly even split between the growth fund and the certificates of deposit would be appropriate. As the money market fund increases in value (interest earned), a portion of the money market fund could be invested in short term (six-month) certificates of deposit to provide a slightly higher rate of return.

## PORTFOLIO STRUCTURE AFTER FIVE YEARS

| Investment | Present Portfolio | Restructured Portfolio | Assets after 5* Years |
|---|---|---|---|
| Certificate of Deposit | $10,000 | | $17,500 |
| Passbook Saving | 2,000 | | |
| Options Trading Account | 3,000 | | |
| Money Market Fund | | 5,000 | 10,200 |
| Capital Growth Mutual Fund | | 5,000 | 45,000 |
| Real Estate Growth Partnership | | 5,000 | 26,400 |
| Total | $15,000 | $15,000 | $99,100 |

*These values are based on the restructured portfolio, plus investments over the five years, plus interest, dividends, and capital appreciation.

Assumptions: Money Market returns 7%
CD returns 8%
Growth Fund returns 14%
Real Estate returns 15% on equity

By the time this young couple is ready to start a family, they will have built a portfolio that can provide for lump sum expenses associated with raising children.

The real estate growth partnerships will begin to sell properties at the time the family is bearing children. Lump sum returns from the sale of the property can be expected over a four- to seven-year period beginning in 1990. If these distributions are not needed for current expenses, they could provide the basis for custodial accounts for the children.

# CHAPTER 6

# Model Portfolio for a Young Family

## CURRENT INFORMATION

| | |
|---|---|
| Marital Status: | Married |
| Employment Status: | Computer Center Manager ($77,000) |
| | Part Time Registered Nurse ($10,000) |
| Ages: | Late Thirties |
| Residence: | Value $117,000 |
| Mortgage Balance: | $68,000 |
| Dependents: | Ages 12, 10, 7 |
| Taxable Income: | $58,000 |
| Marginal Tax Bracket: | 38% |
| Annual Amount Saved: | $15,000 |

## EXPECTED CHANGES IN PRESENT SITUATION

This couple expects to receive an 8 percent increase in the manager's salary annually for the next five years. A 6 percent salary increase is projected for the nurse.

The couple does not expect any additional children. The present residence should be adequate for the next 5-10 years. Annual savings of $15,000 should decrease modestly until the children complete college.

## PRESENT PORTFOLIO

| | |
|---|---|
| Certificate of Deposit | $ 60,000 |
| Money Market Account | 8,000 |
| Common Stock Account | 23,000 |
| IRA Accounts at Bank | 12,000 |
| Vested Value of Company Retirement Plan | 27,000 |
| Total Investment Assets | $130,000 |

## FINANCIAL GOALS EVALUATION

Investors must "value" several different investment goals by numbering them on a scale from 1 to 10. By assigning a low number (1-3), investors indicate a very low investment priority. By assigning a high number (8-10), they indicate a major priority for the next five-year period.

Investors can use the same number more than once; for example, the number 3 might be used four times. This shows several investment goals have a similar priority for the individual.

Most often couples will agree on the relative values. On occasion a difference of opinion arises. Typically, an average of the two values then is used for financial planning.

| Financial Goal | Value Assigned by Investors | Value Assigned by Authors |
|---|---|---|
| Current Income | 2 | 2 |
| Liquidity | 5 | 4* |
| Safety of Principal | 8 | 7* |
| Capital Growth | 6 | 7* |
| Educational Funding | 9 | 10* |
| Life Insurance Coverage | 2 | 2 |
| Hedge Against Inflation | 4 | 4 |
| Retirement Income | 4 | 4 |
| Speculative Gains | 5 | 3* |
| Tax Reduction | 7 | 7 |

*Represents a change from current goals.

## ANALYSIS OF INVESTMENT GOALS

The highest goals, assigned by the couple, in order are educational funding, safety of principal, and tax reduction.

This couple has worked hard and saved regularly for several years. They fear any loss of capital because they can see very large educational expenses beginning in five years when the oldest child enters college.

They realize that the 38 percent marginal tax bracket on taxable income restricts the return from "safe money" investments, but they feel compelled to make sure they keep what they have earned and saved. Below the authors show the present portfolio and a suggested restructured portfolio.

## RESTRUCTURED PORTFOLIO

| Investment | Present Portfolio | Restructured Portfolio |
|---|---|---|
| Certificate of Deposit | $ 60,000 | |
| Money Market Account | 8,000 | $ 8,000 |
| Common Stock Account | 23,000 | |
| IRA Accounts at Bank | 12,000 | |
| Vested Value of Company Retirement Plan | 27,000 | 27,000 |
| Municipal Bond Trusts | | 53,000 |
| Zero-Coupon Government Bonds | | 30,000 |
| IRA Variable Annuity | | 12,000 |
| Total Investment Assets | $130,000 | $130,000 |

This portfolio restructuring should eliminate $6,000 of taxable interest income by cashing in the certificates of deposit.

The municipal bond trusts provide tax free income and can be purchased with separate insurance coverage to provide increased safety. The average maturity can be maintained at 9 to 11 years. This will prevent any major fluctuations of principal due to changes in interest rates. The expected tax free yield is 7.5 percent, which would equal a return of 12.1 percent on a taxable investment for this couple.

Zero-coupon government bonds should be purchased in custodial accounts for the children. By using the children's social security numbers, the annual interest earned will be taxable income to the children, not the parents. These bonds are free from default risk, and the maturities can be scheduled to coincide with the college funding needs.

By changing to a variable annuity for IRA investments, the couple can seek moderate growth of capital while not paying taxes on either the dividends or the capital gains. The variable annuity also guarantees that if one spouse dies, the surviving spouse receives with no delay all original principal as guaranteed, plus earnings.

If possible, the company retirement plan should also be managed for modest growth. Just as in the IRA case, the money will not be taxable for many years. The couple does not need to maintain the personal common stock portfolio if each partner can control growth oriented stocks in retirement accounts. Future commitment of funds should be as follows.

## SCHEDULE OF FUTURE COMMITMENTS

| Investment Outlet | 1986 | 1987 | 1988 | 1989 | 1990 | Total |
|---|---|---|---|---|---|---|
| IRA Variable Annuity | $ 4,000 | $ 4,000 | $ 4,000 | $ 4,000 | $ 4,000 | $20,000 |
| Municipal Bonds | 5,000 | 5,000 | 5,000 | 5,000 | 5,000 | 25,000 |
| Government Zeros | 6,000 | 6,000 | 6,000 | 6,000 | 6,000 | 30,000 |
| Total Invested By Year | $15,000 | $15,000 | $15,000 | $15,000 | $15,000 | $75,000 |

The couple anticipates approximately $15,000 of investable cash flow annually. This money should be proportioned among the three suggested investments for the next 5 years.

The family circumstances are not expected to change meaningfully for the next five years until college expenses begin. The municipal bonds and children's custodial accounts will provide some tax relief, while the IRA in the variable annuity and the company retirement plan will provide some long-term growth of capital for the portfolio.

## PORTFOLIO STRUCTURE AFTER FIVE YEARS

| Investment | Present Portfolio | Restructured Portfolio | Assets after 5* Years |
|---|---|---|---|
| Certificate of Deposit | $ 60,000 | | |
| Money Market Account | 8,000 | $ 8,000 | $ 11,200 |
| Common Stock Account | 23,000 | | |
| IRA Accounts at Bank | 12,000 | | |
| Vested Value of Company Retirement Plan | 27,000 | 27,000 | 67,180 |
| Municipal Bonds | | 53,000 | 105,000 |
| Zero-Coupon Bonds | | 30,000 | 79,600 |
| IRA Variable Annuity | | 12,000 | 46,559 |
| Total | $130,000 | $130,000 | $309,539 |

*These values are based on the restructured portfolio, plus investments over the five years, plus interest, dividends, capital gains, and company contributions to the retirement fund.

Assumptions: Money Market returns 7%
Municipal Bonds returns 7.5%
Zero-Coupon Bonds returns 10%
IRA returns 12%
Retirement Plan returns 20% per year including contributions

The calculation for the five-year growth of the zero-coupon bonds was based on all bonds being purchased and held for the oldest daughter that enters college in five years. Actual value should be slightly higher than the number calculated, because the other two children will not be ready to enter college at the end of the five years.

The family will have close to $80,000 saved toward college expenses by the time the first daughter is ready to enter college. By selecting a variety of maturities, the zero-coupon bonds can be arranged to supply cash as needed over a selected time period. The entire $80,000 would not need to mature the first year she enters college.

# CHAPTER 7

# Model Portfolio
# for Empty Nesters

## CURRENT INFORMATION

| | |
|---|---|
| Marital Status: | Married |
| Employment Status: | Sales Manager ($77,000) |
| | Homemaker |
| Ages: | Mid-Fifties |
| Residence: | Value $147,000 |
| Mortgage Balance: | $8,000 |
| Dependents: | None remaining at home |
| Taxable Income: | $62,000 |
| Marginal Tax Bracket: | 42% |
| Annual Amount Saved: | $25,000 |

## EXPECTED CHANGES IN PRESENT SITUATION

This couple expects to receive an 8 percent increase in the manager's salary for the next five years.

The couple does not expect any additional children, although they plan to help fund their grandchildren's education. The present residence may be sold during the next 12 months, as it is much larger than the couple needs.

Annual savings of $25,000 should remain steady for the next five years.

## PRESENT PORTFOLIO

| | |
|---|---|
| Certificate of Deposit | $ 15,000 |
| Money Market Account | 8,000 |
| Common Stock Account | 3,000 |
| IRA Accounts at Bank | 12,000 |
| Vested Value of Company Retirement Plan | 527,000 |
| Total Investment Assets | $565,000 |

## FINANCIAL GOALS EVALUATION

Investors must "value" several different investment goals by numbering them on a scale from 1 to 10. By assigning a low number (1-3), investors indicate a very low investment priority. By assigning a high number (8-10), they indicate a major priority for the next five-year period.

Investors can use the same number more than once; for example, the number 3 might be used four times. This shows several investment goals have a similar priority for the individual.

Most often couples will agree on the relative values. On occasion a difference of opinion arises. Typically, an average of the two values then is used for financial planning.

| Financial Goal | Value Assigned by Investors | Value Assigned by Authors |
|---|---|---|
| Current Income | 4 | 4 |
| Liquidity | 7 | 5* |
| Safety of Principal | 8 | 8* |
| Capital Growth | 4 | 6* |
| Educational Funding | 6 | 6 |
| Life Insurance Coverage | 2 | 2 |
| Hedge Against Inflation | 4 | 4 |
| Retirement Income | 10 | 10 |
| Speculative Gains | 1 | 1 |
| Tax Reduction | 6 | 8* |

*Represents a change from current goals.

## ANALYSIS OF INVESTMENT GOALS

The highest goals, assigned by the couple, in order are retirement income, safety of principal, and liquidity. Of secondary importance are tax reduction and educational funding for grandchildren.

This couple has worked hard and saved regularly for several years. They have kept pace with the demands of managing a household and substantial educational expenses for several years. They now have all the educational expenses behind them and want to focus on a happy retirement, scheduled to begin seven years from now. They fear any loss of capital, because they can see the need for a substantial retirement income for their favorite hobby, travel.

They realize that the 42 percent marginal tax bracket on taxable income restricts the return from "safe money" investments but feel compelled to make sure they keep what they have earned and saved.

Lastly, a vast portion of total net worth is tied to the husband's company retirement plan. This plan is invested 50 percent in company stock and 50 percent in a balanced stock, bond, and money market portfolio.

The entire company retirement benefits will be taxable income when they are received seven years from now. Upon retirement, the husband may decide to roll the funds over into an IRA account. Money can then be withdrawn on an annual basis as needed, subject to the Internal Revenue Service rules on IRAs. Following is the present portfolio and the authors' suggested restructured portfolio.

## RESTRUCTURED PORTFOLIO

| Investment | Present Portfolio | Restructured Portfolio |
|---|---|---|
| Certificate of Deposit | $ 15,000 | |
| Money Market Account | 8,000 | |
| Common Stock Account | 3,000 | |
| IRA Accounts at Bank | | $ 12,000 |
| Vested Value of Company Retirement Plan | 527,000 | 527,000 |
| Tax Free Money Market Acct. | | 8,000 |
| Municipal Bond Trust | | 18,000 |
| IRA Certif. of Deposit | | 12,000 |
| Total Investment Assets | $565,000 | $565,000 |

This portfolio restructuring should eliminate $2,000 of taxable interest income by cashing in the certificates of deposit and taxable money market account, and switching to a tax free money market fund and other tax advantaged assets.

The municipal bond trusts provide tax free income and can be purchased with separate insurance coverage to provide increased safety. The average maturity can be maintained at 9 to 11 years. This will prevent any major fluctuations of principal due to changes in interest rates. The expected tax free yield is 7.5 percent.

The IRA accounts are safe and secure with the friendly local banker. There is little reason to look for higher rates of return—which accompanied by increased risk—this close (7 years) to retirement.

The very large pool of assets in the retirement plan with the company will produce a substantial taxable income after retirement. The couple is concerned that the stock of the company could decline substantially between now and retirement, decreasing post retirement income. Future commitment of funds should be as follows.

## SCHEDULE OF FUTURE COMMITMENTS

| Investment Outlet | 1986 | 1987 | 1988 | 1989 | 1990 | Total |
|---|---|---|---|---|---|---|
| IRA at Bank | $ 2,000 | $ 2,000 | $ 2,000 | $ 2,000 | $ 2,000 | $ 10,000 |
| Municipal Bonds | 50,000 | 20,000 | 20,000 | 20,000 | 20,000 | 130,000 |
| Government Zeros | 3,000 | 3,000 | 3,000 | 3,000 | 3,000 | 15,000 |
| Real Estate Growth Ptrshp | 100,000 | | | | | |
| Total Invested By Year | $155,000 | $25,000 | $25,000 | $25,000 | $25,000 | $255,000 |

Between now and retirement, proceeds from the sale of the family residence will net a one-time, tax free lump sum of $130,000 after commissions and payment of the small remaining mortgage. These funds are to be placed in a diversified portfolio of real estate partnerships ($100,000) and tax free bonds ($30,000). The strategy is to let the real estate shelter high earned income for the next 4 to 7 years while the tax free bonds accumulate to be used for travel after retirement. It is convenient that the real estate will also begin distributions just before retirement begins.

Our empty nesters have plenty of exposure to the stock market in the company retirement plan. They need to build tax free sources of income outside the plan to help hold the tax burden down after retirement begins. To do this, large purchases of municipal bonds will be made annually.

## PORTFOLIO STRUCTURE AFTER FIVE YEARS

| Investment | Present Portfolio | Restructured Portfolio | Assets after 5* Years |
|---|---|---|---|
| Certificate of Deposit | $ 15,000 | | |
| Money Market Account | 8,000 | | |
| Common Stock Account | 3,000 | | |
| IRA Accounts at Bank | 12,000 | | $ 28,400 |
| Vested Value of Company Retirement Plan | 527,000 | $527,000 | 1,059,000 |
| Tax Free Money Market Acct. | | 8,000 | 10,200 |
| Municipal Bonds | | 18,000 | 182,000 |
| IRA Certif. of Deposit | | 12,000 | |
| Zero Coupons (grandchildren) | | | 20,100 |
| Real Estate | | | 201,100 |
| Total | $565,000 | $565,000 | $1,500,800 |

*These values are based on the restructured portfolio, plus investments over the five years, plus interest, dividends, and capital gains.

Assumptions:  Money Market returns 5%
Municipal Bonds return 7.5%
Zero-Coupon Bonds return 10%
IRA returns 10%
Real Estate returns 15%
Retirement Plan returns 15% (including contributions)

Our couple is well situated for retirement. They have over $500,000 in assets that will produce primarily tax free income and just over $1,000,000 in assets that will produce taxable income. What a dilemma to have!

# CHAPTER 8

# Model Portfolio for a Retiring Couple

## CURRENT INFORMATION

| | |
|---|---|
| Marital Status: | Married |
| Employment Status: | Foreman Assembly Plant ($27,000) |
| | Part Time Teacher's Aide ($6,000) |
| Ages: | Mid-Sixties |
| Residence: | Value $67,000 |
| Mortgage Balance: | None |
| Dependents: | None remaining at home |
| Taxable Income: | $28,000 |
| Marginal Tax Bracket: | 26% |
| Annual Amount Saved: | $8,000 |

## EXPECTED CHANGES IN PRESENT SITUATION

This couple is ready to retire next month.

The couple does not expect any additional children. The present residence should be adequate for the foreseeable future.

## PRESENT PORTFOLIO

| | |
|---|---|
| Certificate of Deposit | $ 60,000 |
| Money Market Account | 8,000 |
| IRA Accounts at Bank | 12,000 |
| Vested Value of Company Retirement Plan | 167,000 |
| Total Investment Assets | $227,000 |

## FINANCIAL GOALS EVALUATION

Investors must "value" several different investment goals by numbering them on a scale from 1 to 10. By assigning a low number (1-3), investors indicate a very low investment priority. By assigning a high number (8-10), they indicate a major priority for the next five-year period.

Investors can use the same number more than once; for example, the number 3 might be used four times. This shows several investment goals have a similar priority for the individual.

Most often couples will agree on the relative values. On occasion a difference of opinion arises. Typically, an average of the two values then is used for financial planning.

| Financial Goal | Value Assigned by Investors | Value Assigned by Authors |
|---|---|---|
| Current Income | 10 | 10 |
| Liquidity | 8 | 6* |
| Safety of Principal | 10 | 10 |
| Capital Growth | 2 | 2 |
| Educational Funding | 1 | 1 |
| Life Insurance Coverage | 2 | 2 |
| Hedge Against Inflation | 6 | 6 |
| Retirement Income | 10 | 10 |
| Speculative Gains | 1 | 1 |
| Tax Reduction | 1 | 1 |

*Represents a change from current goals.

## ANALYSIS OF INVESTMENT GOALS

The highest goals, assigned by the couple, in order are current retirement income, safety of principal, retirement income, and a secondary concern with liquidity and inflation hedging.

This couple has saved regularly for several years. They fear any loss of capital, because they can see the need for continuing income for their years of retirement.

Taxes are not a major factor for this couple; income is the primary concern. Following is the present portfolio and the authors' suggested restructured portfolio.

## RESTRUCTURED PORTFOLIO

| Investment | Present Portfolio | Restructured Portfolio |
|---|---|---|
| Certificate of Deposit | $ 60,000 | $ 78,000 |
| Money Market Account | 8,000 | 27,000 |
| IRA Accounts at Bank | 12,000 | 12,000 |
| Vested Value of Company Retirement Plan | 167,000 | |
| Annuity Contract (Indexed Annuity) | | 100,000 |
| Total Investment Assets | $227,000 | $217,000* |

*Total does not equal "Present Portfolio." This is due to taxes paid on retirement plan distribution.

Our couple elected to receive the distribution of retirement plan assets as a lump sum. They paid taxes on the distribution based on the 10-year forward averaging option. This resulted in a net distribution after taxes of $157,000.

Our couple will use six-month and one-year certificates of deposit at a local bank and the bank money market account. The commitment to the money market account and the certificates of deposit will provide the liquidity requirements and safety of principal this couple seeks.

The large contribution to an annuity contract is in the form of an indexed annuity. (See the Appendix to Chapter 17.) The couple wants a guaranteed minimum interest rate and a hedge from inflation at the same time. The indexed annuity will meet this need, because it offers a guaranteed minimum interest rate and adjustments according to a well-known published index. Future income scheduled should be as follows.

## SCHEDULE OF FUTURE INCOME

| Investment Outlet | 1986 | 1987 | 1988 | 1989 | 1990 | Total |
|---|---|---|---|---|---|---|
| Annuity | | | $ 6,800 | $ 6,800 | $ 6,800 | $20,400 |
| IRA acct Bank | $ 6,800 | $ 6,800 | | | | 13,600 |
| Certificates | 6,200 | 6,200 | 6,200 | 6,200 | 6,200 | 31,000 |
| Money Market | 2,000 | 2,000 | 2,000 | 2,000 | 2,000 | 10,000 |
| Total Received Each Year | $15,000 | $15,000 | $15,000 | $15,000 | $15,000 | $75,000 |

Our couple has targeted $15,000 annually as a beginning spendable cash requirement.

They will receive income from the money market and certificates of deposit each month.

For the first two years they elected to cash the IRA accounts at the bank. This provides taxable income; the annuity contract continues to grow on a tax deferred basis until income is needed.

Beginning in year three the couple will elect to make an annual withdrawal from the indexed annuity. The annuity will continue to earn interest, this interest is more than enough to offset the annual amount withdrawn.

## PORTFOLIO STRUCTURE AFTER FIVE YEARS

| Investment | Present Portfolio | Restructured Portfolio | Assets after 5th Years |
|---|---|---|---|
| Certificate of Deposit | $ 40,000 | $ 78,000 | $ 78,000 |
| Money Market Account | 8,000 | 27,000 | 27,000 |
| IRA Accounts at Bank | 12,000 | 12,000 | 0 |
| Vested Value of Company Retirement Plan | 167,000 | | |
| Annuity Contract (Indexed Annuity) | | 100,000 | 136,200 |
| Total | $227,000 | $217,000 | $241,239 |

Assumptions:   Money Market returns 7%
                     Indexed Annuity returns 10%
                     IRA returns 9%
                     CDs return 8%

The couple has kept the assets very safe, produced an acceptable level of income, and is sensitive to inflation, should it accelerate.

At the same time, actual total assets have grown slightly. Our couple might be able to afford that special trip to Hawaii next year.

# PART 3

# Low-Risk
# Investments

# CHAPTER 9

# Money Market Funds

## DESCRIPTION

A *money market fund* is a portfolio of short term securities designed to provide the investor with immediate access to his or her money. The securities held by the money market fund usually consist of United States government securities, short term debt obligations of large corporations, and debt obligations from large financial institutions. Interest earned in a money market fund is credited daily.

## STRENGTHS

Money market funds offer investors liquidity and safety of principal. Money market funds' interest rates rise as interest rates in general move upward.

## WEAKNESS

Money market funds pay a floating rate of interest. Money market fund interest rates decline when interest rates fall. Over time, the rate of return on a money market fund is unlikely to be as high as the rate of return on common stocks, bonds, or other investments.

## UNIQUE FEATURES

Checks can be written against assets invested in most money market funds. Some restrictions usually apply to such check writing privileges. (Example: No checks can be written in amounts less than $500). By far the major attraction of money market funds is the ability to access investment funds immediately while earning a competitive floating rate of return.

## TAX CONSEQUENCES

Money market funds are available that invest only in securities issued by states and municipalities. These funds are called *tax free money market funds*. All of the interest on a tax free money market fund is exempt from federal government taxation.

Some tax free money market funds invest only in securities from one state. This makes the income exempt from that state's income tax as well as federal tax. For states having high state income tax rates such as New York and California, funds of this type make good sense.

All regular money market funds are federally taxable as interest income to the investor.

## WHERE AND HOW TO BUY

Money market funds are available from all major securities firms, many mutual fund management companies, and some insurance companies.

Money market funds are purchased in $1 units. Most funds require a minimum initial investment of $500 or more. The unit value is always $1.

Advertisements appear in all the major financial publications for money market funds. Investors can contact any brokerage firm to open a money market account or open one directly through the money market firm.

Table 9-1 is a representation of the daily quotation section of money market funds as it appears in the newspaper. The first column is the highest yield the fund has achieved at any time during the past 52 weeks. The second column is the lowest yield the fund has achieved within that time period. The name of the fund appears in column 3; the high, low, and closing yields for the past week are in columns 4, 5, and 6, respectively. The last column is the change in yield from the previous day.

Table 9-1. Newspaper Format for Money Market Fund Daily Quotations

| Yr High | Yr Low | Name | Wk High | Wk Low | Last | Chg |
|---|---|---|---|---|---|---|
| 9.68 | 6.35 | AMEV Fd | 7.22 | 7.20 | 7.22 | +.05 |
| 7.48 | 6.99 | AARP | 7.16 | 7.12 | 7.16 | −.03 |
| 9.39 | 6.89 | ActiveAssetGovt | 7.03 | 6.92 | 6.97 | −.03 |
| 10.05 | 7.30 | ActiveAssetMoney | 7.37 | 7.35 | 7.35 | −.01 |
| 9.55 | 7.05 | AlexBrownCash | 7.46 | 7.40 | 7.41 | +.02 |
| 9.99 | 7.04 | AlexBrownGovt | 7.47 | 7.35 | 7.37 | +.08 |
| . | . | . | . | . | . | . |
| . | . | . | . | . | . | . |
| . | . | . | . | . | . | . |
| 9.38 | 7.04 | Fidelity Cash Reserves | 7.44 | 7.43 | 7.44 | +.03 |
| 9.05 | 7.12 | Fidelity Daily Income | 7.46 | 7.35 | 7.46 | +.13 |
| 9.18 | 7.33 | Fidelity Govt. Portfolio | 7.98 | 7.85 | 7.85 | +.07 |
| 9.42 | 7.41 | Fidelity Domestic Portfolio | 7.70 | 7.69 | 7.70 | +.01 |
| 5.36 | 4.16 | Fidelity Mass. MMKT. | 4.34 | 4.29 | 4.34 | |
| 9.07 | 7.07 | Fidelity MM U.S. Treasury | 7.78 | 7.63 | 7.63 | +.13 |
| 8.89 | 7.07 | Fidelity U.S. Government | 7.44 | 7.39 | 7.41 | −.06 |

## HOW TO SELL

Money market funds can be liquidated by writing a check against invested funds; by written request to the fund manager; or, in some cases, by telephone request.

## TRANSACTION COSTS

Money market funds are available without front-end charges or commissions. A very small management fee is charged by the fund manager for all services rendered. Typically this fee is less than one- half percent of the investor's fund assets.

## PORTFOLIO FIT

Money market funds are used in almost every investment portfolio. Any investment funds that are not committed to other types of investments can be held temporarily in a money market fund. The investor may wish to accumulate reserves in the money market fund for future investments.

## SOURCES OF ADDITIONAL INFORMATION

Listings of money market funds are provided by sources such as Weisenberger Mutual Fund Survey. Included are the name of the fund and such data as total assets in the fund, average percent yield for the last 12 months, and average percent yield for the last 30 days.

Of special interest to investors is the types of the assets the money market fund holds. The safest of all assets are the U.S. government securities. A large percentage of the fund assets may be held in the form of commercial paper (short-term corporate obligations). Some of the money may even be invested in European certificates of deposit or Euro-dollar deposits.

An investor seeking the safest possible money market fund should select a fund that invests only in U.S. government securities. Investors seeking the highest yield usually look at funds that have longer average maturities and that invest in securities other than those issued by the federal government.

## COMMENTS

Money market funds are a versatile tool for all investors. They combine convenience, liquidity, and a fair rate of return. A money market fund should hold part of the emergency cash funds at the foundation of any investment portfolio. Money market funds are available in several special varieties. Government guaranteed money market funds invest only in securities guaranteed by the U.S. government. Tax free money market funds invest only in securities issued by states and municipalities. High tax-bracket investors should consider a tax free money market fund, even though these funds provide a lower yield.

**Exhibit 9-1.   Low Risk: Money Market Mutual Funds**

**INVESTMENT PROFILE**

| INVESTMENT CHARACTERISTICS | Excellent | Good | Average | Poor | None |
|---|---|---|---|---|---|
| Liquidity | ✓ | | | | |
| Safety of Principal | ✓ | | | | |
| Price Stability | ✓ | | | | |
| Reinvestment Protection | | | | ✓ | |
| Growth of Capital | | | ✓ | | |
| Cash Income | | | ✓ | | |
| Growth of Income | | | | | ✓ |
| Inflation Hedge | | ✓ | | | |
| Tax Advantaged | | | | | ✓* |

**Liquidity**—the ability to quickly realize cash from the sale at fair market value

**Safety of Principal**—the principal is safe from bankruptcy or default

**Price Stability**—the market value of the asset does not change in value

**Reinvestment Protection**—protection against reinvesting cash flow at lower rates as interest rates decline

**Growth of Capital**—the original investment increases over time to create capital gains

**Cash Income**—the cash income relative to treasury bills returns

**Growth of Income**—the ability of the cash income stream to increase over time

**Inflation Hedge**—the ability of total return (cash income plus capital gains) to keep pace with inflation over time

**Tax Advantaged**—the ability to reduce or defer current federal income taxes

*Some money market mutual funds may invest in tax free short-term securities and provide an average tax shelter.

# CHAPTER 10

# Money Market Accounts

## DESCRIPTION

*Money market accounts* are deposit accounts at financial institutions. These institutions include banks, savings and loan associations, and some credit unions.

This type of account offers a floating interest rate and provides the investor with immediate access to his or her money.

Minimum balance requirements vary, depending on the type of account and the type of institution selected. As a general rule of thumb, investors can expect slightly higher interest rates from savings and loan associations and credit unions than they will find at commercial banks. Investors are cautioned that there is a great deal of variance from one geographic location to another throughout the United States. In some areas, commercial banks may offer better rates and terms for money market accounts.

In addition, not all financial institutions return canceled checks or canceled negotiable orders of withdrawal (NOWs) to investors using a money market account.

Money market accounts compete directly with money market funds, discussed in Chapter 9 of this book. The main difference between them is their source (financial institutions versus securities brokerage firms) and the type of insurance they carry.

## STRENGTHS

Money market accounts offer investors safety of principal and liquidity. These accounts are very similar to money market funds, with the important strength that they are covered by insurance at commercial banks (*Federal Deposit Insurance Corporation*) and savings and loan associations (*Federal Savings and Loan Insurance Corporation*). This insurance coverage is of importance to investors seeking a very high degree of safety of principal.

During periods of rising interest rates, money market accounts show rising rates of return for investors.

## WEAKNESS

Money market accounts pay a floating rate of interest. Money market accounts' interest rates decline when interest rates fall. Over the long term, the rate of return on a money market account probably will not be as high as the rate of return on stocks, bonds, or other investments.

## UNIQUE FEATURES

Investors can write checks against assets invested in money market accounts. The terms of these check writing privileges vary substantially from one financial institution to another. Several restrictions are common. Typically there is a limit to the number of checks that are permitted each month and the minimum amount of a check.

## TAX CONSEQUENCES

Money market accounts pay interest that is fully taxable as interest income for federal income tax purposes. The interest earned is also subject to state and local taxes in states and municipalities that levy such taxes.

## WHERE AND HOW TO BUY

Money market accounts are available from all major banks, savings and loan associations, mutual savings banks, and credit unions.

Money market accounts are purchased in any amount. Most accounts require a minimum initial investment of between $500 and $2500. Investors should compare accounts available in any given geographic area for the features that best meet the individual's needs.

## HOW TO SELL

Money market accounts can be liquidated by writing a check against invested funds or by written request to the financial institution.

## TRANSACTION COSTS

Money market accounts are available without front-end charges or commissions. A monthly service charge may be assessed by the financial institution. The terms of this monthly service charge vary substantially among different institutions.

## PORTFOLIO FIT

Money market accounts can be used in almost every investment portfolio. Any investment funds that are not committed to other types of investments can be held in a money market account. The investor may wish to accumulate reserves in the money market account for future investments.

## SOURCES OF ADDITIONAL INFORMATION

Each financial institution has a complete brochure available for depositors to review prior to opening a money market account.

A listing of money market accounts from the Dallas Times Herald appears in Table 10-1. Similar tables can be found in most local newspapers.

## COMMENTS

Money market accounts are a versatile tool for all investors. They combine convenience, liquidity, and a fair rate of return for a low-risk security. A money market account or money market fund can be used in conjunc-

**Table 10-1.   Newspaper Format for Money Market
Account Quotations (October, 1985)**

| Money Market Account | Rate | Yield | Minimum |
|---|---|---|---|
| *Savings and Loans* | | | |
| Vernon Savings | 8.25 | 8.60 | $2,500 |
| Paris Savings | 8.25 | 8.57 | 2,500 |
| Gill Savings | 8.25 | 8.54 | 2,500 |
| Independent American Savings | 8.00 | 8.44 | 2,500 |
| Nowlin Savings | 8.00 | 8.32 | 1,000 |
| Commerce Savings | 8.00 | 8.32 | 1,000 |
| NorthPark Savings | 8.00 | 8.30 | 1,000 |
| Western Savings | 7.75 | 8.17 | 1,000 |
| Benjamin Franklin Savings | 7.75 | 8.03 | 2,000 |
| Commodore Savings | 7.75 | 7.98 | 1,000 |
| Savings of America | 7.50 | 7.76 | 2,500 |
| Richardson Savings & Loan | 7.50 | 7.76 | 2,500 |
| Murray Savings | 7.50 | 7.76 | 2,500 |
| Bright Banc | 7.50 | 7.76 | 1,000 |
| First Texas Savings | 7.50 | 7.76 | 1,000 |
| Sunbelt Savings | 7.75 | NA | 1,000 |
| *Banks* | | | |
| First City Bank of Dallas | 7.05 | 7.28 | 1,000 |
| Republic Bank Dallas | 7.00 | 7.25 | 1,000 |
| NorthPark National Bank | 7.00 | 7.23 | 2,500 |
| BancTexas Dallas | 7.00 | 7.23 | 2,500 |
| MBank Preston | 6.80 | 7.03 | 2,500 |
| Allied Lakewood Bank | 6.80 | 7.02 | 2,500 |
| InterFirst Banks | 6.80 | 7.01 | 2,500 |
| MBank Dallas | 6.75 | 6.98 | 2,500 |
| Texas Commerce Bk-Dallas | 6.80 | NA | 1,000 |

*Source: Dallas Times Herald*, November 4, 1985.

tion with an investment portfolio to balance risk and hold short-term liquid assets until they are needed for other investment opportunities.

Many investors "chase yields" on money market accounts and money market funds. This yield chasing involves switching assets frequently from one financial institution to another. Generally these investors are trying to maximize the yield on their investment assets. In reality these investors have a narrow outlook; they seek only liquidity and current yield to form a portfolio that has a higher total return. A portfolio that invests only in money market accounts or money market funds is not a true investment portfolio.

**Exhibit 10-1.   Low Risk: Money Market Accounts**

**INVESTMENT PROFILE**

| INVESTMENT CHARACTERISTICS | Excellent | Good | Average | Poor | None |
|---|---|---|---|---|---|
| Liquidity | ✓ | | | | |
| Safety of Principal | ✓ | | | | |
| Price Stability | ✓ | | | | |
| Reinvestment Protection | | | | ✓ | |
| Growth of Capital | | | ✓ | | |
| Cash Income | | | ✓ | | |
| Growth of Income | | | | | ✓ |
| Inflation Hedge | | | ✓ | | |
| Tax Advantaged | | | | | ✓ |

**Liquidity**—the ability to quickly realize cash from the sale at fair market value

**Safety of Principal**—the principal is safe from bankruptcy or default

**Price Stability**—the market value of the asset does not change in value

**Reinvestment Protection**—protection against reinvesting cash flow at lower rates as interest rates decline

**Growth of Capital**—the original investment increases over time to create capital gains

**Cash Income**—the cash income relative to treasury bills returns

**Growth of Income**—the ability of the cash income stream to increase over time

**Inflation Hedge**—the ability of total return (cash income plus capital gains) to keep pace with inflation over time

**Tax Advantaged**—the ability to reduce or defer current federal income taxes

# CHAPTER 11

# Certificates of Deposit

## DESCRIPTION

*Certificates of deposit* (commonly referred to as *CDs*) are time deposits with financial institutions. These certificates entitle the investor to the receipt of interest. The length of maturity, the interest rate paid, and the size of the certificate are established by the issuing institution. In recent years federal government regulations of deposits of this nature have been virtually eliminated.

Two types of certificates of deposit are available: negotiable and nonnegotiable.

Negotiable certificates of deposit have a minimum investment requirement of $100,000. Both the interest rate and maturity date of these "jumbo" certificates of deposit can be negotiated between the depositor and the issuing institution. The majority have maturities of 4-6 months.

Nonnegotiable certificates of deposit are categorized according to minimum investment size, time until maturity, and interest rate in accordance with the terms fixed by the issuing institution.

Table 11-1 presents the interest rates paid on large negotiable six-month certificates of deposit from 1978 to 1985. The rate cited is an annual average.

## STRENGTHS

The greatest advantage of certificates of deposit is the government insurance that is available to investors on their invested funds. Certificates of

**Table 11-1.  Interest
Rates on Six-Month CDs**

| Year | Rate |
| --- | --- |
| 1978 | 8.61% |
| 1979 | 11.44 |
| 1980 | 10.89 |
| 1981 | 15.77 |
| 1982 | 12.57 |
| 1983 | 9.27 |
| 1984 | 10.68 |
| 1985 | 8.08* |

*Average for first six months
of 1985.
*Source: Federal Reserve Bul-
letin*, selected issues.

deposit also are available in a wide variety of maturities to meet many
different needs of investors.

## WEAKNESSES

Certificates of deposit offer no capital appreciation potential. They lock in
a fixed rate of return that often disappoints investors during periods of
rising interest rates. This same "locked-in rate syndrome" causes many
investors to engage in second guessing the interest rate market. Many
times the people waiting to see whether rates will go up or down, miss
excellent investment opportunities.

Nonnegotiable Certificates of deposit also contain penalty provisions
that may significantly lower the rate of return if an investor needs access to
funds prior to maturity of the certificate.

## UNIQUE FEATURES

The most unique feature of a certificate of deposit is the insurance normally associated with the product. Many investors remember bank defaults of the Great Depression and rely on the insured CD to protect their
savings. It is interesting to note that there have been many failures of

financial institutions in the 1980s, and most depositors have been protected by the insurance offered by corporations associated with the federal government. Federal insurance on a CD covers up to $100,000 of loss.

The insurance is offered by the Federal Deposit Insurance Corporation (FDIC) and the Federal Savings and Loan Insurance Corporation (FSLIC). These two organizations charge member banks and savings and loan associations an insurance premium for the insurance coverage.

## TAX CONSEQUENCES

All certificates of deposit are fully taxable. Every agency of government, (federal, state and local) that levies an income tax considers interest earned on a certificate of deposit as taxable income.

## WHERE AND HOW TO BUY

Virtually all financial institutions provide certificates to the investing public. Banks, savings and loan associations, mutual savings banks, and credit unions all offer a broad variety of certificates of deposit. It is important to point out that securities brokerage firms now offer certificates of deposit to their clients. Many times these CDs carry a slightly higher interest rate than traditional certificates of deposit offered by financial institutions.

An investor need only visit a local branch of a financial institution to purchase a certificate of deposit. Some CDs are even offered by mail to investors.

Brokerage firm CDs are actually issued by a financial institution, include the same insurance coverage associated with traditional CDs, and offer very competitive interest rates. The brokerage firms make these certificates of deposit available on a daily basis for the investing public.

A sampling of recent interest rates available on selected maturities on certificates of deposit is presented in Table 11-2.

From Table 11-2, investors can see that yields on certificates vary at different financial institutions even though maturities may be equal.

## HOW TO SELL

Traditional nonnegotiable certificates of deposit are normally held to maturity to avoid the early withdrawal penalty imposed by financial institu-

Table 11-2.   Certificates of Deposit

# HIGH YIELD SAVINGS

Small minimum balance, generally $500 to $2,500

| Savings Money Market Accounts | Rate | Yield | Six Months Savings CDs | Rate | Yield |
|---|---|---|---|---|---|
| Custom Svgs, Pikesville Md ............. | 8.63% | 9.15% | Colonial National, Wilm Del ............ | 8.38% | 8.87% |
| Citisavings, San Antonio Texas ....... | 8.38% | 8.74% | Savings of America, Dallas .............. | 8.50% | 8.87% |
| Seguin Svgs, Seguin, Texas ............. | 8.35% | 8.71% | Century Svgs, Baytown Texas .......... | 8.50% | 8.87% |
| Franklin Svgs, Ottawa Ks ................ | 8.25% | 8.60% | First Federal, New Orleans ............ | 8.50% | 8.87% |
| Gulf Federal, Metairie La ................ | 8.25% | 8.57% | Beach Svgs, Huntington Bch Ca ........ | 8.38% | 8.86% |

| 30-Day Savings CDs | Rate | Yield | One Year Savings CDs | Rate | Yield |
|---|---|---|---|---|---|
| Century Svgs, Baytown Texas .......... | 8.25% | 8.60% | Capital City Svgs,Austin Texas ........ | 9.25% | 9.58% |
| Charter Svgs,Corp Chris Texas ....... | 8.50% | 8.50% | Financial Svgs, Dallas .................... | 9.00% | 9.44% |
| Benjamin Franklin, Houston ........... | 8.10% | 8.41% | Spindletop Svgs,Beaumont Texas .... | 9.00% | 9.41% |
| Dixie Federal, New Orleans ............. | 8.00% | 8.33% | Meridian Svgs, Arlington Texas ....... | 9.00% | 9.31% |
| Citisavings, San Antonio Texas ........ | 8.13% | 8.25% | Unity Svgs, Beverly Hills Ca ............. | 9.00% | 9.30% |

| 60-Day Savings CDs | Rate | Yield | 2½ Years Savings CDs | Rate | Yield |
|---|---|---|---|---|---|
| Charter Svgs,Corp Chris Texas ........ | 8.50% | 8.50% | Time Svgs, San Francisco ................ | 9.54% | 10.00% |
| Benjamin Franklin, Houston ............ | 8.10% | 8.41% | Spindletop Svgs,Beaumont Texas .... | 9.50% | 9.96% |
| Commonwealth Svgs, Houston ......... | 8.40% | 8.40% | Colonial National, Wilm Del ............ | 9.25% | 9.83% |
| Citisavings, San Antonio Texas ........ | 8.13% | 8.25% | Berkley Federal, Norfolk Va ............ | 9.35% | 9.81% |
| Community Fed, San Marino Ca ....... | 7.95% | 8.19% | Maryland Fed, Hyattsville Md .......... | 9.20% | 9.78% |

| 90-Day Savings CDs | Rate | Yield | 5 Years Savings CDs | Rate | Yield |
|---|---|---|---|---|---|
| Colonial National, Wilm Del ,........... | 8.38% | 8.87% | Spindletop Svgs,Beaumont Texas ..... | 10.15% | 10.54% |
| Citisavings, San Antonio Texas ........ | 8.38% | 8.64% | Delta Svgs, Kenner La ................... | 10.00% | 10.52% |
| Century Svgs, Baytown Texas ......... | 8.25% | 8.60% | South Bay Svgs, Costa Mesa Ca ...... | 9.88% | 10.52% |
| Beach Svgs, Huntington Bch Ca ....... | 8.13% | 8.59% | Baltimore County, Perry Hall Md .... | 10.00% | 10.51% |
| Dixie Federal, New Orleans ............. | 8.20% | 8.54% | Alliance Svgs, Houston ................... | 9.90% | 10.27% |

# HIGH YIELD JUMBOS

Large minimum balance, generally $100,000.

| Jumbo Money Market Accounts | Rate | Yield | Six Months Jumbo CDs | Rate | Yield |
|---|---|---|---|---|---|
| Custom Svgs, Pikesville Md ............. | 8.63% | 9.15% | Farmers Svgs, Davis Ca ................ | 9.13% | 9.13% |
| Seguin Svgs, Seguin Texas .............. | 8.50% | 8.87% | Universal Svgs, Chickasha Ok ......... | 9.13% | 9.13% |
| First Federal, New Orleans ............ | 8.50% | 8.87% | Victor Fed, Muskogee Ok ................ | 9.00% | 9.12% |
| Guaranty Federal, Dallas ............... | 8.75% | 8.75% | Benjamin Franklin, Houston ............ | 8.75% | 9.04% |
| Citisavings, San Antonio Texas ........ | 8.38% | 8.74% | Meridian Svgs, Arlington Texas ........ | 9.00% | 9.00% |

| 30-Day Jumbo CDs | Rate | Yield | One Year Jumbo CDs | Rate | Yield |
|---|---|---|---|---|---|
| Benjamin Franklin, Houston ........... | 8.40% | 8.73% | Centennial Svgs, Santa Rosa Ca ........ | 9.50% | 9.50% |
| Southwest Svgs, Los Angeles .......... | 8.25% | 8.63% | Southwest Svgs, Los Angeles ............ | 9.00% | 9.44% |
| Victor Federal, Muskogee Ok ........... | 8.50% | 8.62% | Alliance Svgs, Houston ................... | 9.10% | 9.42% |
| Franklin Svgs, Ottawa Ks ............... | 8.50% | 8.50% | Meridian Svgs, Arlington Texas ........ | 9.38% | 9.38% |
| Commonwealth Svgs, Houston ......... | 8.50% | 8.50% | Benjamin Franklin, Houston ............ | 9.00% | 9.31% |

| 60-Day Jumbo CDs | Rate | Yield | 2½ Years Jumbo CDs | Rate | Yield |
|---|---|---|---|---|---|
| Victor Fed, Muskogee Ok ................ | 8.75% | 8.87% | Centennial Svgs, Santa Rosa, Ca ...... | 10.00% | 10.00% |
| Commonwealth Svgs, Houston ......... | 8.80% | 8.80% | Home Svgs, Midland Texas .............. | 9.75% | 9.75% |
| Benjamin Franklin, Houston ............ | 8.40% | 8.73% | Southwest Svgs, Los Angeles ............ | 9.25% | 9.71% |
| Farmers Svgs, Davis Ca ................. | 8.65% | 8.65% | Baltimore County, Perry Hall Md .... | 9.25% | 9.69% |
| Southwest Svgs, Los Angeles ........... | 8.25% | 8.63% | Alliance Svgs, Houston ................... | 9.30% | 9.63% |

| 90-Day Jumbo CDs | Rate | Yield | 5 Years Jumbo CDs | Rate | Yield |
|---|---|---|---|---|---|
| Victor Fed, Muskogee Ok ................ | 9.00% | 9.12% | Baltimore County, Perry Hall Md ..... | 10.00% | 10.51% |
| Farmers Svgs, Davis Ca ................. | 8.85% | 8.85% | Alliance Svgs, Houston ................. | 9.90% | 10.28% |
| Benjamin Franklin, Houston ........... | 8.50% | 8.77% | Southwest Svgs, Los Angeles ............ | 9.75% | 10.26% |
| Southwest Svgs, Los Angeles ........... | 8.38% | 8.77% | Peoples Svgs, Llano Texas .............. | 10.25% | 10.25% |
| Commonwealth Svgs, Houston ......... | 8.75% | 8.75% | National Permanent, Washington DC | 9.75% | 10.24% |

Source: MASTERFUND INC., New York.
Banxquote is a registered trademark
and service mark of MASTERFUND INC.

Reprinted with permission.

tions. Should an investor need to liquidate a certificate of deposit prematurely a penalty of up to six months interest earned is not uncommon in the industry.

In case an investor does need funds, certificates of deposit purchased through a securities brokerage firm may offer investors an advantage over traditional CDs. The brokerage firm is normally willing to purchase the CDs back from investors at "market prices." If interest rates have risen slightly from the date of purchase the brokerage firm may offer less than one dollar for each dollar originally invested in the CD. On the other hand, in the event interest rates declined, an investor could receive more than the original amount invested in the CD. At any rate, the investor does not suffer the automatic penalty that is imposed by the financial institutions.

## TRANSACTION COSTS

Certificates of deposit incur no front-end fees or charges when purchased from a traditional financial institution.

Certificates of deposit issued by brokerage firms have no front-end fees, commissions, or costs of any type. The lack of brokerage firm fees is not magic. The brokerage firms are paid a placement fee by the issuing financial institution for placing the certificates with their clients. This in no way influences the interest rate or terms received by the client. In fact, the costs saved by the financial institution (rent on a branch office, labor costs, overhead expenses, advertising, and so on) often enable the securities brokerage firm to offer certificates of deposit that pay a slightly higher interest rate than those offered by a traditional branch office of a financial institution.

## PORTFOLIO FIT

Certificates of deposit are typically purchased by two types of investors. The first group is attempting to accumulate funds for a major purchase or significant future expenditure. Examples include young people saving to purchase a home and even younger people saving for future educational expenses. The second group comprises mostly investors seeking safety of principal, regular income to meet living expenses, and convenience of a local financial institution.

## SOURCES OF ADDITIONAL INFORMATION

Additional information about certificates of deposit is available from all issuers of the product. Many financial institutions and most major brokerage firms offer descriptive brochures about certificates of deposit.

Additional information concerning the insurance coverage may be obtained from the agencies that provide the insurance. Most of these brochures are available from the product suppliers. An investor needs only to call any of the suppliers to receive a wealth of descriptive material on certificates of deposit.

## COMMENTS

Investors considering the use of certificates of deposit can thank the U.S. government for rescinding many of the regulations formerly associated with the product. The introduction of new methods of distribution (securities brokerage firms) and flexible terms have enhanced this investment vehicle in recent years. As competition expands in the financial industry, further changes in this product can be expected. Many experts in the field expect that CD investors will be offered a participatory bonus based on the earnings of the financial institution in future years. These bonus payments will be in addition to the guaranteed rate of return offered on the face amount of the certificate of deposit.

Two additional items need to be reviewed concerning the new channels of distribution for CDs. The securities brokerage firms that provide CDs to clients issued the certificates of deposit in "book entry form." This means that no special piece of paper is issued in the name of the investor. Rather, the securities firm reflects the ownership of the certificate of deposit each month on a statement furnished to the customer. Second, many times the interest earned on a brokerage firm CD is automatically credited to a money market account at the brokerage firm. Many clients see this as an added advantage.

**Exhibit 11-1.   Low Risk: Non-Negotiable Certificates of Deposit**

**INVESTMENT PROFILE**

| INVESTMENT CHARACTERISTICS | Excellent | Good | Average | Poor | None |
|---|---|---|---|---|---|
| Liquidity | | | | ✓ | |
| Safety of Principal | ✓ | | | | |
| Price Stability | ✓ | | | | |
| Reinvestment Protection | | LT | ST | | |
| Growth of Capital | | | | | ✓ |
| Cash Income | | ✓ | | | |
| Growth of Income | | | | | ✓ |
| Inflation Hedge | | | ST | LT | |
| Tax Advantaged | | | | | ✓ |

**Liquidity**—the ability to quickly realize cash from the sale at fair market value

**Safety of Principal**—the principal is safe from bankruptcy or default

**Price Stability**—the market value of the asset does not change in value

**Reinvestment Protection**—protection against reinvesting cash flow at lower rates as interest rates decline

**Growth of Capital**—the original investment increases over time to create capital gains

**Cash Income**—the cash income relative to treasury bills returns

**Growth of Income**—the ability of the cash income stream to increase over time

**Inflation Hedge**—the ability of total return (cash income plus capital gains) to keep pace with inflation over time

**Tax Advantaged**—the ability to reduce or defer current federal income taxes

LT = Long-term non-negotiable certificates.
ST = Short-term non-negotiable certificates.

**Exhibit 11-2.   Low Risk: Negotiable Certificates of Deposit**

**INVESTMENT PROFILE**

| INVESTMENT CHARACTERISTICS | Excellent | Good | Average | Poor | None |
|---|---|---|---|---|---|
| Liquidity | ✓ | | | | |
| Safety of Principal | ✓ | | | | |
| Price Stability | ✓ | | | | |
| Reinvestment Protection | | | | ✓ | |
| Growth of Capital | | | | | ✓ |
| Cash Income | | ✓ | | | |
| Growth of Income | | | | | ✓ |
| Inflation Hedge | | | ✓ | | |
| Tax Advantaged | | | | | ✓ |

**Liquidity**—the ability to quickly realize cash from the sale at fair market value

**Safety of Principal**—the principal is safe from bankruptcy or default

**Price Stability**—the market value of the asset does not change in value

**Reinvestment Protection**—protection against reinvesting cash flow at lower rates as interest rates decline

**Growth of Capital**—the original investment increases over time to create capital gains

**Cash Income**—the cash income relative to treasury bills returns

**Growth of Income**—the ability of the cash income stream to increase over time

**Inflation Hedge**—the ability of total return (cash income plus capital gains) to keep pace with inflation over time

**Tax Advantaged**—the ability to reduce or defer current federal income taxes

# CHAPTER 12

# Treasury Bills

## DESCRIPTION

A *treasury bill (T-bill)* is a short-term United States government debt obligation. A treasury bill is purchased at a discount from face value. Upon maturity the investor receives the full face value of the T-bill. The interest rate earned by the investor is calculated based on the discount from face value. The larger the discount the higher the interest rate earned.

Treasury bills are sold for maturities of up to one year. The most common maturities at the time of issuance are three months and six months. Treasury bills are available with maturities of one week to one year in the secondary market provided by U.S. government securities dealers. As old T-Bills approach maturity, the Federal Reserve sells new maturities every week.

The following example demonstrates how to calculate the effective rate of return on a treasury bill.

An investor asks her banker or broker to purchase a treasury bill that matures at a face value of $10,000 six months from today. The investor is aware that treasury bills are sold at a discount from face value. Her supplier quotes a price of 95 (95 percent of face value). This means a $10,000 face value treasury bill will cost $9,500. Thus, the investor will receive $500 in interest as the difference between $9,500 and $10,000. The time period for the return, in this case, is six months (180 days).

The formula used to calculate the effective return is:

$$\frac{\text{Interest}}{\$10,000 - \text{Interest}} \times \frac{\text{Days in the year*}}{\text{Days treasury bill is outstanding}}$$

*For financial calculations, 360 days is normally used.

Using this example:

$$\text{Effective Rate of Return} = \frac{\$500}{\$10,000 - \$500} \times \frac{360}{180}$$

$$= \frac{\$500}{\$9500} \qquad \times 2$$

$$= .0526315 \qquad \times 2$$

$$\text{Effective Rate of Return} = .105263 \text{ or } 10.526\%$$

## STRENGTHS

Treasury bills are considered the safest of all investments. Investors consider the U.S. government to be without credit risk. Treasury bills are very liquid.

During periods of rising interest rates, treasury bill rates adjust very quickly to increases in inflation.

## WEAKNESSES

Because treasury bills are riskless, the rate of return is not as high as other investments of similar maturities (for example, certificates of deposit, described in Chapter 11). The rate of return on a treasury bill is fixed from the date of purchase to the date of maturity. However, because the maturity length is always less than one year and can be as short as a few days, investors may not be able to reinvest their money at the same rate each time they purchase T-bills. Over time, the rate of return on treasury bills is unlikely to be as high as the rate of return on investments of longer maturities or higher risk.

## UNIQUE FEATURES

Treasury bills are extremely safe. They offer a very liquid security for short-term investment requirements. T-bills are one of the few securities issued at a discount from face value.

## TAX CONSEQUENCES

Although the income on an investment in treasury bills comes entirely in the form of a capital gain, the tax authorities treat the income as ordinary income and not as a capital gain. All income from U.S. government securities is exempt from state and local income taxes.

## WHERE AND HOW TO BUY

The U.S. government supplies treasury bills at a weekly auction. Payment for T-bills must generally accompany the order if it is placed through a Federal Reserve bank. Payment can be made in U.S. currency, matured treasury securities, or by checks issued directly by a financial institution. Personal checks are not acceptable.

If treasury bills are purchased through a brokerage firm or bank trust department, the investor's account will be debited on the settlement date for the amount of the purchase.

Treasury bills are issued with a minimum denomination of $10,000 and in increments of $5,000 thereafter. T-bills are always issued in *book entry* form. Book entry form means that the purchaser's ownership of the treasury bills is recorded in a book entry account at the U.S. Treasury Department. The purchaser receives a receipt rather than an engraved certificate as evidence of the purchase. This method of recording ownership protects the purchaser against loss, theft, or counterfeiting of ownership documents.

Each week, three-month and six-month T-bills are sold on a competitive bid basis. Many financial institutions and brokerage firms submit bids on behalf of clients for a nominal fee. More typically, they will simply buy previously issued and outstanding $10,000 treasury bills for their customers. Generally these firms also offer recordkeeping of the treasury bills and will collect the proceeds for the client upon maturity of the T-Bill.

## HOW TO SELL

Treasury bills can be held until maturity or sold in the secondary market. This is a competitive bid market maintained by many securities dealers around the country.

## TRANSACTION COSTS

The purchase of treasury bills from the Federal Reserve is free of charges. Brokerage firms and financial institutions charge a minimum fee (usually $25) to purchase treasury bills. All sales of treasury bills prior to maturity must be processed by a brokerage firm or financial institution. The Federal Reserve does not repurchase treasury bills from individuals. All sales through a brokerage firm or financial institution are done on a net basis to the client. The client receives the amount quoted by a securities dealer without additional commission charges.

An investor wishing to liquidate treasury bills should solicit multiple bids from several brokerage firms and financial institutions to minimize transaction costs.

In reality, most treasury bills are held to maturity by individual investors.

## PORTFOLIO FIT

Treasury bills are most commonly used by investors seeking a short-term security with a high degree of safety. This investment is often used before funds are committed to a longer-term investment. Some very cautious investors simply depend on the safety of the United States government security to protect their investment assets. Many money market funds purchase treasury bills.

## SOURCES OF ADDITIONAL INFORMATION

Quoted prices and yields for treasury bills are available in the major financial publications and in many local newspapers. An example of quotations is presented in Table 12-1.

The *bid* price is the percentage discount from face value that a dealer requires to buy treasury bills from an investor. The *asked* price is the percentage discount from face value an investor would pay when purchasing a treasury bill.

The Federal Reserve banks also have a brochure available to treasury bill investors. It is titled *United States Treasury Securities Basic Information* and is available free of charge through any Federal Reserve bank.

**Table 12-1. Newspaper Format for Treasury Bill Quotations**

| Due | Bid | Ask | Yield |
| --- | --- | --- | --- |
| 1986 | | | |
| 2-27 | 6.50 | 6.38 | 6.47 |
| 3- 6 | 6.92 | 6.84 | 6.95 |
| 3-13 | 6.91 | 6.85 | 6.97 |
| 3-20 | 6.91 | 6.85 | 6.98 |
| 3-27 | 6.77 | 6.71 | 6.84 |
| 4- 3 | 6.98 | 6.92 | 7.07 |
| 6-19 | 7.04 | 6.98 | 7.24 |
| 7-24 | 7.10 | 7.06 | 7.37 |
| 1987 | | | |
| 1-87 | 7.10 | 7.08 | 7.55 |
| 2-87 | 7.06 | 7.04 | 7.54 |

Also, the appendix to Chapter 13, ''Treasury Notes,'' contains a list of all Federal Reserve banks.

## COMMENTS

Treasury bills are often owned by large institutional investors. However, for some individual investors treasury bills offer excellent safety and a fair rate of return. Investors in high tax brackets may enjoy the safety treasury bills afford, but may be forced to achieve a higher after tax rate of return in other investments.

**Exhibit 12-1.   Low Risk: Treasury Bills**

**INVESTMENT PROFILE**

| INVESTMENT CHARACTERISTICS | Excellent | Good | Average | Poor | None |
|---|---|---|---|---|---|
| Liquidity | ✓ | | | | |
| Safety of Principal | ✓ | | | | |
| Price Stability | ✓ | | | | |
| Reinvestment Protection | | | | ✓ | |
| Growth of Capital | | | | | ✓ |
| Cash Income | | | ✓ | | |
| Growth of Income | | | | | ✓ |
| Inflation Hedge | | | ✓ | | |
| Tax Advantaged | | | | ✓* | |

**Liquidity**—the ability to quickly realize cash from the sale at fair market value

**Safety of Principal**—the principal is safe from bankruptcy or default

**Price Stability**—the market value of the asset does not change in value

**Reinvestment Protection**—protection against reinvesting cash flow at lower rates as interest rates decline

**Growth of Capital**—the original investment increases over time to create capital gains

**Cash Income**—the cash income relative to treasury bills returns

**Growth of Income**—the ability of the cash income stream to increase over time

**Inflation Hedge**—the ability of total return (cash income plus capital gains) to keep pace with inflation over time

**Tax Advantaged**—the ability to reduce or defer current federal income taxes

*Interest on Treasury bills is exempt from state and local taxes.

# CHAPTER 13

# Treasury Notes

## DESCRIPTION

A *treasury note (T-note)* is an intermediate term U.S. government obligation. A treasury note is purchased at a par value of $1,000 or multiples thereof. Treasury notes are available at the time of original issue in maturities from 2 to 10 years. Over time the notes move closer to maturity, and this permits the investor to select virtually any maturity date between the present time and 10 years. The interest rate earned by the investor is fixed at the time the treasury note is sold.

Investors should be aware that the prices quoted in the financial press are listed in increments of 1/32 of a dollar. Table 13-1 illustrates the newspaper format for T-note quotations.

For example, the 9.00 percent note due September of 1987 is bid 100.27 asked 100.31. The yield is 8.42 percent. The *bid* is the price the securities brokerage firm will pay for a given treasury note. The *asked* price is the price at which they will sell the treasury note to investors.

An investor wishing to buy the note would pay $1009.6875 (100.31) per $1,000 face value. In these listings, 100.31 means 100 and 31/32 dollars per $100 of face value.

An investor selling the same note would receive $1,008.4375 per $1,000 face value or 100 and 27/32 dollars per $100 of face value.

The difference between $1,009.6875 and $1,008.4375 is the *spread* ($1.250 per $1,000 face) or profit for the securities firm providing the market in the security.

## STRENGTHS

Treasury notes, like other U.S. government issues, are considered to be free of credit risk. T-notes are very liquid.

**Table 13-1.    Newspaper Format for Treasury Note Quotations**

| Mat. Date | Bid | Asked | Bid Chg. | Yield |
|-----------|-----|-------|----------|-------|
| 8-7/8s, 7-87 | 100.22 | 100.26 | +.2 | 8.34 |
| 8-7/8s, 8-87 | 100.20 | 100.24 | −.1 | 8.41 |
| 12-3/8s, 8-87 | 106.5 | 106.9 | ... | 8.37 |
| 13-3/4s, 8-87 | 106.10 | 106.14 | +.1 | 8.37 |
| 9s, 9-87 | 100.27 | 100.31 | ... | 8.42 |

## WEAKNESS

Because treasury notes are riskless, the rate of return is not as high as other investments of similar maturities (for example, certificates of deposit, described in Chapter 11). The rate of return on a treasury note is fixed from the date of purchase to the date of maturity. However, because the maturity length can be up to 10 years in the future, an investor may see some limited fluctuation in the principal value of his investment as interest rates rise and fall in the open market. This interest rate risk should not be confused with default risk. All U.S. government obligations are considered to be without default risk.

## UNIQUE FEATURES

Treasury notes are extremely safe. Investors can choose T-notes for intermediate-term investment requirements that fall between short-term treasury bills (that mature in less than a year) and long-term government bonds (with a 30-year maturity). Interest payments on treasury notes are paid semi-annually.

## TAX CONSEQUENCES

All interest earned on investments in treasury notes is fully taxable for federal income tax purposes as interest income.

Interest earned on treasury notes is exempt from state and local income taxes.

## WHERE AND HOW TO BUY

The U.S. government supplies treasury notes at quarterly auctions held each February, May, August, and November.

Delivery of the notes and payment for them is usually scheduled the next week.

T-notes are issued in *book entry form* with a minimum denomination of $1,000. The book entry method means that the purchaser's ownership of treasury notes is recorded in an account at the Treasury Department. The purchaser receives a receipt rather than an engraved certificate as evidence of the purchase. This method of recording ownership protects the purchaser against loss, theft, or counterfeiting of ownership documents.

Each quarter treasury notes are sold on a competitive bid basis. Smaller investors may enter a noncompetitive bid in amounts up to $1 million. These noncompetitive bids are guaranteed to be filled at the average interest rate of all competitive bidders. Bids for treasury notes may be submitted at any Federal Reserve bank or branch.

A list of all the Federal Reserve banks and branches appears in the appendix at the end of this chapter.

Some financial institutions and brokerage firms submit bids on behalf of clients for a nominal fee. For practical purposes, the small investor can bypass the bidding process and simply buy or sell existing treasury notes through a financial institution or brokerage firm. Generally these firms also offer safekeeping of the treasury notes and will collect the proceeds for the client upon maturity of the T-notes.

## HOW TO SELL

Treasury notes can be held until maturity or sold in the secondary market. This is a competitive bid market maintained by many securities dealers and financial institutions around the country. Federal Reserve banks will not repurchase treasury notes from investors.

If an investor sells a treasury note prior to the scheduled maturity, he or she will be credited with interest that has accrued since the most recent semiannual interest payment date.

## TRANSACTION COSTS

The Federal Reserve banks do not charge investors any fees for T-notes purchased through the Federal Reserve system.

All transactions involving treasury notes (both purchase and sale) performed for a client of a brokerage securities firm are done on a net basis. (See discussion of transaction costs for treasury bills to review the concept of net basis.) It would be prudent for an investor considering a treasury note transaction to consult with several brokerage firms to receive a competitive bid or offer for the T-notes.

## PORTFOLIO FIT

Treasury notes are most commonly used by investors seeking a medium-term security with a high degree of safety. This investment is often used before funds are committed to a longer term investment (for example, accumulating funds to purchase a retirement home). Some very cautious investors simply depend on the safety of the U.S. government security to protect their investment assets.

## SOURCES OF ADDITIONAL INFORMATION

The Treasury Department publishes a booklet entitled "United States Treasury Securities—Basic Information" that is very helpful for investors. Any Federal Reserve bank cited in the appendix to this chapter should have copies available.

## COMMENTS

Most treasury notes are owned by large institutional investors. However, for some individual investors treasury notes offer excellent safety and a fair rate of return. Most individual investors find it convenient to use the services of a brokerage firm or financial institution's trust department to purchase and hold treasury notes due to the purchase and delivery procedures involved. Investors in high tax brackets may enjoy the safety treasury notes afford but may be forced to consider alternative investments in municipal securities to achieve a higher after tax rate of return.

# APPENDIX

| *Federal Reserve Office* | *Address and Telephone Number(s)* |
|---|---|
| Atlanta | 104 Marietta Street, N.W.<br>Atlanta, Georgia 30301<br>(404) 586-8500 |
| Birmingham Branch | (205) 252-3141 |
| Jacksonville Branch | (904) 632-4400 |
| Miami Branch | (305) 591-2065 |
| Nashville Branch | (615) 259-4006 |
| New Orleans Branch | (504) 586-1505 |
| Boston | 600 Atlantic Avenue<br>Boston, Massachusetts 02106<br>(617) 973-3000 |
| Chicago | 230 South LaSalle Street<br>P.O. Box 834<br>(312) 322-5322 |
| Detroit Branch | (313) 961-6880 |
| Cleveland | 1455 East Sixth Street<br>P.O. Box 6387<br>Cleveland, Ohio 44101<br>(216) 579-2000 |
| Cincinnati Branch | (513) 721-4787 |
| Pittsburgh Branch | (412) 261-7800 |
| Dallas | 400 S. Akard<br>Dallas, Texas 75222<br>(214) 651-6111 |
| Kansas City | 925 East Grand Avenue<br>Kansas City, Missouri 64198<br>(816) 881-2000 |
| Denver Branch | (303) 534-5500 |
| Oklahoma City Branch | (405) 235-1721 |
| Omaha Branch | (402) 341-3610 |
| Minneapolis | 250 Marquette Avenue<br>Minneapolis, Minnesota 55480<br>(612) 340-2345 |
| Helena Branch | (406) 442-3860 |
| New York | 33 Liberty Street<br>Federal Reserve P.O. Station<br>New York, New York 10045<br>(212) 791-5000 |
| Buffalo Branch | (716) 849-5000 |

| | |
|---|---|
| Philadelphia | 100 North 6th Street<br>Philadelphia, Pennsylvania 19106<br>(215) 574-6000 |
| Richmond | 701 East Byrd Street<br>P.O. Box 27622<br>Richmond, Virginia 23261<br>(804) 643-1250 |
| Baltimore Branch | (301) 539-6552 |
| Charlotte Branch | (704) 373-0200 |
| St. Louis | 411 Locust Street<br>P.O. Box 442<br>St. Louis, Missouri 63166<br>(314) 444-8444 |
| Little Rock Branch | (501) 372-5451 |
| Louisville Branch | (502) 587-7351 |
| Memphis Branch | (901) 523-7171 |
| San Francisco | 101 Market Street<br>San Francisco, California 94105<br>(415) 974-2000 |
| Los Angeles Branch | (213) 683-8323 |
| Portland Branch | (503) 221-5900 |
| Salt Lake City Branch | (801) 355-3131 |
| Seattle Branch | (206) 442-1377 |

**Exhibit 13-1.  Low Risk: Treasury Notes**

**INVESTMENT PROFILE**

| INVESTMENT CHARACTERISTICS | Excellent | Good | Average | Poor | None |
|---|---|---|---|---|---|
| Liquidity | √ | | | | |
| Safety of Principal | √ | | | | |
| Price Stability | | √ | | | |
| Reinvestment Protection | | | LT | ST | |
| Growth of Capital | | | | | √ |
| Cash Income | | | √ | | |
| Growth of Income | | | | | √ |
| Inflation Hedge | | | √ | | |
| Tax Advantaged | | | | √* | |

**Liquidity**—the ability to quickly realize cash from the sale at fair market value

**Safety of Principal**—the principal is safe from bankruptcy or default

**Price Stability**—the market value of the asset does not change in value

**Reinvestment Protection**—protection against reinvesting cash flow at lower rates as interest rates decline

**Growth of Capital**—the original investment increases over time to create capital gains

**Cash Income**—the cash income relative to treasury bills returns

**Growth of Income**—the ability of the cash income stream to increase over time

**Inflation Hedge**—the ability of total return (cash income plus capital gains) to keep pace with inflation over time

**Tax Advantaged**—the ability to reduce or defer current federal income taxes

*Interest on Treasury Notes is exempt from state and local taxes.
LT = Long-term T-notes.
ST = Short-term T-notes.

# CHAPTER 14

# Short-Term Municipal Securities

## DESCRIPTION

This chapter considers all fixed-income financial instruments with maturities up to five years issued by governmental units other than the U.S. government. Investors need to be aware of these securities as alternatives to taxable investments. (Long-term municipal securities are discussed in Chapter 25, ''Long-Term Municipal Bonds.'') Examples of municipal governmental issuers include states, counties and parishes, cities, school districts, and special taxation districts.

Short-term municipal securities are debt obligations of state and local governments. These *munibonds* are issued in increments of $5,000 face value.

## STRENGTHS

Short-term municipal securities have the advantage of being totally free from federal government taxation. In addition, short-term municipal securities have very little price risk for investors. The market price for short term municipal securities fluctuates very little.

## WEAKNESS

The main weakness of short-term municipal securities is the relatively low current yield available on the securities. This is in part because the securities are exempt from federal taxation.

## Table 14-1. Taxable Equivalent Yield Table

| Federal Tax Bracket | Tax-Exempt Yield Equivalents | | | | | | | | | |
|---|---|---|---|---|---|---|---|---|---|---|
|  | 8.75% | 9.00% | 9.25% | 9.50% | 9.75% | 10.00% | 10.25% | 10.50% | 10.75% | 11.00% |
| 28% | 12.15 | 12.50 | 12.85 | 13.19 | 13.54 | 13.89 | 14.24 | 14.58 | 14.93 | 15.28 |
| 30 | 12.50 | 12.86 | 13.21 | 13.57 | 13.93 | 14.29 | 14.64 | 15.00 | 15.36 | 15.71 |
| 33 | 13.06 | 13.43 | 13.81 | 14.18 | 14.55 | 14.93 | 15.30 | 15.67 | 16.04 | 16.42 |
| 34 | 13.26 | 13.64 | 14.02 | 14.39 | 14.77 | 15.15 | 15.53 | 15.91 | 16.29 | 16.67 |
| 38 | 14.11 | 14.52 | 14.92 | 15.32 | 15.73 | 16.13 | 16.53 | 16.94 | 17.34 | 17.74 |
| 42 | 15.09 | 15.52 | 15.95 | 16.38 | 16.81 | 17.24 | 17.67 | 18.10 | 18.53 | 18.97 |
| 45 | 15.91 | 16.36 | 16.82 | 17.27 | 17.73 | 18.18 | 18.64 | 19.09 | 19.55 | 20.00 |
| 48 | 16.83 | 17.31 | 17.79 | 18.27 | 18.75 | 19.23 | 19.71 | 20.19 | 20.67 | 21.15 |
| 49 | 17.16 | 17.65 | 18.14 | 18.63 | 19.12 | 19.61 | 20.10 | 20.59 | 21.08 | 21.57 |
| 50 | 17.50 | 18.00 | 18.50 | 19.00 | 19.50 | 20.00 | 20.50 | 21.00 | 21.50 | 22.00 |

## UNIQUE FEATURES

A wide variety of maturities are available to investors who decide to use short-term municipal securities as an alternative to taxable fixed-income investments such as certificates of deposit or treasury bills.

Each individual issue of municipal bonds is totally free from federal government taxation; that is, the interest paid by the municipality to the investor is not taxed as income for the investor's federal form 1040. However, interest from municipal bonds is used to calculate the tax due on social security payments by retired citizens receiving social security.

## TAX CONSEQUENCES

By far the most important feature of short-term municipal securities is the tax free nature of the interest earned. Most states also exempt interest earned on municipal bonds issued within that state from state income taxes. For example, if an investor living in Belvidere, Illinois purchased bonds issued by the City of Chicago, the bonds would be "double tax exempt"—their yields would not be taxed by the State of Illinois or the federal government. If a resident of Madison, Wisconsin owned the same bond, the yields would be exempt from federal taxes, but they would be taxable by the State of Wisconsin. A tax equivalent yield chart is presented in Table 14-1.

To read this chart, investors must first know their *marginal tax bracket*, or the percentage of tax computed on the "last dollars earned"—

that amount over the minimum in the taxpayer's tax bracket. Of these last earned dollars, what percentage will go to pay federal government taxes? Investors can determine their marginal tax bracket for this year's tax schedules by looking up their taxable income range in the federal tax schedules, then looking across the row at the percent listed next to the tax owed. The percent is the marginal tax bracket—the percentage of tax paid on the amount earned over the lowest amount in the tax range.

For convenience, Table 14-1 includes an approximate listing of the marginal tax bracket under the column Federal Tax Bracket. Investors can simply scan down the left-hand column to the correct marginal bracket, then read across the top of the table to the current yield on tax exempt bonds (the boldface percentage listed under Tax Exempt Yield Equivalents). By tracing down the percent column that the tax free bond will pay and across the row of their marginal tax bracket until the row and column intersect, investors can see a second percentage at the point of intersection. This is the yield a *taxable* investment would have to pay to match the tax free bond's yield.

Take an example of an investor in the 42 percent marginal tax bracket. She is considering whether to buy a tax exempt bond that earns 9 percent. She reads down the 9.00% column of the table and across the 42 federal tax bracket row. The point of intersection is the cell containing 15.52. This means that this investor would need to earn 15.52 percent on a taxable investment (such as CDs, which pay interest that is taxed) just to match the 9 percent tax free yield.

An investor must achieve a substantially higher return from a taxable investment in order to match the aftertax return available on a tax free municipal bond.

## WHERE AND HOW TO BUY

Short- and medium-term municipal securities initially are issued by cities, towns, counties, states, and special taxation districts.

As time passes, bonds that originally were issued for maturities of as long as 25 years move closer to their scheduled maturity date. These bonds then become suitable for investors seeking tax free income without the interest rate risk associated with longer maturities of fixed-income instruments.

Once the short- and medium-term municipal securities are issued, investors must purchase these bonds from traditional securities firms or, in some cases, from a bank trust department.

Occasionally investors are able to purchase short-term municipal securities immediately upon issue by the particular municipality involved. These securities are offered at par value ($5,000 per bond) to investors. No commission is charged to investors purchasing new issues.

The municipality involved typically hires a securities firm to serve as underwriter of the bond issue. Each maturity will pay a stated rate of interest to the owner. All municipal bonds pay interest twice each year. The interest payment dates vary depending on the particular issue.

One special note is in order for investors seeking to buy municipal securities at the time they are underwritten. Short-term municipal securities are very difficult to purchase in small increments (less than $100,000) at the time they are first issued. Typically these bonds will be purchased as a complete block by a commercial bank for the bank portfolio. However, an investor should have little difficulty in purchasing these issues in smaller amounts once they are outstanding.

New issues of municipal bonds are sold to investors by making available all the pertinent information in a document called a *prospectus*. The prospectus contains a very detailed description of the bonds, the sources of revenue available to make the interest payments due to the investor and information about the particular uses for the money raised by the bond. As a practical matter, investors very rarely see a printed prospectus prior to requesting the bonds from the underwriter. The prospectus generally is available a few days after the order is given to the underwriter. An investor can always revoke an order after he or she receives and reviews the prospectus.

It is fortunate that an active secondary market exists for short-term municipal securities. Virtually all securities dealers regularly buy and sell these securities for clients. Each firm posts the bonds it has available every business day. Typically clients are welcome to drop by a broker's office and review the inventory of municipal bonds available.

Some investors rely on their brokers to review the list frequently to find selected issues of bonds that meet the particular credit quality, geographic location, and maturity requirements of the investor.

Most short-term municipal securities are purchased by investors with the assistance of a seasoned stockbroker. Often a particularly desirable offering may last only a few hours—or even less—in inventory of a brokerage firm. If investors have previously discussed the type of security they want with their broker, the broker may be able to do an excellent job of purchasing the choicest securities offered that meet the clients' requirements.

Mutual funds that purchase only tax-free municipal securities are also a way in which an investor can buy a diversified portfolio of municipals.

## HOW TO SELL

Investors should note that large issues of municipal securities are more liquid than very small issues of municipal securities. The spread between bid and offered prices posted by securities dealers is generally larger on small issues than on large issues of a municipal security. Investors should "shop their bonds" among several possible buyers. A good broker typically shops the bonds for his or her clients. An example is:

ISSUE: Austin Texas Mortgage Revenue Bonds Due 9-1-1993
Insured by Federal Savings and Loan Insurance Corporation
Rated AAA by Standard and Poor's
Interest rate 9.00%
$10,000 face amount
Interest payment dates January 1 and July 1

| Firm | Bid |
|---|---|
| XYZ Securities | $101 |
| ABC Investments | 99 |
| RTY Services | 102 |

Investors would deliver their bonds to RTY Services, because RTY is offering to pay $10,200 for the bonds. The low bid belongs to ABC Investments at $9,900.

All short-term municipal securities are traded with accrued interest. Using the previous example, if investors purchase the bond on March 1st, they will have to pay the seller of the bond two months worth of interest at the time the bond is traded. Of course, the new owners collect a full six-month interest payment on July 1st. In this example, a buyer of the Austin, Texas bond would pay $10,200 for the bond and another $150 for accrued interest or a total of $10,350.00.

## TRANSACTION COSTS

Short-term municipal securities are available as new issue bonds without sales charges. The issuing municipality pays the brokerage firm or bank a placement fee.

Short-term municipal securities can be purchased in the open market. The bonds will trade on a net basis. The brokerage firm will offer the bonds to investors at a "net" price that includes any fees for the brokerage firm. Investors should shop among several brokerage firms and banks to achieve the most favorable terms.

It is noteworthy that these securities are available in the form of *unit investment trusts*. Unit investment trusts are often more convenient for investors with less than $100,000 in a particular portfolio. Unit investment trusts offer professional selection and a diversified portfolio of bonds—all in convenient $1,000 size units.

## PORTFOLIO FIT

Short-term municipal securities provide tax free income for high tax-bracket investors who are concerned with stability of principal.

Typically, these investors are very concerned with safety and do not want the risks associated with longer maturity bonds.

Short-term municipal securities are an excellent alternative to certificates of deposit for high tax-bracket investors.

## SOURCES OF ADDITIONAL INFORMATION

All short-term municipal securities are rated by the credit rating agencies of Standard & Poor's Corporation and Moody's Credit Reporting Service. A basic outline of the credit rating system for municipal bonds appears in Table 14-2. Investors generally do not buy municipal bonds rated below A without personal knowledge of the particular circumstances surrounding a specific issue.

## COMMENTS

Short-term municipal securities offer a very acceptable alternative to investors in high federal income tax brackets. A well diversified portfolio of

**Table 14-2.  Standard & Poor's Rating Definitions for Corporate and
Municipal Bonds**

| Term | Definition |
|---|---|
| Debt rating | A current assessment of the creditworthiness of an obligor for a specific obligation. This assessment may take into consideration obligors such as guarantors, insurers, or lessees. The ratings are based, in varying degrees, on the following:<br>I. Likelihood of default-capacity and willingness of the obligor as to the timely payment of interest and repayment of principal in accordance with the terms of the obligation;<br>II. Nature of and provisions of the obligation;<br>III. Protection afforded by, and relative position of, the obligation in the event of bankruptcy, reorganization, or other arrangement under the laws of bankruptcy and other laws affecting creditors' rights. |
| AAA | Debt rated AAA has the highest rating assigned by Standard & Poor's. Capacity to pay interest and repay principal is extremely strong. |
| AA | Debt rated AA has a very strong capacity to pay interest and repay principal and differs from the higher rated issues only in small degree. |
| A | Debt rated A has a strong capacity to pay interest and repay principal, although it is somewhat more susceptible to the adverse effects of changes in circumstances and economic conditions than debt in higher rated categories. |
| BBB | Debt rated BBB is regarded as having an adequate capacity to pay interest and repay principal. Whereas it normally exhibits adequate protection parameters, adverse economic conditions or changing circumstances are more likely to lead to a weakened capacity to pay interest and repay principal for debt in this category than in higher rated categories. |
| BB, B, CCC, CC | Debt rated BB, B, CCC, and CC is regarded, on balance, as predominantly speculative with respect to capacity to pay interest and repay principal in accordance with the terms of the obligation. BB indicates the lowest degree of speculation and CC the highest degree of speculation. While such debt will likely have some quality and protective characteristics, these are outweighed by large uncertainties or major risk exposures to adverse conditions. |
| C | The rating C is reserved for income bonds on which no interest is being paid. |
| D | Debt rated D is in default, and payment of interest and/or repayment of principal is in arrears. |

**Table 14-2.   (Continued)**

| Term | Definition |
|---|---|
| Plus(+) or Minus(−) | The ratings from "AA" to "B" may be modified by the addition of a plus or minus sign to show relative standing within the major rating categories. |
| L | The letter L indicates that the rating pertains to the principal amount of those bonds where the underlying deposit collateral is fully insured by the Federal Savings & Loan Insurance Corp. or the Federal Deposit Insurance Corp. |
| Bond Investment Quality Standards | Under present commercial bank regulation issued by the Comptroller of the Currency, bonds rated in the top four categories (AAA, AA, A, BBB, commonly known as "Investment Grade" ratings) are generally regarded as eligible for bank investment. In addition, the Legal Investment Laws of various states may impose certain rating or other standards for obligations eligible for investment by savings banks, trust companies, insurance companies and fiduciaries generally. |

*Source: Standard & Poor's Bond Guide.* Reprinted with permission.

these securities can provide steady, balanced income free from federal taxation without the interest rate risk of long-term debt instruments, whose yields suffer if interest rates rise.

In recent years special insurance from a consortium of large insurance companies has been added to these securities. The insurance companies guarantee that all interest and principal will be paid exactly when due to the investor. This insurance has made municipal bonds palatable to even the most risk-averse investors.

Why more investors do not take advantage of municipal securities, especially the insured variety, is puzzling. Many investors seeking safety of principal, steady income, and very little interest rate risk should look at short-term municipal securities.

It is important to note that this investment is commonly available in the form of unit investment trusts. Investors should read Chapter 29, "Unit Investment Trusts," for more details. Unit investment trusts make investments in short-term tax free bonds especially convenient to purchase by investors with under $100,000.

**Exhibit 14-1. Low Risk: Short-Term Municipal Securities**

**INVESTMENT PROFILE**

| INVESTMENT CHARACTERISTICS | Excellent | Good | Average | Poor | None |
|---|---|---|---|---|---|
| Liquidity | | √ | | | |
| Safety of Principal | | * | | | |
| Price Stability | √ | | | | |
| Reinvestment Protection | | | | √ | |
| Growth of Capital | | | | | √ |
| Cash Income | | | √ | | |
| Growth of Income | | | | | √ |
| Inflation Hedge | | | | √ | |
| Tax Advantaged | √ | | | | |

**Liquidity**—the ability to quickly realize cash from the sale at fair market value

**Safety of Principal**—the principal is safe from bankruptcy or default

**Price Stability**—the market value of the asset does not change in value

**Reinvestment Protection**—protection against reinvesting cash flow at lower rates as interest rates decline

**Growth of Capital**—the original investment increases over time to create capital gains

**Cash Income**—the cash income relative to treasury bills returns

**Growth of Income**—the ability of the cash income stream to increase over time

**Inflation Hedge**—the ability of total return (cash income plus capital gains) to keep pace with inflation over time

**Tax Advantaged**—the ability to reduce or defer current federal income taxes

*Safety of principal depends on the rating the bond receives as well as whether the bonds are insured or not.

# CHAPTER 15

# Whole Life Insurance

## DESCRIPTION

*Whole (permanent) life insurance* is a combination of a death benefit plus the accumulation of cash value over the life of the policy. Whole life insurance provides monetary protection for an investor's beneficiary. In the event that the insured (investor) does not die prematurely, whole life insurance offers a cash value accumulation for future years. Investors who purchase a *term* life insurance policy, on the other hand, receive only death benefits without the cash value feature of whole life insurance.

## STRENGTHS

Whole life insurance provides a large source of funds in the event of the investor's untimely demise. Whole life insurance avoids the costs and delays of probate (the legal settlement of an estate) often associated with other assets.

The proceeds of a life insurance policy are not taxable as income to the investor in the event of death. However, the proceeds are included in the value of the estate for estate tax purposes.

## WEAKNESS

Whole life insurance has historically been characterized by high costs and low investment rates of return. High front-end commission structures have prevented whole life insurance from offering competitive rates of return with alternative investments.


## UNIQUE FEATURES

Most unique features of whole life insurance center on *protection,* not *investment.* Continued insurance premiums can be paid by the insurance company in case the insured becomes disabled. Additional dependent coverage is available on some policies and guaranteed future insurability is available to the insured with many policies.

In addition, many policies offer the owner the right to borrow against the cash value of the policy at below-market interest rates.


## TAX CONSEQUENCES

The best news about whole life insurance involves several special tax treatments accorded life insurance contracts. First, and possibly most important, all accumulations of cash value in a life insurance contract grow on a tax deferred basis. For example, if cash value increases from $1,000 to $1,100 during a calendar year, none of the $100 increase is subject to federal income taxes.

Proceeds paid out by the insurance company as death benefits are not taxable as income to the insured or to the beneficiary. The amount of the benefits is included in calculating estate taxes. The proceeds of the policy are paid directly to the named beneficiary of the policy and escape the costs of probate as well.


## WHERE AND HOW TO BUY

Virtually hundreds of insurance companies offer whole life insurance policies in the United States and other countries. These firms are heavily advertised in the telephone directory, newspaper, television, radio, and other media. Prospective whole life insurance buyers should use caution and shop the market carefully before purchasing policies. Many times the most aggressively marketed products are not the best value.

All insurance companies are represented by agents. These agents may have an office in a public building, or they may work out of their home.

Typically, the agent assists the individual by completing the application forms for life insurance. In some cases a physical examination may be required. Individuals can elect to have their insurance premiums deducted automatically from their checking accounts by the insurance company. This service is called an *automatic debit*. Other methods of premium payment include annual and semiannual invoices from the insurance company.

## HOW TO SELL

When they reach retirement age, many owners of whole life insurance elect to convert the accumulated cash value of their insurance policy into an annuity contract. These investments are explained in Chapter 17, "Annuity Contracts." One other very popular method of partial liquidation of a whole life insurance policy is borrowing against the cash value of the policy. Over the course of several years, a policy owner builds up hundreds or even thousands of dollars worth of cash value. This money can be borrowed from the insurance company at an interest rate listed in the terms of the policy. Because interest rates have risen dramatically in recent years, many whole life insurance investors find it advantageous to borrow the cash value of their policy from the insurance company and invest the cash in alternative investments. Many whole life insurance policies issued in the 1950s, 1960s, and early 1970s permit owners to borrow against their cash value for as little as 5 or 6 percent interest.

## TRANSACTION COSTS

Whole life insurance transaction costs are not specifically identified by the insurance company. These costs are contained within the premium paid by the purchaser of the policy. A purchaser of whole life insurance does not receive any itemized statement of sales commissions, insurance company front-end charges, or other policy costs. These costs vary significantly from one company to another. It is not uncommon to have as much as 65 percent or more of the first year's premium payment paid out to the agent as sales commission. Additional "trailer commissions" are paid each year to the selling agent. These commissions are much more modest, ranging from 2 to 5 percent of the premium paid. It should be obvious that money invested in whole life insurance suffers a serious disadvantage because of the high transaction costs of the product.

## PORTFOLIO FIT

Whole life insurance achieves very few specific investment goals. Perhaps the best application of whole life insurance as an investment is for those investors who lack the discipline to invest regularly. Whole life insurance can and does act as a "forced savings account." Generally speaking, an investor would be better off purchasing variable life insurance or term insurance policies and investing the balance of the funds in a well-managed mutual fund.

## SOURCES OF ADDITIONAL INFORMATION

All insurance companies that offer whole life insurance make brochures available to prospective customers. Publications such as *Moody's Bank and Finance Manual* list hundreds of the largest U.S. life insurance companies.

A very important independent source of information about insurance companies is *Best's Insurance Reports*. A. M. Best company is an independent analyst of the insurance industry. A. M. Best has provided these independent ratings since 1899. The best rating system evaluates insurance companies based on the following vital areas: competent underwriting, control of expenses, adequate reserves, and sound investments. Best issues six quality ratings. The A+ and A ratings are considered excellent. The middle ratings are B+ (very good), B (good), and C+ (fairly good). The C (fair) rating is the lowest. Investors definitely should request a copy of the Best's rating report on a company before buying a policy from that company. Typically, investors should only consider insurance companies rated A+ or A by this independent rating service.

## COMMENTS

Whole life insurance should not be considered an investment. Rather, whole life insurance is simply a product that does not measure up against other investments. Thus, investors may wish to consider annuities, variable annuities, or mutual funds in conjunction with term life insurance protection as an alternative to whole life insurance.

**Exhibit 15-1.   Low Risk: Whole Life Insurance**

**INVESTMENT PROFILE**

| INVESTMENT CHARACTERISTICS | Excellent | Good | Average | Poor | None |
|---|---|---|---|---|---|
| Liquidity | | | | ✓ | |
| Safety of Principal | ✓ | | | | |
| Price Stability | | | | | N.A. |
| Reinvestment Protection | | | | | N.A. |
| Growth of Capital | | | | ✓ | |
| Cash Income | | | | ✓ | |
| Growth of Income | | | ✓ | | |
| Inflation Hedge | | | | ✓ | |
| Tax Advantaged | | | ✓ | | |

**Liquidity**—the ability to quickly realize cash from the sale at fair market value

**Safety of Principal**—the principal is safe from bankruptcy or default

**Price Stability**—the market value of the asset does not change in value

**Reinvestment Protection**—protection against reinvesting cash flow at lower rates as interest rates decline

**Growth of Capital**—the original investment increases over time to create capital gains

**Cash Income**—the cash income relative to treasury bills returns

**Growth of Income**—the ability of the cash income stream to increase over time

**Inflation Hedge**—the ability of total return (cash income plus capital gains) to keep pace with inflation over time

**Tax Advantaged**—the ability to reduce or defer current federal income taxes

# CHAPTER 16

# Universal (Variable) Life Insurance

## DESCRIPTION

*Universal (variable) life insurance* is a life insurance product with features similar to a combination of term insurance and an annuity. *Term insurance* offers death benefits in the event of the demise of the insured and nothing else. It is the least costly form of insurance protection. An *annuity* offers a tax deferred investment that pays market rates of interest.

## STRENGTHS

A policy holder generally can restructure his or her policy to increase or reduce the level of insurance protection provided. The investor is also able to restructure the premium payment provisions of the policy to allow for better cash flow management within the family budget. Universal life insurance offers a "money market" rate of return on accumulated cash values. While this is generally an improvement over whole life insurance, it is only marginally competitive with other low-risk investments over the long term.

## WEAKNESSES

Universal life insurance is a permanent life insurance type product. Because it is a permanent life product, it carries the disadvantages of high front-end costs. The returns expected in a universal life insurance policy

**113**

should be no higher than a typical money market fund or treasury bill investment.

## UNIQUE FEATURES

Universal life insurance combines all the traditional insurance benefits available in whole life insurance policies with a money market fund return on funds accumulated in the cash value portion of the policy. Whole life insurance does not offer this floating rate of return on cash value.

The borrowing provisions of a variable life policy are not as favorable as the below-market interest rates offered on loans to owners of whole life insurance policies. Interest rates on variable life insurance policies are generally near market interest rates.

## TAX CONSEQUENCES

The best news about universal life insurance involves several special tax treatments accorded life insurance contracts. First, and possibly most important, all accumulations of cash value in a life insurance contract grow on a tax deferred basis. For example, if cash value increases from $1,000 to $1,100 during a calendar year, none of the $100 increase is subject to federal income taxes. If a policy owner borrows against this cash value, he or she has not created a taxable exchange. All $1,100 could be borrowed from the insurance company, and none of the money would need to be reported on that year's federal income tax return.

Proceeds paid out by the insurance company as death benefits are not taxable as income to the insured or to the beneficiary. The benefit amount *is* included in calculating estate taxes. The proceeds of the policy are paid directly to the named beneficiary of the policy and escape the costs of probate. Over a long period of time, universal life insurance provides a reasonable return on an investor's money. The fact that the cash value in an insurance policy grows on a tax deferred basis offsets the fact that the front-end charges are high on insurance policies. This compounding of the federal government's tax dollars adds significantly to the return achieved with these policies.

## WHERE AND HOW TO BUY

Virtually hundreds of insurance companies offer universal life insurance policies in the United States and other countries. These firms are heavily advertised in the telephone directory, newspaper, television, radio, and other media. Any prospective universal life insurance buyer should compare several companies' plans carefully. Often the most heavily marketed products are not the best value.

Agents represent insurance companies to clients; they may have offices in public buildings or they may work from their home. Some companies or policies require a physical examination prior to accepting an application. Individuals often have their insurance premiums deducted automatically from their checking accounts by the insurance company through an *automatic debit*. Other investors prefer to pay premiums annually or semiannually when invoiced by the insurance company.

## HOW TO SELL

When they attain retirement age, many people with universal life insurance elect to convert the accumulated cash value of their insurance policy into an annuity contract. These investments are explained in Chapter 17, ''Annuity Contracts.'' One other very popular means to partially liquidate a universal life insurance policy is to borrow against the cash value of the policy. Over the course of several years policies accrue hundreds or thousands of dollars worth of cash value. This money can be borrowed from the insurance company at an interest rate listed in the policy.

## TRANSACTION COSTS

Universal life insurance transaction costs are not specifically identified by the insurance company. These costs are contained within the premium paid by the purchaser. A purchaser of universal life insurance does not receive any itemized statement of sales commissions, insurance company front-end charges, or other policy costs. These costs vary significantly from one company to another. It is not uncommon for more than 45 percent of the first year's premium payment to paid out as sales commissions to the agent. Additional *trailer commissions* are paid each year to the selling agent. These commissions are much more modest, ranging from 2 to 5 percent of the premium paid. Obviously, money invested in universal life insurance suffers a serious disadvantage because of its high transaction costs.

## PORTFOLIO FIT

The uses of universal life insurance within a traditional investment portfolio are limited. If investors need the discipline of paying life insurance premiums regularly, they should select universal life insurance, because it generally provides better investment results than a traditional whole life contract. This is especially true during periods of high inflation.

## SOURCES OF ADDITIONAL INFORMATION

All insurance companies that offer universal life insurance prepare brochures for prospective customers. A very important independent source of information about insurance companies is *Best's Insurance Reports*. A. M. Best Company is an independent analyst of the insurance industry. A. M. Best has provided these independent ratings since 1899. The best rating system evaluates insurance companies based on the following vital areas: competent underwriting, control of expenses, adequate reserves, and sound investments. Best's evaluates insurance companies against a scale of six quality ratings. A+ and A are considered excellent. The average ratings are B+ (very good), B (good), and C+ (fairly good). C (fair) is the lowest rating. Investors should first request a copy of the Best's rating report on a company before buying a policy from that insurance firm. Typically, investors should only consider insurance companies rated A+ or A by this independent rating service.

## COMMENTS

Universal life insurance is not a pure investment. Life insurance fulfills a very important role in financial planning for all individuals. Universal life insurance is simply a product that provides more insurance protection than investment rewards. It is a simple fact that it is more profitable for an insurance company to sell a universal life insurance product (or a whole life insurance product) than term insurance and an annuity contract.

During the late 1970s and early 1980s billions of dollars were borrowed by owners of insurance policies against their cash value. Often an investor could double the rate of return on his investment by placing their accumulated cash values in a simple bank certificate of deposit. This large outflow of funds literally forced the insurance industry to improve the products it offers to the investing public.

Universal life insurance is the new generation product for the 1980s. It is likely that further changes will occur in the insurance industry. Many insurance companies have adopted the strategy of purchasing other investment companies to retain the share of the financial services market they enjoyed in the 1950s and 1960s. The authors believe one of the best "new" insurance products available is the variable annuity. Variable annuities are discussed in Chapter 22.

**Exhibit 16-1.   Low Risk: Universal (Variable) Life Insurance**

**INVESTMENT PROFILE**

| INVESTMENT CHARACTERISTICS | Excellent | Good | Average | Poor | None |
|---|---|---|---|---|---|
| Liquidity | | ✓ | | | |
| Safety of Principal | ✓ | | | | |
| Price Stability | | | | | N.A. |
| Reinvestment Protection | | | ✓ | | |
| Growth of Capital | | ✓ | | | |
| Cash Income | | | ✓ | | |
| Growth of Income | | | | | ✓ |
| Inflation Hedge | | | ✓ | | |
| Tax Advantaged | | ✓ | | | |

**Liquidity**—the ability to quickly realize cash from the sale at fair market value

**Safety of Principal**—the principal is safe from bankruptcy or default

**Price Stability**—the market value of the asset does not change in value

**Reinvestment Protection**—protection against reinvesting cash flow at lower rates as interest rates decline

**Growth of Capital**—the original investment increases over time to create capital gains

**Cash Income**—the cash income relative to treasury bills returns

**Growth of Income**—the ability of the cash income stream to increase over time

**Inflation Hedge**—the ability of total return (cash income plus capital gains) to keep pace with inflation over time

**Tax Advantaged**—the ability to reduce or defer current federal income taxes

# CHAPTER 17

# Annuity Contracts

## DESCRIPTION

An *annuity contract* (or a *single-premium deferred annuity*) is a contract between an investor and a life insurance company. These contracts are similar to a certificate of deposit with a financial institution. The insurance company promises to pay a minimum rate of interest to the investor for a specific period of time. All interest that is credited to the investor's account is totally tax deferred for as long as the contract is owned by the investor. Tax deferral can significantly increase an investor's total dollar return on investment.

## STRENGTHS

Annuity contracts are guaranteed by the issuing insurance company. The assets of the insurance company back each dollar the investor places in the contract. Investors have more assets securing the annuity contract than they have invested in the contract. Annuity contract earnings are totally deferred from federal income taxes until the funds are withdrawn from the contract. A special strength of annuity contracts is the special death benefit provision. The annuity contract has no pure life insurance attached to the contract; however, in the event of the death of the annuitant all proceeds from the contract are paid directly to the named beneficiary. All of these proceeds are free from probate (the legal proceedings that are necessary to settle an estate) and the costs associated with probate. Annuity contracts are offered to investors without any sales charges, commissions, or front-end fees.

## WEAKNESS

Most annuity contracts have an early withdrawal penalty. This penalty is similar to the early withdrawal penalties attached by financial institutions to certificates of deposit. The insurance company must have some assurance that the investor will use the annuity contract for a minimum period of time (usually four to six years). Because of this assurance, the insurance company is able to offer a very competitive rate on funds invested in the annuity contract. Typically the withdrawal penalty is approximately 5 percent of the amount invested. This penalty is totally eliminated at the end of the stated period of time. The withdrawal provisions are generally not a major consideration for investors if they are using the annuity contract for the long-term portfolio requirements it is designed to meet.

## UNIQUE FEATURES

By far the most attractive feature of the annuity contract is the deferral of income from federal taxation. Investors should note that a tax *deduction on the investment* is not created by an investment in an annuity as it is in an individual retirement account. Only the tax *deferral on the earnings* is the same as for an IRA.

Annuity contracts provide a degree of liquidity for investors who may need to use a portion of their investment from time to time. Almost all annuity contracts provide for "partial withdrawals" on an annual basis. These withdrawals typically are approximately 10 percent of the contract value. For example, an investor has a $100,000 annuity contract that earns 10 percent interest annually. At the end of one year the investor may need to withdraw some money for personal reasons. The investor normally will be able to withdraw about $11,000 without penalties of any kind from the insurance company (10 percent of the policy total value of $110,000).

| | |
|---|---|
| Amount Invested | $100,000 |
| Year One Interest | 10,000 |
| Total Contract Value | $110,000 |
| 10% partial withdrawal privilege | $ 11,000 |

This withdrawal will be treated as taxable interest income to the investor to the extent that cash received is earned income. Any return of principal is not taxable to the investor.

Another aspect that is often overlooked by investors (and investment advisers) is the elimination of the interest rate risk posed by other fixed-income investments. The insurance company assumes the interest rate risk in an annuity contract, since it guarantees the investor's principal at all times.

All insurance companies are rated for financial security by Best's Insurance Ratings Company, an independent rating company that specializes in examining the current financial situation of all insurance companies. Furthermore, each insurance company must pass a rigorous examination by the state insurance department of each state in which it conducts business. The state insurance department must preapprove all annuity contracts to be offered by the insurance company in a particular state.

## TAX CONSEQUENCES

As has been previously discussed, annuity contracts earn interest that is deferred from federal income taxes until the contract is totally or partially liquidated. Tax deferral is a powerful investment tool that makes more sense to investors as their the tax brackets rise.

If a partial distribution is requested, the proceeds are taxable based on the last-earned, first-taxed principle.

| | | |
|---|---|---|
| Investment | $100,000 | |
| Interest earned | 21,000 | |
| Total contract value | 121,000 | |
| Amount withdrawn | | $25,000 |
| Taxable amount | | 21,000 |
| Nontaxable return of capital | | 4,000 |

In this example, an investor purchases a $100,000 annuity contract. The investor lets his investment grow to $121,000. He then withdraws $25,000.00. For federal income tax purposes, he has taxable income of $21,000 and a return of capital of $4,000. The most important benefit in a tax deferred annuity contract is the fact that money normally paid to the federal government in the form of taxes on interest income stays in the contract and earns more interest each year. Exhibit Table 17-1 shows how important tax deferral can become.

It becomes obvious that for accumulation oriented investors seeking safety of principal, a tax deferred annuity contract is a very impressive investment.

**Exhibit 17-1.   Difference in Funds Accrued between Taxable and Tax Deferred, Compounding Yields**

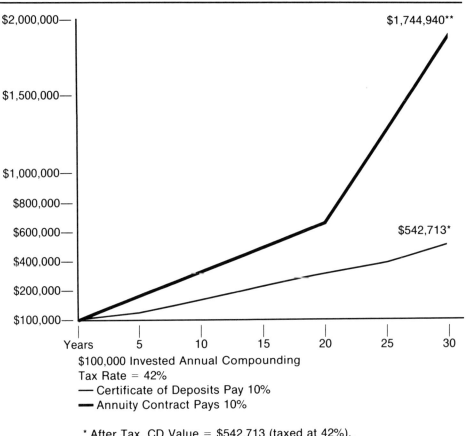

\* After Tax, CD Value = $542,713 (taxed at 42%).
\*\* After Tax, Annuity Value = $1,054,065 (taxed at 42%).

One other important aspect of the tax code that applies to annuity contracts is the tax free exchange privilege. Section 1035 of the Internal Revenue Code provides for tax free exchanges of monies from one annuity contract to another. Suppose an investor purchases an annuity contract in 1986 at a rate of 10 percent. Five years later in 1991 interest rates move up to 15 percent. The investor can move his money into a new annuity contract that pays substantially higher interest rates without penalty from the Internal Revenue Service. (For an even better method, see the appendix to this chapter, which discusses indexed annuity products.)

## WHERE AND HOW TO BUY

Many major insurance companies offer annuity contracts. Often these contracts are more actively marketed by securities dealers than by actual insurance agents. Rates and terms of the contracts vary slightly from one company to another, but the structure, tax and death benefit advantages, and income provisions remain essentially the same.

Annuity contracts can be purchased in any dollar amount over a stated minimum, usually $5,000. An application form is required, which includes some simple personal and health information. Rarely is any physical examination required on investments of less than $100,000. Within three to four weeks of submitting the completed application, the investor receives the annuity contract from the insurance company.

## HOW TO SELL

Liquidation of an annuity contract may take several forms. An investor can, at any time, request a complete lump sum distribution of the contract. Typically the insurance company will comply with this type of request within five business days. Partial withdrawals may be made several times during the life of the contract. Again, the investor typically initiates this request in writing to the insurance company. Some companies may accept telephone liquidation requests.

Another very popular form of liquidation is *annuitization* of the contract. In this case, the investor elects to take the proceeds of the contract in monthly payments over a period of years.

If the proceeds of the contract are intended to provide retirement income, this can be a very beneficial option for investors. The investors instruct the insurance company to provide a monthly income for the rest of their lives or a particular period of time, or both.

There are many options available to investors if they elect to annuitize. Perhaps the most important thing to remember is that the investors can change the terms of liquidation at any time. The decision made at the time the annuity contract is purchased is in no way binding on investors. This added flexibility can be important for investors if their personal situations change unexpectedly.

In the event of death, the annuity contract is self-liquidating. The named beneficiary or beneficiaries receive the proceeds of the contract without any insurance company penalties or probate costs. As in the case of annuitization options, the beneficiary of the policy can be changed at any time.

A qualified professional will be able to discuss the proper selection of liquidation terms with the investor as the need arises. It should be mentioned that not all annuitization rates are the same. Investors should shop for annuitization rates just as they shop for investment (or accumulation) rates when they purchase the annuity contract.

A higher annuitization rate will not be expressed as a percentage rate; rather, the insurance companies will quote a monthly payment guaranteed for a certain period of time. All else being equal, the company quoting the highest monthly payment should be selected.

## TRANSACTION COSTS

Annuity contracts are generally available with no transaction costs. There are no sales charges, commissions, or management fees associated with an annuity contract. Investor should shop around for annuity contract rates. Rates offered by various insurance companies are competitive. Rate differences of more than .5 percent are rare for equal accumulation periods. An example is:

Company A     10% guaranteed for one year
Company B     10.25% guaranteed for one year
Company C      9.75% guaranteed for one year

Initially, the investor would select company B. Most policies provide for a bailout clause that enables the investor to withdraw all money if the interest rate for future years drops more than 1 percent below the original rate.

## PORTFOLIO FIT

Investors seeking to accumulate funds over the long term for a definite future purpose should consider an annuity contract. Typical applications include retirement funding, college education for children and grandchildren, and special purchases for recreational endeavors. Interest rates are comparable or even higher than those paid by traditional financial institutions, and all interest earned is tax deferred. These contracts can be used to provide a lifetime of income if desired by the investor.

Investors generally buy annuity contracts because they believe that at the time they want to withdraw money from the contract they will be in a lower tax bracket. The money accumulates tax deferred while they are employed and while they are in a substantially higher tax bracket than they expect to be after they retire.

## SOURCES OF ADDITIONAL INFORMATION

Brochures are available from virtually every securities dealer that markets annuity contracts. Most insurance agents also have information on annuity contracts. These contracts are not highly advertised to the public. It may require a bit of leg work on the part of investors to find an investment executive with experience in annuity contracts, but the extra effort could be most rewarding.

## COMMENTS

Annuity contracts are possibly the most overlooked of all safe money investments. The insurance industry has established a very successful track record for investors in annuity contracts. These contracts are very often "undersold" by both insurance agents and securities dealers for four reasons. First, a special license is required in most states to sell annuity contracts. Second, and by far more important, annuity contracts pay very modest placement fees (generally only 4 percent of the amount invested) to the salespeople that explain them to investors. Third, there is little (if any) advertising to attract investor attention by the insurance companies supplying the product. Fourth, a slightly complicated product structure requires substantial time to be spent explaining annuity contracts to investors. All of these factors have kept annuity contracts out of view by the investment public.

A great deal of money invested in other forms of long-term, safe investments would be better invested in tax deferred annuity contracts.

The appendix to this chapter discusses a relatively new and very special type of annuity contract that may significantly alter the product mix in many investment portfolios in the future.

The indexed annuity contract (discussed fully in the appendix) is clearly an investment that is designed for inflationary times. Inflation has ravaged fixed-income investments of the past 20 years. Indexed annuity contracts eliminate the old interest rate guessing game so many investors have had to play.

Indexed annuity investors do not worry about how long they should "tie up" their funds. The insurance company will pay a competitive rate of return and eliminate interest rate risk at the same time. Why should investors pay current federal income taxes, assume interest rate risk on their principal, generate commissions by changing maturities in a bond portfolio, and constantly worry about interest rate changes when an indexed annuity contract is available at no cost? The indexed annuity contract may not be a perfect investment, but it does come close for accumulation oriented investors.

## APPENDIX

No investment is entirely inflation proof; however, indexed annuity contracts may come the closest of all of the recently marketed investments. Indexed annuity contracts have all the same basic characteristics of regular annuity contracts.

The unique feature of indexed annuity contracts is the adjustable interest rate feature. In addition to receiving a guaranteed base rate of interest, investors can earn substantially above the base rate in the event that interest rates climb in future years. For example, an investor owns an indexed annuity contract guaranteed to pay 10 percent interest for 3 years. In addition to the 10 percent base rate, an investor may earn more if the selected index moves above 10 percent. This index is normally a well-known, published interest rate such as the 90-day Treasury bill rates or a long-term bond index rate. Every quarter (sometimes every year) the index is checked. If the index rate is higher than the base rate, the investor receives the index rate for the next 90 days. If the base rate is higher, the base rate is credited to the annuity contract. Exhibit 17-2 illustrates this concept.

Note that the dashes indicate the rate actually paid at any point in time. The actual rate can be higher than 10 percent when Treasury bill rates are above 10 percent but never lower than 10 percent when Treasury bill rates are below 10 percent. Thus, the rate starts at 10 percent, then rises above 10 percent in years 2 and 3. Even though rates decline to 8

## Exhibit 17-2.  Indexed Annuity Contract Payments

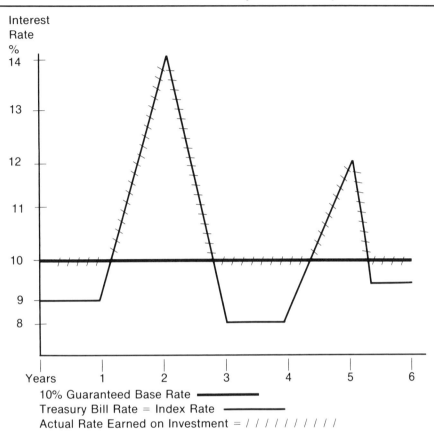

10% Guaranteed Base Rate ━━━━━━
Treasury Bill Rate = Index Rate ━━━━━
Actual Rate Earned on Investment = / / / / / / / / / /

percent in year 4, the guaranteed rate of 10 percent is paid. It briefly goes up to 12 percent, in year 5, but at the end of year six (the last year), it is down to 10 percent.

As shown in Exhibit 17-2, the investor is protected by the index during periods of high inflation. Investors have the assurance of earning a competitive rate of interest at all times. Typically investors will receive the guaranteed base rate for five or six years. At that time the investors will be offered a new base rate by the insurance company. If investors believe they can find better terms elsewhere, they simply move their funds to a different investment. All the federal income tax provisions apply to indexed annuity contracts just as they do to regular annuity contracts, including the tax free exchange privilege.

**Exhibit 17-3.  Low Risk: Annuity Contracts (AC)**

**INVESTMENT PROFILE**

| INVESTMENT CHARACTERISTICS | Excellent | Good | Average | Poor | None |
|---|---|---|---|---|---|
| Liquidity | | | | √ | |
| Safety of Principal | | √ | | | |
| Price Stability | | | | | N.A. |
| Reinvestment Protection | | √ | | | |
| Growth of Capital | | √ | | | |
| Cash Income | | √ | | | |
| Growth of Income | | | | √ | |
| Inflation Hedge | | | | √ | |
| Tax Advantaged | | √ | | | |

**Liquidity**—the ability to quickly realize cash from the sale at fair market value

**Safety of Principal**—the principal is safe from bankruptcy or default

**Price Stability**—the market value of the asset does not change in value

**Reinvestment Protection**—protection against reinvesting cash flow at lower rates as interest rates decline

**Growth of Capital**—the original investment increases over time to create capital gains

**Cash Income**—the cash income relative to treasury bills returns

**Growth of Income**—the ability of the cash income stream to increase over time

**Inflation Hedge**—the ability of total return (cash income plus capital gains) to keep pace with inflation over time

**Tax Advantaged**—the ability to reduce or defer current federal income taxes

### Exhibit 17-4.   Low Risk: Indexed Annuity Option
### INVESTMENT PROFILE

| INVESTMENT CHARACTERISTICS | Excellent | Good | Average | Poor | None |
|---|---|---|---|---|---|
| Liquidity | | | | √ | |
| Safety of Principal | | √ | | | |
| Price Stability | | | | | N.A. |
| Reinvestment Protection | | | | √ | |
| Growth of Capital | | √ | | | |
| Cash Income | | √ | | | |
| Growth of Income | | √ | | | |
| Inflation Hedge | | √ | | | |
| Tax Advantaged | | √ | | | |

**Liquidity**—the ability to quickly realize cash from the sale at fair market value

**Safety of Principal**—the principal is safe from bankruptcy or default

**Price Stability**—the market value of the asset does not change in value

**Reinvestment Protection**—protection against reinvesting cash flow at lower rates as interest rates decline

**Growth of Capital**—the original investment increases over time to create capital gains

**Cash Income**—the cash income relative to treasury bills returns

**Growth of Income**—the ability of the cash income stream to increase over time

**Inflation Hedge**—the ability of total return (cash income plus capital gains) to keep pace with inflation over time

**Tax Advantaged**—the ability to reduce or defer current federal income taxes

# PART 4

# Moderate-Risk Investments

# CHAPTER 18

# Blue Chip Stocks

## DESCRIPTION

*Blue chip stocks* represent globally recognized corporations. There are over 100 companies that qualify as blue chip stocks. However, companies in the Dow Jones Industrial average are often associated with the title "blue chips."

The *Dow Jones Industrial Average* is a market index of 30 industrial companies that represent the major industries, such as oil, steel, autos, chemicals, paper, and retail.

As companies merge or are acquired, they are deleted from the index, and new companies are added. For example, in November 1985, Phillip Morris Inc. and McDonald's Corporation replaced General Foods and American Brands. General Foods was acquired by Phillip Morris. Since Phillip Morris is a large tobacco company, American Brands (also a tobacco company) was deleted to keep from overweighting the index with the tobacco industry.

Table 18-1 is a listing of the Dow Jones Industrial stocks that details the absolute percentage increases and annual compounded rates of return for all 30 stocks from December 31, 1974 to December 31, 1984. While table 18-1 does not include the sizable stock market gains (30 percent) during 1985 and early 1986, it does point out that selecting the "right" stocks is very important.

The Consumer Price Index has had a compounded annual rate of return of 7.73 percent over this same time period. Some of these stocks are no longer considered "blue chip" because of industry problems and market share erosion due to competitive factors.

**Table 18-1. Annual Percentage Increases and Annual Compounded Rates of Return for Dow Jones Industrial Stocks**

| | Percentage Changes in the Dow Jones Industrial Stocks 12/31/74–12/31/84 | Annual Compounded Rate of Return |
|---|---|---|
| 1. Westinghouse Electric | +422.5% | 17.98% |
| 2. United Technologies | +342.9 | 16.05 |
| 3. American Brands | +324.8 | 15.56 |
| 4. Woolworth, F.W. | +294.7 | 14.72 |
| 5. General Electric | +239.3 | 12.99 |
| 6. General Foods | +212.6 | 12.07 |
| 7. IBM | +193.2 | 11.36 |
| 8. American Express | +192.6 | 11.33 |
| 9. Chevron Corporation | +180.9 | 10.88 |
| 10. Exxon Corporation | +178.5 | 10.79 |
| 11. General Motors | +161.8 | 10.10 |
| 12. Aluminum Company of America | +147.7 | 9.49 |
| 13. Owens-Illinois | +138.5 | 9.08 |
| Consumer Price Index | +110.6 | 7.73 |
| 14. Goodyear Tire & Rubber | +101.9 | 7.28 |
| 15. Allied Corporation | + 82.4 | 6.19 |
| 16. American Can | + 74.1 | 5.70 |
| 17. Minnesota Mining & Mfg | + 70.5 | 5.48 |
| 18. AT&T | + 65.5 | 5.17 |
| 19. Texaco Inc. | + 63.5 | 5.04 |
| 20. duPont de Nemours | + 61.0 | 4.88 |
| 21. International Paper | + 50.7 | 4.19 |
| 22. Merck & Co. | + 41.6 | 3.54 |
| 23. Procter & Gamble | + 39.9 | 3.41 |
| 24. Sears, Roebuck & Co. | + 31.6 | 2.78 |
| 25. Eastman Kodak | + 14.3 | 1.35 |
| 26. United States Steel | + 3.1 | .3 |
| 27. Union Carbide | − 11.2 | −1.18 |
| 28. Bethlehem Steel | − 29.7 | −3.46 |
| 29. Inco Limited | − 42.4 | −5.37 |
| 30. International Harvester | − 58.9 | −8.51 |
| Average Annual 10-Year Return | | 6.64% |
| Compound Return | | 6.42% |

Table 18-2 shows the change in value of the Dow Jones Industrial Average from 1975 to 1984. This table shows the percentage change by quarter as well as earnings and dividend data for the entire Dow Jones Industrial Average.

Blue chip stocks are noted for the ability to grow and pay dividends to investors. These companies often are involved in multiple industries or many different segments of the same broad industry. An example of the latter is General Electric Corporation in the electronics industry. Blue chip stocks are seldom able to match the performance of a true high-growth stock simply because of the large size of the blue chip company and the number of shares it has issued.

A blue chip stock is best recognized for its ability to consistently earn a good return on assets and investor's capital. While not as consistent as a public utility company, the blue chip stock operates in a less regulated environment and earns a higher overall rate of return than does a utility company.

Exhibit 18-1 is a reprint of a Standard & Poor's Corporation Stock Report on International Business Machines Corporation. IBM—or "Big Blue" as it is called—is a widely recognized blue chip stock. Similar information on thousands of other common stocks can be found in Standard & Poor's Stock Reports for companies traded on The New York Stock Exchange, The American Stock Exchange, or the over-the-counter market.

## STRENGTHS

Blue chip stocks' strength rest on the vast amount of capital available to the company for use in the expansion of business. A blue chip company may be able to act quickly to commit human and financial resources in response to a special business opportunity.

From an investment perspective, blue chip stocks are very liquid investments that offer long-term growth and modest income.

## WEAKNESSES

For an individual, blue chip stocks may not meet a specific investment goal. Rather than providing high growth, blue chip stocks offer moderate growth. Blue chip stocks do not offer exceptionally high income; the divi-

### Table 18-2.   Barron's 10-Year History of Dow Jones Stock Averages

## Quarterly Dow Jones Industrial Stock Average

The table below lists the earnings (losses) of the Dow Jones Industrial Average based upon generally accepted accounting principles. The P/E ratio for the DJI correctly reflects deficit/negative earnings for the 1982 September and December quarters. The 1984 December 12-months dividend reflects $1.87½ GM dividend distribution value of one share of class E common for each 20 shares of common held. N.A.-Not available. d-Deficit.

| Year | Quarter Ended | | Clos. Avg. | Qtrly Chg. | | % Chg. | | Qtrly Earns | 12-Mth Earns | P/E Ratio | 12-Mth Divs | Divs Yield | Payout Ratio |
|---|---|---|---|---|---|---|---|---|---|---|---|---|---|
| 1984 | Dec. | 31 | 1211.57 | + | 4.86 | + | 0.40 | N.A. | N.A. | N.A. | 60.63 | 5.00 | N.A. |
| | Sept. | 28 | 1206.71 | + | 74.31 | + | 6.56 | 29.06 | 106.11 | 11.2 | 58.41 | 4.84 | .5402 |
| | June | 29 | 1132.40 | − | 32.49 | − | 2.79 | 35.02 | 102.07 | 11.1 | 57.67 | 5.00 | .5650 |
| | Mar. | 30 | 1164.89 | − | 93.75 | − | 7.45 | 30.12 | 87.38 | 13.3 | 56.39 | 4.84 | .6453 |
| 1983 | Dec. | 30 | 1258.64 | + | 25.51 | + | 2.07 | 13.89 | 72.45 | 17.4 | 56.33 | 4.47 | .7775 |
| | Sept. | 30 | 1233.13 | + | 11.17 | + | 0.91 | 23.04 | 56.12 | 30.0 | 54.59 | 4.43 | .9727 |
| | June | 30 | 1221.96 | + | 91.93 | + | 8.13 | 20.33 | 11.59 | 105.4 | 54.65 | 4.42 | 4.0635 |
| | Mar. | 31 | 1130.03 | + | 83.49 | + | 7.98 | 15.19 | 9.52 | 118.7 | 54.10 | 4.79 | 5.6828 |
| 1982 | Dec. | 31 | 1046.54 | + | 150.29 | + | 16.77 | d2.44 | 9.15 | 114.4 | 54.14 | 5.17 | 5.9169 |
| | Sept. | 30 | 896.25 | + | 84.32 | + | 10.38 | d21.49 | 35.15 | 25.5 | 55.55 | 6.20 | 1.5804 |
| | June | 30 | 811.93 | − | 10.84 | − | 1.32 | 18.26 | 79.90 | 10.2 | 55.84 | 6.88 | .6989 |
| | Mar. | 31 | 822.77 | − | 52.23 | − | 5.97 | 14.82 | 97.13 | 8.5 | 56.28 | 6.84 | .5794 |
| 1981 | Dec. | 31 | 875.00 | + | 25.02 | + | 2.94 | 23.56 | 113.71 | 7.7 | 56.22 | 6.42 | .4944 |
| | Sept. | 30 | 849.98 | − | 126.90 | − | 12.99 | 23.26 | 123.32 | 6.9 | 56.18 | 6.61 | .4539 |
| | June | 30 | 976.88 | − | 26.99 | − | 2.69 | 35.49 | 128.91 | 7.6 | 55.98 | 5.73 | .4266 |
| | Mar. | 31 | 1003.87 | + | 39.88 | + | 4.14 | 31.40 | 123.60 | 8.1 | 54.99 | 5.48 | .4449 |
| 1980 | Dec. | 31 | 963.99 | + | 31.57 | + | 3.39 | 33.17 | 121.86 | 7.9 | 54.36 | 5.64 | .4461 |
| | Sept. | 30 | 932.42 | + | 64.50 | + | 7.43 | 28.85 | 111.58 | 8.4 | 53.83 | 5.77 | .4824 |
| | June | 30 | 867.92 | + | 82.17 | + | 10.46 | 30.18 | 116.40 | 7.5 | 52.81 | 6.08 | .4537 |
| | Mar. | 31 | 785.75 | − | 52.99 | − | 6.32 | 29.66 | 120.77 | 6.5 | 52.10 | 6.63 | .4314 |
| 1979 | Dec. | 31 | 838.74 | − | 39.93 | − | 4.54 | 22.89 | 124.46 | 6.7 | 50.98 | 6.08 | .4096 |
| | Sept. | 28 | 878.67 | + | 36.69 | + | 4.36 | 33.67 | 136.26 | 6.4 | 51.45 | 5.85 | .3776 |
| | June | 29 | 841.98 | − | 20.20 | − | 2.34 | 34.55 | 128.99 | 6.5 | 50.35 | 5.98 | .3903 |
| | Mar. | 30 | 862.18 | + | 57.17 | + | 7.10 | 33.35 | 124.10 | 6.9 | 49.48 | 5.74 | .3987 |
| 1978 | Dec. | 29 | 805.01 | − | 60.81 | − | 7.02 | 34.69 | 112.79 | 7.1 | 48.52 | 6.03 | .4302 |
| | Sept. | 29 | 865.82 | + | 46.87 | + | 5.72 | 26.40 | 101.59 | 8.5 | 47.42 | 5.48 | .4668 |
| | June | 30 | 818.95 | + | 61.59 | + | 8.13 | 29.66 | 91.37 | 9.0 | 46.74 | 5.71 | .5115 |
| | Mar. | 31 | 757.36 | − | 73.81 | − | 8.88 | 22.04 | 89.23 | 8.5 | 46.53 | 6.14 | .5215 |
| 1977 | Dec. | 30 | 831.17 | − | 15.94 | − | 1.88 | 23.49 | 89.10 | 9.3 | 45.84 | 5.51 | .5145 |
| | Sept. | 30 | 847.11 | − | 69.19 | − | 7.55 | 16.18 | 89.86 | 9.4 | 44.73 | 5.28 | .4978 |
| | June | 30 | 916.30 | − | 2.83 | − | 0.31 | 27.52 | 97.18 | 9.4 | 43.85 | 4.79 | .4512 |
| | Mar. | 31 | 919.13 | − | 85.52 | − | 8.51 | 21.91 | 95.51 | 9.6 | 42.63 | 4.64 | .4463 |
| 1976 | Dec. | 31 | 1004.65 | + | 14.46 | + | 1.46 | 24.25 | 96.72 | 10.4 | 41.40 | 4.12 | .4280 |
| | Sept. | 30 | 990.19 | − | 12.59 | − | 1.27 | 23.50 | 95.81 | 10.3 | 38.90 | 3.93 | .4060 |
| | June | 30 | 1002.78 | + | 3.33 | + | 0.33 | 25.85 | 90.68 | 11.1 | 38.10 | 3.80 | .4202 |
| | Mar. | 31 | 999.45 | + | 147.04 | + | 17.25 | 23.12 | 81.87 | 12.2 | 36.88 | 3.69 | .4565 |
| 1975 | Dec. | 31 | 852.41 | + | 58.53 | + | 7.37 | 23.34 | 75.66 | 11.3 | 37.46 | 4.39 | .4951 |
| | Sept. | 30 | 793.88 | − | 85.11 | − | 10.72 | 18.37 | 75.47 | 10.5 | 38.28 | 4.82 | .5072 |
| | June | 30 | 878.99 | + | 110.84 | + | 12.61 | 17.04 | 83.83 | 10.5 | 38.66 | 4.40 | .4612 |
| | Mar. | 31 | 768.15 | + | 151.91 | + | 24.65 | 16.91 | 93.47 | 8.2 | 38.56 | 5.02 | .4125 |

## Exhibit 18-1. Standard & Poor's Stock Report on IBM

# Int'l Business Machines 1210

NYSE Symbol IBM    Options on CBOE (Jan-Apr-Jul-Oct)    In S&P 500

| Price | Range | P-E Ratio | Dividend | Yield | S&P Ranking |
|---|---|---|---|---|---|
| Oct. 21'85 | 1985 | | | | |
| 127½ | 138¼–117⅜ | 13 | 4.40 | 3.5% | A+ |

### Summary

IBM is the world's largest manufacturer of computers and information processing equipment and systems, ranging from microcomputers to large-scale mainframes. Earnings for 1986 are expected to recover sharply, primarily reflecting the first full year of shipments of a new high-end mainframe and strong demand for personal computers; a stable dollar would also be beneficial.

### Current Outlook

Earnings for 1986 are projected at $13.00 a share, up from the $10.75 estimated for 1985.

The $1.10 quarterly dividend is the minimum expectation.

Gross income growth should be in excess of 15% in 1986, reflecting the first full year of shipments of the new 3090-200 mainframe and high-end storage devices and strong demand for personal computers. Sales of mid-range processors could continue to be restrained by the temporary saturation of the market, weak capital spending, and the lack of networking capabilities. A stable or weaker dollar would have a substantial positive effect on sales. Margins are likely to widen with the greater volume and productivity improvement programs.

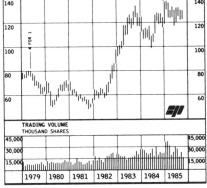

### Gross Income (Billion $)

| Quarter: | 1986 | 1985 | 1984 | 1983 |
|---|---|---|---|---|
| Mar. | --- | 9.77 | 9.59 | 8.29 |
| Jun. | --- | 11.43 | 11.20 | 9.59 |
| Sep. | --- | 11.70 | 10.66 | 9.41 |
| Dec. | --- | --- | 14.50 | 12.90 |
| | --- | --- | 45.94 | 40.18 |

Revenues for the nine months ended September 30, 1985 rose 4.6%, year to year; sales increased 12%, service revenues were up 17%, but rental income declined 38%. Pretax earnings fell 12%. After taxes at 43.7% in each period, net income was also down 12%. Share earnings were $6.31, versus $7.22.

### Capital Share Earnings ($)

| Quarter: | 1986 | 1985 | 1984 | 1983 |
|---|---|---|---|---|
| Mar. | E2.65 | 1.61 | 1.97 | 1.62 |
| Jun. | E3.00 | 2.30 | 2.65 | 2.22 |
| Sep. | E3.00 | 2.40 | 2.60 | 2.14 |
| Dec. | E4.35 | E4.44 | 3.55 | 3.06 |
| | E1.300 | E10.75 | 10.77 | 9.04 |

### Important Developments

Oct. '85—IBM said that orders in the third quarter showed strong growth, year to year, led by high-end processors and storage, typewriters, and personal computers. Separately, IBM unveiled its local area network; it will use existing telephone lines and will cost about $800 to hook up each personal computer. Details on how Systems/36 office minicomputers, mainframes and other IBM products are to be attached were not disclosed, but the partial announcement could remove some of the confusion over future communications standards currently depressing demand for computers. A vector processor option for the new 3090 mainframe was also introduced, which should aid IBM's expansion in the scientific engineering market, and availability of the four processor 3090-400 mainframe was moved up to the fourth quarter of 1986 from the second quarter of 1987.

**Next earnings report due in mid-January.**

### Per Share Data ($)

| Yr. End Dec. 31 | 1984 | 1983 | 1982 | 1981 | 1980 | 1979 | 1978 | 1977 | 1976 | 1975 |
|---|---|---|---|---|---|---|---|---|---|---|
| Book Value | 41.79 | 38.02 | 33.13 | 30.66 | 28.18 | 25.64 | 23.14 | 21.39 | 21.15 | 19.05 |
| Earnings | 10.77 | 9.04 | 7.39 | 5.63 | 6.10 | 5.16 | 5.32 | 4.58 | 3.99 | 3.34 |
| Dividends | 4.10 | 3.71 | 3.44 | 3.44 | 3.44 | 3.44 | 2.88 | 2.50 | 2.00 | 1.62½ |
| Payout Ratio | 38% | 41% | 47% | 62% | 56% | 67% | 54% | 54% | 50% | 49% |
| Prices—High | 128½ | 134¼ | 98 | 71½ | 72¾ | 80½ | 77½ | 71½ | 72⅛ | 56⅞ |
| Low | 99 | 92¼ | 55⅝ | 48⅜ | 50⅜ | 61⅛ | 58¾ | 61⅛ | 55⅞ | 39⅜ |
| P/E Ratio— | 12–9 | 15–10 | 13–8 | 13–9 | 12–8 | 16–12 | 15–11 | 16–13 | 18–14 | 17–12 |

Data as orig. reptd. Adj. for stk. div(s). of 300% Jun. 1979. E-Estimated.

Standard NYSE Stock Reports
Vol. 52/No. 207/Sec. 8

**October 28, 1985**
Copyright © 1985 Standard & Poor's Corp. All Rights Reserved

Standard & Poor's Corp.
25 Broadway, NY, NY 10004

## Exhibit 18-1. (Continued)

# 1210      International Business Machines Corporation

### Income Data (Million $)

| Year Ended Dec. 31 | Revs. | Oper. Inc. | % Oper. Inc. of Revs. | Cap. Exp. | Depr. | Int. Exp. | Net Bef. Taxes | Eff. Tax Rate | Net Inc. | % Net Inc. of Revs. |
|---|---|---|---|---|---|---|---|---|---|---|
| 1984 | 45,937 | 14,704 | 32.0% | 6,276 | 3,473 | 408 | [2]11,623 | 43.4% | 6,582 | 14.3% |
| 1983 | 40,180 | 13,262 | 33.0% | 4,930 | 3,673 | [3]390 | [2] 9,940 | 44.8% | 5,485 | 13.7% |
| 1982 | 34,364 | 11,199 | 32.6% | 6,685 | 3,143 | 514 | [2] 7,930 | 44.4% | [1]4,409 | 12.8% |
| 1981 | 29,070 | 8,926 | 30.7% | 6,845 | 2,899 | 480 | [2] 5,988 | 44.8% | 3,308 | 11.4% |
| 1980 | 26,213 | 8,102 | 30.9% | 6,592 | 2,362 | [1]325 | [2] 5,897 | 39.6% | 3,562 | 13.6% |
| 1979 | 22,863 | 7,215 | 31.6% | 5,991 | 1,970 | 140 | 5,553 | 45.8% | 3,011 | 13.2% |
| 1978 | 21,076 | 7,265 | 34.5% | 4,046 | 1,824 | 55 | 5,798 | 46.3% | 3,111 | 14.8% |
| 1977 | 18,133 | 6,657 | 36.7% | 3,395 | 1,999 | 40 | 5,092 | 46.6% | 2,719 | 15.0% |
| 1976 | 16,304 | 5,928 | 36.4% | 2,518 | 1,858 | 45 | 4,519 | 46.9% | 2,398 | 14.7% |
| 1975 | 14,437 | 5,245 | 36.3% | 2,439 | 1,822 | 63 | 3,721 | 46.5% | 1,990 | 13.8% |

### Balance Sheet Data (Million $)

| Dec. 31 | Cash | Current Assets | Current Liab. | Ratio | Total Assets | Ret. on Assets | Long Term Debt | Common Equity | Total Cap. | % LT Debt of Cap. | Ret. on Equity |
|---|---|---|---|---|---|---|---|---|---|---|---|
| 1984 | 4,362 | 20,375 | 9,640 | 2.1 | 42,808 | 16.4% | 3,269 | 26,489 | 31,815 | 10.3% | 26.4% |
| 1983 | 5,536 | 17,270 | 9,507 | 1.8 | 37,243 | 15.6% | 2,674 | 23,219 | 26,606 | 10.1% | 25.2% |
| 1982 | 3,300 | 13,014 | 8,209 | 1.6 | 32,541 | 14.1% | 2,851 | 19,960 | 23,134 | 12.3% | 22.9% |
| 1981 | 2,029 | 10,303 | 7,320 | 1.4 | 29,586 | 11.7% | 2,669 | 18,161 | 21,082 | 12.7% | 19.0% |
| 1980 | 2,112 | 9,925 | 6,526 | 1.5 | 26,703 | 13.9% | 2,099 | 16,453 | 18,734 | 11.2% | 22.7% |
| 1979 | 3,771 | 10,851 | 6,445 | 1.7 | 24,530 | 13.3% | 1,589 | 14,961 | 16,690 | 9.5% | 21.2% |
| 1978 | 4,031 | 10,321 | 5,810 | 1.8 | 20,771 | 15.7% | 286 | 13,494 | 13,889 | 2.1% | 24.0% |
| 1977 | 5,407 | 10,073 | 5,209 | 1.9 | 18,978 | 15.0% | 256 | 12,618 | 12,962 | 2.0% | 21.7% |
| 1976 | 6,156 | 9,920 | 4,082 | 2.4 | 17,723 | 14.4% | 275 | 12,749 | 13,088 | 2.1% | 19.8% |
| 1975 | 4,768 | 8,115 | 3,363 | 2.4 | 15,531 | 13.4% | 295 | 11,416 | 11,756 | 2.5% | 18.4% |

Data as orig. reptd. **1.** Reflects accounting change. **2.** Incl. equity in earns. of nonconsol. subs. **3.** Net of interest income.

## Business Summary

IBM is the largest manufacturer of data processing equipment and systems. Industry segment contributions in recent years:

| Gross revenues | 1984 | 1983 |
|---|---|---|
| Processors/peripherals | 51% | 54% |
| Office products | 21% | 20% |
| Programs/maint./other | 24% | 23% |
| Federal systems | 4% | 3% |

Sales provided 65% of revenues in 1984, rentals 14%, and services 21%. Foreign operations contributed 40% of revenues and 39% of profits.

Processors manipulate data through the operation of a stored program. Peripherals include printers, copiers, storage and telecommunication devices. Office products include small business computers, intelligent workstations and typewriters. Program products include applications and systems software. Other revenues are derived from supplies and unit record equipment, and education and testing materials. The Federal systems group serves U.S. government space, defense and other agencies.

IBM owns a 19% stake in Intel Corp., a major semiconductor manufacturer.

## Dividend Data

Dividends have been paid since 1916. A dividend reinvestment plan is available.

| Amt. of Divd. $ | Date Decl. | Ex-divd. Date | Stock of Record | Payment Date |
|---|---|---|---|---|
| 1.10 | Oct. 23 | Oct. 31 | Nov. 7 | Dec. 10'84 |
| 1.10 | Jan. 28 | Feb. 6 | Feb. 13 | Mar. 9'85 |
| 1.10 | Apr. 29 | May 3 | May 9 | Jun. 10'85 |
| 1.10 | Jul. 30 | Aug. 8 | Aug. 14 | Sep. 10'85 |

Next dividend meeting: late Oct. '85.

## Finances

Expenditures for research, development and engineering amounted to $4.2 billion ($9.1% of gross income) in 1984.

## Capitalization

**Long Term Debt:** $2,583,000,000, incl. $1.29 billion of 7 7/8% debs. conv. into com. at $153.66 a share.

**Capital Stock:** 614,349,392 shs. ($1.25 par). Institutions hold approximately 50%. Shareholders of record: 792,506.

**Office**—Armonk, New York 10504. **Tel**—(914) 765-1900. **Stockholder Relations Dept**—590 Madison Ave., NYC 10022. **Tel**—(212) 407-4000. **Chrmn**—J. R. Opel. **Pres & CEO**—J. F. Akers. **Secy**—J. H. Grady. **Treas**—J. W. Rotenstreich. **Investor Contact**—J. M. Heatley. **Dirs**—J. F. Akers, S. D. Bechtel, Jr., G. B. Beitzel, H. Brown, J. E. Burke, F. T. Cary, W. T. Coleman, Jr., T. F. Frist, Jr., P. R. Harris, C. A. Hills, A. Houghton, Jr., N. deB. Katzenbach, R. W. Lyman, W. H. Moore, J. R. Munro, J. R. Opel, D. P. Phypers, P. J. Rizzo, W. W. Scranton, I. S. Shapiro, C. Vance. **Transfer Agents**—Company's NYC & Chicago offices. **Registrars**—Morgan Guaranty Trust Co., NYC; First National Bank, Chicago; Montreal Trust Co., Montreal & Toronto. **Incorporated** in New York in 1911.

dends received are modest, and prices can demonstrate severe fluctuations over a 5 to 10 year period.

## UNIQUE FEATURES

Perhaps the most unique feature of blue chip stocks is the depth of management and strong capital positions held by these large, international companies. Investors often are willing to pay a premium price for blue chip stocks because of these features.

## TAX CONSEQUENCES

The same dividend exclusion is available on blue chip stocks for investors as on other company's dividends. Up to $100 of dividends may be excluded from taxation for an individual investor. This amount doubles to $200 for couples filing a joint tax return.

In addition to these tax factors, investors need to be aware of the consequences of selling a blue chip stock. According to the Internal Revenue Service, a stock asset qualifies for capital gains treatment. If an investor has held the stock for at least six months, 60 percent of any gain on sale of the asset above the cost basis is excluded from taxation. That means only 40 percent of the gain is included in taxable income. Long-term capital gains are given perhaps the best possible tax treatment of any income subject to tax.

Short-term capital gains are recognized on the profitable sale of blue chip stock owned for less than six months and one day. The entire amount of the gain above the cost basis in the stock is taxable as ordinary income.

Investors that sell blue chip stock for a long-term capital loss (with a holding period over six months) are subject to the maximum tax *disadvantage* for their loss. Only 50 percent of the loss can be used as a deduction to offset gross income, while the remaining 50 percent cannot be used at all. This simply means that one-half of a net long-term capital loss is deductible and the other half is lost forever.

Short-term capital losses for the blue chip stock investor are not as unfortunate as long-term losses. The entire amount of a short-term capital loss is deductible on a dollar for dollar basis from gross income. This loss is subject to an annual limit of $3,000. Amounts in excess of $3,000 can be carried over to future years.

Investors that sell blue chip stocks and recognize a long-term capital loss will be permitted to utilize up to a maximum of $6,000 to offset $3,000 of gross income in any one year. The balance of the long term capital loss in excess of $6,000 must be carried forward to future tax years.

Investors need to be aware that in reality a special process of combining these gains and losses into a "net capital position" takes place for income tax reporting purposes. Because of this net effect, all of an investor's transactions involving capital gains and losses must be considered as a whole. This can include many transactions in addition to investments in blue chip stocks.

Investors should acquire the advice of a qualified taxation professional in the strategic decision process of tax reduction or minimization.

## WHERE AND HOW TO BUY

Blue chip stocks can be purchased from any licensed securities dealer.

In addition to the traditional purchase of blue chip stocks through a securities dealer, investors may have the option to reinvest any dividends paid by the company into additional shares of common stock. When investors notify either the company or their brokers of wish to reinvest dividends, dividend reinvestment accounts are opened that cycle income back into stock purchases automatically. In such plans, investors receive the added benefit of being able to purchase fractional shares.

These shares are held for the investors in the designated accounts by the stock transfer agent of the company. Typically this stock transfer agent is a large bank or trust company.

A few companies also offer the ability to add additional contributions to the dividend reinvestment account. Investors simply send checks for the additional amount they wish to reinvest.

The company then purchases more common stock for those investors. Typically the company is willing to perform these reinvestment and additional investment services without charge to the investor or for a fee of $5 or less.

## HOW TO SELL

Blue chip stocks can be liquidated through any licensed securities dealer.

In some dividend reinvestment plans, the trustee of the plan may be authorized to liquidate shares on behalf of the plan participants. Participants in reinvestment plans always have the option of having the shares of stock transferred and mailed to them.

## TRANSACTION COSTS

Investors should note that not all securities dealers charge the same fees for services performed. *Full-service brokerage firms* provide important services for clients over and above the actual execution of a simple buy or sell order. *Discount brokerage firms* specialize in offering the lowest possible cost transactions. An individual investor should review the level of service he or she requires and select a securities dealer accordingly.

## PORTFOLIO FIT

Blue chip stocks are by far the most widely owned securities. Ownership may take several different forms. Employees of the blue chip company participate in employee stock ownership plans. Individual investors enjoy the dividends and growth afforded by blue chip stocks. In addition, pension plans regularly commit considerable portions of retirement funds to ownership of these stable stocks.

Only the most risk-averse investors fail to own these securities. Even though individual investors may not own blue chip stocks in a personal portfolio, it is highly probable that their pension plan, mutual fund, or professionally managed trust portfolio includes several blue chip stocks.

Many investors should ask themselves if the direct ownership of a blue chip stock is really necessary. Investors with large percentages of their net worth invested in company pension plans and mutual funds that contain blue chip stocks might wish to consider more tax related investments in their personal portfolios. A thorough review of an investor's entire portfolio may reveal the need to increase ownership of either more conservative investments or more risk oriented investments in the personal portfolio to balance the large portion of the investor's pension, IRA, and trust portfolios already positioned in blue chip stocks.

On the opposite end of the spectrum, an investor with a portfolio of very conservative securities (for example, certificates of deposit) may wish to participate in the general growth of the economy by owning blue chip stocks.

## SOURCES OF ADDITIONAL INFORMATION

Investors can call a brokerage firm and ask for research reports on many blue chip stocks. Any public library contains numerous research sources and periodic publications that will provide information on blue chip stocks.

From an individual investor's point of view, investment newsletters and publications from stock brokerage firms offer the most direct information. These sources often contain specific buy-hold-sell recommendations. Most of the other sources furnish an overview of the company and a review of current results but stop short of endorsing ownership of the stock.

## COMMENTS

Blue chip stocks represent the backbone of the investment community. These companies have developed large intracompany management functions to deal with the welfare of employees, the communities in which they are located, and society in general.

Investors in blue chip stocks are generally willing to give up the exceptional rates of growth found in stocks of smaller, less-established companies. While blue chip stocks provide moderate dividend yields, the investor will not attain the high dividend yields of utility stocks. Blue chip stocks are noted for their overall rate of return.

**Exhibit 18-2.  Moderate Risk: Blue Chip Stocks**

**INVESTMENT PROFILE**

| INVESTMENT CHARACTERISTICS | Excellent | Good | Average | Poor | None |
|---|---|---|---|---|---|
| Liquidity | √ | | | | |
| Safety of Principal | | | √ | | |
| Price Stability | | | √ | | |
| Reinvestment Protection | | | √ | | |
| Growth of Capital | | √ | | | |
| Cash Income | | | | √ | |
| Growth of Income | | √ | | | |
| Inflation Hedge | | LT | | ST | |
| Tax Advantaged | | | | | √* |

**Liquidity**—the ability to quickly realize cash from the sale at fair market value

**Safety of Principal**—the principal is safe from bankruptcy or default

**Price Stability**—the market value of the asset does not change in value

**Reinvestment Protection**—protection against reinvesting cash flow at lower rates as interest rates decline

**Growth of Capital**—the original investment increases over time to create capital gains

**Cash Income**—the cash income relative to treasury bills returns

**Growth of Income**—the ability of the cash income stream to increase over time

**Inflation Hedge**—the ability of total return (cash income plus capital gains) to keep pace with inflation over time

**Tax Advantaged**—the ability to reduce or defer current federal income taxes

*If the IRS continues the $100 dividend exclusion, an investor can get a small tax benefit.
LT = Long time periods (5–10 years).
ST = Shorter time periods (1–3 years).

# CHAPTER 19

# Growth Stocks

## DESCRIPTION

*Growth stocks* are defined as companies whose earnings will grow at a significantly higher rate than the economy as a whole. A good rule of thumb would suggest a growth stock should have an earnings per share growth rate of at least double a recognized investment standard—for example, the earnings per share growth rate of the Standard & Poor's 500 index. The Standard & Poor's 500 index compound growth rate for the decade from January 1, 1975 to December 31, 1984 was 5.8 percent.

A growth stock is purchased for increases in the price per share. Typically growth stocks are associated with significant improvements in medical and electronic technology; improved methods of manufacturing; or significant cost reductions in transportation, information processing, and distribution. Periodically other growth stocks may be found in the specialty retailing, pharmaceutical, and emerging biological sectors of the economy.

Listings such as *The Value Line Investment Survey* provide rankings of growth stocks having higher than average growth rates of for the last 10 years.

Exhibit 19-1 is a recap sheet on Hospital Corporation of America taken from Standard & Poor's Corporation Stock Reports. Hospital Corporation of America is one of the high-growth companies frequently cited in growth stock lists.

HCA (the stock symbol for Hospital Corp.) has grown from earnings per share of $.35 in 1974 to $3.35 in 1984. This is over a ninefold increase in just 10 years or a compounded annual rate of 25.3 percent.

**Exhibit 19-1. Standard & Poor's Stock Report on Hospital Corp.**

# Hospital Corp. of America 1157

**NYSE Symbol HCA Options on Pac (Jan-Apr-Jul-Oct) In S&P 500**

| Price | Range | P-E Ratio | Dividend | Yield | S&P Ranking |
|---|---|---|---|---|---|
| Jul. 31'85 | 1985 | | | | |
| 48⅝ | 52¼-36½ | 13 | 0.60 | 1.2% | A+ |

**Summary**

**Hospital Corp. of America is the world's largest hospital management chain, operating more than 400 acute care and psychiatric hospitals in the U.S. and abroad. In July, 1985 HCA withdrew from its planned merger with American Hospital Supply Corp., following the latter firm's acceptance of a higher offer from Baxter Travenol Laboratories and a settlement agreement reached by the three firms.**

## Current Outlook

**Earnings for 1985 are projected at about $4.00 a share, up from 1984's $3.35. Another healthy gain seems in prospect for 1986.**

**Dividends are expected to continue at $0.15 quarterly.**

Net operating revenues should post a healthy gain in 1985, aided by contributions from additional units acquired or constructed, new management contracts, and greater intensity of service. Profitability should benefit from the better volume, improved efficiency and higher other income.

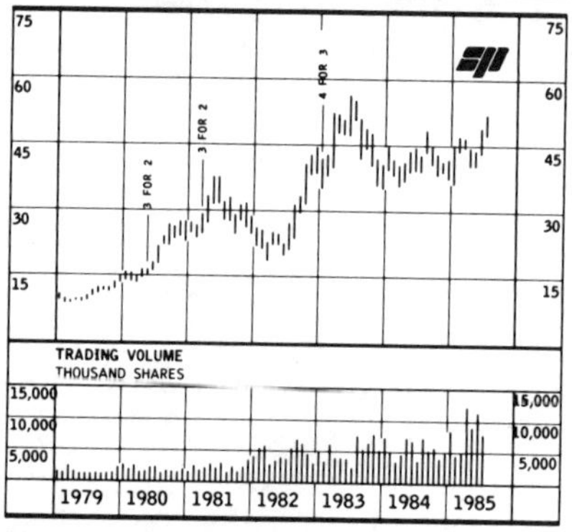


### Net Oper. Revs. (Million $)

| Quarter: | 1985 | 1984 | 1983 | 1982 |
|---|---|---|---|---|
| Mar. | 985 | 879 | 805 | 724 |
| Jun. | 993 | 868 | 802 | 735 |
| Sep. | --- | 853 | 803 | 749 |
| Dec. | --- | 899 | 793 | 769 |
| | --- | 3,499 | 3,203 | 2,977 |

Gross revenues for the six months ended June 30, 1985 increased 12%, year to year, aided contributions from new hospitals and management contracts. Pretax income gained 23%. After taxes at 42.2% in each period, net income also was up 23%, to $2.18 a share from $1.82. Results in the 1985 period included a gain of $0.29 a share from the exchange of Beverly Enterprises stock for convertible debt.

### Common Share Earnings ($)

| Quarter: | 1985 | 1984 | 1983 | 1982 |
|---|---|---|---|---|
| Mar. | 1.16 | 0.98 | 0.81 | 0.65 |
| Jun. | 1.02 | 0.84 | 0.70 | 0.56 |
| Sep. | E0.92 | 0.78 | 0.65 | 0.53 |
| Dec. | E0.90 | 0.75 | 0.64 | 0.52 |
| | E4.00 | 3.35 | 2.80 | 2.25 |

## Important Developments

**Jul. '85**—The company said that its $2.5 billion three-year expansion program remained intact despite its aborted attempt to merge with American Hospital Supply Corp. (AHS). HCA withdrew its plans to merge with AHS following AHS's acceptance of a higher bid from Baxter Travenol Laboratories (BAX) and a settlement agreement reached by the three firms. As part of the accord, AHS will pay HCA $200 million in cash, of which $150 million will be paid on consummation of the BAX/AHS merger and the remaining $50 million will be payable on certain conditions after five years. Also, HCA and AHS agreed to amend HCA's agreement to purchase $325 million annually in supplies from AHS through December, 1988. HCA is now committed to purchase $200 million annually for a 5-year period through 1990.

**Next earnings report due in mid-October.**

### Per Share Data ($)

| Yr. End Dec. 31 | 1984 | 1983 | 1982 | [1]1981 | [1]1980 | 1979 | 1978 | 1977 | 1976 | 1975 |
|---|---|---|---|---|---|---|---|---|---|---|
| Book Value | **18.52** | 15.61 | 12.41 | 8.29 | 7.28 | 6.54 | 4.91 | 4.25 | 3.68 | 3.08 |
| Earnings | **3.35** | 2.80 | 2.25 | 1.67 | 1.30 | 1.01 | 0.80 | 0.65 | 0.55 | 0.45 |
| Dividends | **0.50** | 0.40 | 0.33 | 0.25½ | 0.20 | 0.16¾ | 0.12⅜ | 0.09 | 0.06½ | 0.04½ |
| Payout Ratio | **15%** | 14% | 16% | 16% | 15% | 18% | 15% | 14% | 12% | 10% |
| Prices—High | **48¾** | 56⅝ | 44⅞ | 38 | 27⅞ | 14⅞ | 11½ | 6⅞ | 5¾ | 5⅜ |
| Low | **35¾** | 35⅜ | 18⅝ | 23¾ | 13½ | 8⅝ | 5⅝ | 4½ | 4⅛ | 1¾ |
| P/E Ratio— | **15-11** | 20-13 | 20-8 | 23-14 | 21-10 | 15-9 | 14-7 | 10-7 | 11-7 | 12-4 |

Data as orig. reptd. Adj. for stk. div(s). of 33⅓% Jan. 1983, 50% Mar. 1981, 50% Jun. 1980, 33% Sept. 1978, 25% Oct. 1977. 1. Reflects merger or acquisition. E-Estimated.

Standard NYSE Stock Reports
Vol. 52/No. 151/Sec. 11

**August 7, 1985**
Copyright © 1985 Standard & Poor's Corp. All Rights Reserved
Standard & Poor's Corp.
25 Broadway, NY, NY 10004

Copyright © 1985 Standard & Poor's Corp. All rights reserved. Reprinted with permission.

**Table 19-1.   NASDAQ Industrial Index 1973–1985**

| Year | High | Low | Close | Annual % Change |
|------|------|------|-------|-----------------|
| 1973 | 136.97 | 80.15 | 83.57 | −36.9 |
| 1974 | 89.78 | 54.21 | 56.46 | −32.4 |
| 1975 | 93.79 | 57.22 | 80.95 | +43.4 |
| 1976 | 100.12 | 81.44 | 100.12 | +23.7 |
| 1977 | 109.43 | 96.29 | 109.43 | + 9.3 |
| 1978 | 155.79 | 101.91 | 126.85 | +15.9 |
| 1979 | 175.18 | 126.88 | 175.18 | +38.1 |
| 1980 | 274.70 | 145.03 | 261.36 | +49.2 |
| 1981 | 283.03 | 204.62 | 229.29 | −12.3 |
| 1982 | 281.64 | 177.70 | 273.58 | +19.3 |
| 1983 | 408.42 | 270.55 | 323.68 | +18.3 |
| 1984 | 336.16 | 250.18 | 260.73 | −19.5 |
| 1985 | 330.17 | 258.85 | 330.17 | +26.6 |

## STRENGTHS

Growth stocks have the ability to grow faster than the economy, thereby serving as an inflation hedge over the long term. Over 5- to 10-year holding periods, significant long-term capital gains can accumulate.

Since growth stocks are more likely to be found trading over-the-counter, the NASDAQ index would be a means of demonstrating the long term performance of the smaller high growth companies.

The data in Table 19-1 illustrates this. This table displays the National Association of Security Dealers Industrial Stock Index for the 13 years from 1973 to 1985.

## WEAKNESSES

Growth stocks provide very little dividend income. These are high-risk companies dependent on high growth rates to sustain a high stock price. If growth declines, the stock price could fall dramatically.

## UNIQUE FEATURES

Growth stocks offer investors the ability to earn above-average returns on invested capital. Many times a high-growth company is able to reinvest

#### Table 19-2.   Tandy Corporation's 10-Year Growth

Stock price on January 1, 1975 = $11.50.

| November 28, 1975 | Tandy Corporation spins off Tandycraft and Tandy Brands. Each shareholder receives one share of TandyCraft for each two shares of Tandy Corporation owned and one share of TandyBrands for each ten shares of Tandy Corporation owned. |
| January 9, 1976 | Tandy Corporation stock split 2:1 |
| June 30, 1978 | Tandy Corporation stock split 2:1 |
| December 31, 1980 | Tandy Corporation stock split 2:1 |
| May 29, 1981 | Tandy Corporation stock split 2:1 |

*Corporations Divested From Tandy*

| May 16, 1977 | TandyCraft stock split 2:1 |
| September 30, 1977 | TandyCraft dividend $1.75 (in the form of 9% debentures) |
| September 30, 1978 | TandyCraft dividend $1.00 (in the form of 9% debentures) |
| December 31, 1977 | Tandy Brands spins off Stafford Lowden on the basis of one Stafford Lowden share for each 4 Tandy Brands shares owned. |
| September, 1979 | TandyCraft spins off Color Tile Inc. on the basis of one share of Color Tile for each share of TandyCraft owned. |
| January 2, 1980 | Color Tile stock splits 2:1 |

most of the profits earned from operations. Reinvested funds expand operations and generate improvements through research and development of related new products. This reinvestment results in a compounding effect for the investor. Over a period of several years, a modest investment can "grow with the company" into a sizable capital position.

The following illustration is an example of a growth stock investment. Table 19-2 illustrates Tandy Corporation from January 1, 1975 until December 31, 1984.

An investment in 100 shares of Tandy Corporation would have cost $1,150 on January 2, 1975. As of December 31, 1984 that $1,150.00 would be worth $24,321 of various securities. This works out to an annualized compound rate of return of 35.68 percent!

Tandy Corporation is a very large retailer of consumer electronics. The major operation is the Radio Shack chain of electronics stores. The spin-off operations include handycrafts, home improvements, and specialty retail operations.

Over a 10-year period, an investor would have experienced a 2,114 percent increase on the initial investment.

The most basic assumption for growth stock investors is that future growth characteristics and growth rates can be accurately determined through financial, marketing, and economic analysis. To the extent that this is valid, an investor needs to be prepared to devote considerable time to the study and evaluation of a broad variety of companies and industries.

Investors are cautioned that the ability to select a truly successful growth stock from the thousands of companies available today is a very risky endeavor. Many nesteggs have been depleted—if not completely destroyed—by individuals seeking another Tandy Corporation, Xerox, or the next IBM.


## TAX CONSEQUENCES

The same dividend exclusion is available on growth stocks for investors as on other dividends. Up to $100 of dividends may be excluded from taxation for an individual investor. This amount doubles to $200 for couples filing joint tax returns.

In addition to the tax factors already discussed, investors need to be aware of the consequences upon sale of stocks.

The Internal Revenue Service considers stock sales in its capital gains treatment. This means that if investors hold stock for six months and one day (or longer), 60 percent of any gain on sale of the asset above the cost basis is excluded from taxation. Gains from the sale of stock at that point are considered long-term. Only 40 percent of the gain is included in taxable income. This is perhaps the most advantageous treatment for taxable yields.

Short-term capital gains are recognized on the profitable sale of growth stock owned for less than six months and one day. The entire amount of the gain above the cost basis of the stock is taxable as ordinary income.

Investors who sell growth stock for a long-term capital loss (that is, the investors hold stock for more than six months and then sell it at a loss) have the greatest disadvantage for the tax treatment of their investment. Only 50 percent of the loss can be used as a deduction to offset gross income, while the remaining 50 percent cannot be used at all. This simply means that one-half of a net long-term capital loss is deductible, and the other half is not tax deductible. Investors that sell stock and recognize a long-term capital loss will be permitted to use up to a maximum of $6,000 to offset $3,000 of gross income in any one year. The balance of the long term capital loss in excess of $6,000 must be carried forward to future tax years.

Short-term capital loss tax treatments for the stock investor are not as unfortunate as long-term losses. The entire amount of a short-term capital loss is deductible on a dollar-for-dollar basis from gross income. Annual deductions against ordinary income arising from capital losses are subject to an annual limit of $3,000. Amounts in excess of $3,000 can be carried over to future years.

Investors should learn about the special process of combining these gains and losses into a "net capital position." This takes place for income tax reporting purposes. Because of this net effect, all of an investor's transactions involving capital gains and losses must be considered as a whole. This can include many transactions in addition to investments in growth stocks.

The advice of a qualified taxation professional is invaluable in strategic tax reduction or minimization.

## WHERE AND HOW TO BUY

Growth stocks can be purchased from any licensed securities dealer.

In addition to the traditional purchase of growth stocks through a securities dealer, investors may have the option to reinvest any dividends paid by the company into additional shares of common stock. Investors notify the company or their brokers of their preference to reinvest dividends. The firm opens a dividend reinvestment account to receive yields from the existing shares.

These yields purchase more shares, which are held in the designated account by the stock transfer agent of the company. Typically this stock transfer agent is a large bank or trust company.

Many companies also offer the ability to add additional contributions of up to $1,000 monthly to the dividend reinvestment account. Investors simply send in checks for the additional amount to be reinvested.

The company then purchases more common stock for those investors. Typically the company is willing to perform these reinvestment and additional investment services without charge to the investors.

## HOW TO SELL

Growth stocks can be liquidated through any licensed securities dealer.

In some dividend reinvestment plans, the trustee may be authorized to liquidate a part or all of an investor's shares upon the investor's request. Investors may request the share certificates to be shipped to them at any time.

## TRANSACTION COSTS

Growth stocks may be smaller and less frequently traded stocks found on the National Association of Securities Dealers over-the-counter listings.

The over-the-counter stocks may have a larger spread between the bid and asked price than would be found on the New York Stock Exchange. The effect of the larger spread is an increase in transaction costs for growth stock investors.

Investors should note that not all securities dealers charge the same fees for services performed. *Full-service brokerage firms* provide important services for clients over and above the actual execution of a simple buy or sell order. *Discount stock brokerage firms* specialize in offering the lowest possible cost transactions with no-frills service. An individual investor needs to review the level of service he or she requires and select a securities dealer accordingly.

## PORTFOLIO FIT

Growth stocks are typically owned by a broad variety of investors. Aggressive investors seeking growth of capital will normally commit a high percentage of their portfolios to growth stocks. It would not be surprising for younger investors to hold 50 percent or more of their portfolios in growth stocks.

Pension plans commit a more modest portion of their portfolios to growth stocks. It's not be unusual for pension funds to have just 20 percent of their assets invested in growth stocks.

Investors should remember that before they buy growth stocks, they should ensure that they have adequate funds for short-term emergencies. Growth stocks often must be held for several years to yield significant income; if investors have to sell growth stocks that were purchased relatively recently, the stocks may not have increased in value enough even to cover the broker's commissions!

## SOURCES OF ADDITIONAL INFORMATION

Several good sources of information are available on growth stocks. These include *Barron's, Business Week, Forbes, Fortune, Inc., Investors Daily, The Wall Street Journal,* and many other sources provided by Standard & Poor's Corporation and Value Line. Brokerage firms are also willing to furnish investors with research reports on growth stocks.

From an individual investor's point of view, investment newsletters and publications from stock brokerage firms offer the most direct information. These sources often contain specific buy-hold-sell recommendations. Most of the other sources furnish an overview of the company and a review of current results but stop short of endorsing ownership of the stock.

## COMMENTS

Investors should use caution in the selection of growth stocks. Expertise in selection of growth stocks is at best a very uncertain science, and in practice it is an art.

Growth stocks are undoubtedly one of the most popular topics of investment conversation in modern society. Investors should be aware that very few companies consistently outperform the averages. The selection of individual growth stocks is a high-risk proposition. This risk can be reduced by holding a diversified portfolio of growth stocks.

Our entire economy is structured to induce competition. This competition should cause companies with exceptional products, high rates of growth, and high profitability to attract the most competition. Eventually this competition should slow the high rates of growth enjoyed by the pioneer company in a particular field. (Think of Xerox and the reproduction equipment industry and more recently, Apple Computer in the personal computer market.)

To overcome this competitive pressure, a true growth company must be exceptionally well managed. Company officials must be creative, long-term thinkers who are able to accept a reasonable level of risk when they undertake new company projects.

Investors seeking these special growth situations must be willing to accept some setbacks along the investment path. A true growth stock investor must be exceptionally disciplined. No matter how well a company was projected to perform, when performance does not live up to the expectations, the investor must be willing to recognize a loss and begin searching for a more promising company.

**Exhibit 19-2.   Moderate Risk: Growth Stocks**

**INVESTMENT PROFILE**

| INVESTMENT CHARACTERISTICS | Excellent | Good | Average | Poor | None |
|---|---|---|---|---|---|
| Liquidity | ✓ | | | | |
| Safety of Principal | | | | ✓ | |
| Price Stability | | | | ✓ | |
| Reinvestment Protection | | | | ✓ | |
| Growth of Capital | ✓ | | | | |
| Cash Income | | | | ✓ | |
| Growth of Income | | | | ✓ | |
| Inflation Hedge | LT | | | ST | |
| Tax Advantaged | | | | | ✓* |

**Liquidity**—the ability to quickly realize cash from the sale at fair market value

**Safety of Principal**—the principal is safe from bankruptcy or default

**Price Stability**—the market value of the asset does not change in value

**Reinvestment Protection**—protection against reinvesting cash flow at lower rates as interest rates decline

**Growth of Capital**—the original investment increases over time to create capital gains

**Cash Income**—the cash income relative to treasury bills returns

**Growth of Income**—the ability of the cash income stream to increase over time

**Inflation Hedge**—the ability of total return (cash income plus capital gains) to keep pace with inflation over time

**Tax Advantaged**—the ability to reduce or defer current federal income taxes

*If the IRS continues the $100 dividend exclusion, an investor can get a very small annual tax benefit.
LT = Growth stocks held 5 to 10 years.
ST = Growth stocks held 1 to 3 years.

# CHAPTER 20

# Public Utility Common Stocks

## DESCRIPTION

*Public utility common stock* represents the direct ownership of the assets, earnings, and dividend payments of hundreds of local utility companies in the United States. Because public utility companies provide a service that is considered a necessity and because these companies operate under conditions in which direct competition is not practical, public utility companies are subject to broad regulation by governmental agencies. Historically, public utility common stocks have been exceptionally stable in financial performance. Because of governmental regulation, above-average growth rates are uncommon for these stocks. Most public utility common stocks are noted for the high rates of return received by investors in the form of cash dividends.

## STRENGTHS

The basic strength of public utility common stock is the stability of earnings and dividends of the investment. Over time, investors can receive an increase in income as dividend payments increase.

A noteworthy advantage is the ability of public utility common stock to eventually increase dividends enough to offset the effects of inflation on investors' portfolios.

155

## WEAKNESSES

The greatest risk of ownership of most public utility common stock is generally not a part of the product itself.

Investors require the yield on public utility common stock to be adjusted upward during a time of rising interest rates. The market adjusts by reducing the price of the shares. The market adjusts the price of the utility stocks to keep the current dividend yield competitive with other high-yielding investments, such as bonds.

## UNIQUE FEATURES

Earnings per share for public utility common stock are noted for great stability in both exceptionally strong and exceptionally weak periods of overall economic performance.

This stability stems from the virtually constant, highly predictable demand for the products supplied (electricity, water, and natural gas). A regulated operating environment protects the companies from competition and is designed to produce a targeted return on the investments of the utility companies. This is accomplished by regulating the prices charged for the products sold to consumers. Investors find that this predictable, regulated environment offers a much lower degree of risk than traditional competitive industries.

Dividend reinvestment programs of many utilities allow dividends to automatically purchase shares of stock from the company at as much as a 5 percent discount under market prices.

## TAX CONSEQUENCES

Several special tax treatments may be available to owners of public utility common stock. These include automatic tax-favored reinvestment of dividends, dividend exclusion, return of capital, and lower taxes on capital gains.

The same dividend exclusion is available on public utility common stock for investors as on other company's dividends. Up to $100 of dividends may be excluded from taxation for an individual investor. This amount doubles to $200 for couples filing a joint tax return.

Dividends of some public utility companies may be designated as a return of investor's capital. In such cases, the amount of the dividend designated as return of capital is not taxed at all. Investors must reduce the "cost basis" of their stock by the amount of the capital returned. For example, if an investor owned 100 shares of XYZ utility for a purchase price of $10 per share, and the investor received a $1 dividend that was designated as a return of capital, the investor would have no taxable income. The cost basis per share of the stock would be reduced to $9.

Besides these tax factors, investors should be aware of the consequences of selling public utility stock. The IRS considers public utility common stock capital gains as taxable. If investors hold his stock for more than six months, 60 percent of any capital gain on sale of the stock above the cost basis is excluded from taxation. Only 40 percent of the gain is considered taxable income. This is perhaps the best possible tax treatment for an investment's yields.

Short-term capital gains are recognized on the profitable sale of public utility common stock that was owned for less than six months and one day. The entire amount of the gain above the cost basis in the stock is taxable as ordinary income.

Investors that sell public utility common stock for a long-term capital loss (with a holding period over six months) can use only 50 percent of the loss as a deduction to offset gross income. The other 50 percent of the loss cannot be deducted at all. This means that one-half of a net long term capital loss is deductible and the other half is lost for tax purposes.

Investors that sell public utility common stock and recognize a long-term capital loss can use up to a maximum of $6,000 in losses to offset $3,000 of gross income in any one year. The balance of the long-term capital loss in excess of $6,000 must be carried forward to future tax years.

Short-term capital losses (of stock held less than six months) for the public utility common stock investor are more favorable than long-term losses. The entire amount of a short-term capital loss is deductible from gross income up to an annual maximum of $3,000. Amounts in excess of $3,000 can be carried over to future years.

Investors should know about a special process of combining these gains and losses into a "net capital position" for income tax reporting purposes. Because of this net effect, all of an investor's transactions involving capital gains and losses must be considered as a whole. This can include many transactions in addition to investments in public utility common stocks.

A qualified tax consultant can advise investors best about tax reduction or minimization.

## WHERE AND HOW TO BUY

Public utility common stock is issued by hundreds of local utility companies in the United States and in some other countries as well. Most public utility common stocks are traded on the New York Stock Exchange or the American Stock Exchange. From time to time these companies must raise additional capital to expand their ability to service customers. This additional capital may be raised by issuing additional common stock. Typically this stock is sold by a group of brokerage firms to the public.

When new shares of public utility common stock are sold to raise additional capital for the utility company, a group of securities dealers called an *underwriting syndicate* is formed. This underwriting syndicate consults with the utility company to determine how much stock is to be sold, when the stock will be sold, and at what price the stock will be available. Because almost all of the utility companies are publicly owned, the price of the stock to investors in these newly issued shares is very close to the current price in the stock market.

The advantage for investors in purchasing the stock through the underwriting syndicate stems from the fact that the utility company agrees to pay the underwriting syndicate a placement fee for selling the stock to investors. The underwriting syndicate charges no sales charges or commissions to investors at the time of purchase of new shares of the utility stock.

The use of a dividend reinvestment plan on a regular basis also allows an investor to accumulate capital in addition to dividends in ownership of the utility stock.

To summarize, investors can purchase public utility common stock at any time in open market transactions, or they can purchase public utility common stock when additional shares are sold through a special underwriting syndicate. They can also use dividend reinvestment plans.

## HOW TO SELL

Investors can sell public utility common stock on regular business days through any securities firm. Most public utility common stocks are listed on either the New York Stock Exchange or the American Stock Exchange. These exchanges provide a very liquid market for the shares of public utility companies. Individual investors face very little risk that a willing buyer cannot be found for a public utility common stock position of almost any size.

## TRANSACTION COSTS

As previously discussed, public utility common stock may be purchased at certain times without transaction costs through a special offering of newly issued shares. Typically, the securities firm handling the sale of public utility stock charges a commission for executing the order. Investors are cautioned that not all securities firms have the same commission charges. It may be prudent for an investor to compare charges at various firms prior to selling the stock.

## PORTFOLIO FIT

Public utility common stocks have historically paid a very high percentage of earnings to investors in the form of dividends. These dividends attract such investment groups as retired persons, pension plans, and trust accounts because of they offer relatively secure, steady income.

These groups of investors are seeking a high degree of current income, stability of principal, and the potential for modest growth of their investment over a long holding period.

Over a period of several years, most public utility common stocks have demonstrated the ability to raise the cash dividends paid to stockholders. As the population grows in the geographic area served by the utility company, the company must grow to supply the needed services. As this growth occurs, the regulatory agencies allow the companies to expand earnings. This modest growth of earnings provides the base to expand dividend payments to the owners of public utility common stock.

As owners of public utility common stocks, many retired persons have been able to retain purchasing power in periods of economic inflation. The increases in dividend payments received by owners of utility stocks help to offset price increases of goods and services purchased by consumers. Unfortunately, these dividend increases are not perfectly matched with changing prices during any specific year. Typically the dividend increases paid to shareholders lag behind inflation rate changes by several quarters.

In recent years problems associated with nuclear powered electricity generating plants have caused considerable fluctuations in the price of public utility common stocks. Typically, these utility companies have been involved in the construction and operation of nuclear power facilities. Many investors elect to avoid public utility common stock with nuclear exposure. Less conservative investors appreciate the risk premium that burdens some nuclear utilities. Higher dividend yields are generally available on the public utility common stocks with nuclear involvement.

Exhibits 20-1 and 20-2 show two reports from Standard & Poor's stock guide. Minnesota Power & Light represents a utility company with no nuclear plant exposure. Middle South Utilities has experienced problems with nuclear power generating facilities and as a result has been forced to reduce dividend payments to shareholders. Their comparative trading volume charts show how this dividend reduction has lowered investor interest in Middle South, while volume in Minnesota Power & Light has increased.

## SOURCES OF ADDITIONAL INFORMATION

Investors may call any brokerage firm for research reports. Public utility stocks are widely analyzed by all major brokerage firms. Public libraries maintaining business sections often have research available from *Value Line, Standard & Poors, Moody's* or other investment services.

## COMMENTS

In conclusion, public utility common stock has the same characteristics as other income oriented investments. Fluctuations of principal value can become large if interest rates suffer severe changes.

**Exhibit 20-1.   Standard & Poor's Evaluation of Minnesota Power & Light, a Nonnuclear Powered Electric Utility**

# Minnesota Power & Light     1518

NYSE Symbol MPL

| Price | Range | P-E Ratio | Dividend | Yield | S&P Ranking |
|-------|-------|-----------|----------|-------|-------------|
| May 22'85 | 1985 | | | | |
| 36 | 36¾-29¼ | 8 | 2.76 | 7.7% | A− |

## Summary

This moderate-sized utility serves an important iron mining area, which also has some diversified industry. The predominant fuel used for electric power generation is coal. Internally generated funds are expected to exceed construction expenditures through 1993. No rate increases have been filed since 1981, and MPL has no plans for any before 1987. MPL said in December, 1984 that it planned to derive 25% of its earnings from non-power generating activities by 1992.

## Business Summary

Minnesota Power & Light provides electric service in a 26,000 square-mile area in central and northeastern Minnesota. A subsidiary, Superior Water, Light, & Power (SWL&P), provides electric, water, and gas service in Superior, Wisc., and adjacent areas. Contributions to electric revenues (94% of total revenues in 1984) by customer class in recent years:

| Revenues | 1984 | 1983 | 1982 | 1981 |
|----------|------|------|------|------|
| Residential.......... | 11% | 12% | 12% | 11% |
| Commercial ........ | 10% | 10% | 10% | 9% |
| Industrial............. | 66% | 66% | 65% | 69% |
| Other ................. | 13% | 12% | 13% | 11% |

Revenues from sales to taconite processing customers accounted for 48% of total operating revenues in 1984 and 49% in 1983.

The fuel mix in 1984 was 66% steam (mostly coal), 7% hydro and 27% purchased. The company had received most of its purchased power (408 mw) under a long-term contract with Square Butte Electric Cooperative. However, effective January 1, 1985 Square Butte reduced the company's entitlement to 122 mw. Peak load in 1984 was 1,107 mw and system capability was 1,802 mw (including 408 mw from Square Butte). The capacity margin in 1984 was 39%.

In December, 1984 the company estimated construction expenditures for 1985-93 of $545.5 million (before AFUDC), including $32.9 million for 1985. Internally generated funds were expected to greatly exceed construction expenditures in 1984-93.

Topeka Group, Inc. was formed in 1983 to manage the company's diversification efforts. In December, 1984 MPL said that it was planning to di-

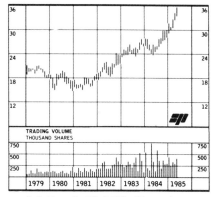

TRADING VOLUME
THOUSAND SHARES

versify to the extent that 25% of its earnings would be derived from non-power activities by 1992.

## Important Developments

**Dec. '84**—MPL projected electric kwh sales over the period 1984-93 would increase 1.4% a year. However, sales for 1985 were expected to decline 1.3%. Gas sales over the same period were expected to fall 4.9% a year. Purchased power was expected to comprise 19% of electric energy sources in 1993, down from 27% in 1984.

**Sep. '84**—The company's Topeka Group subsidiary acquired Universal Telephone, Inc., an operator of telephone, water and wastewater utilities, for $23 million.

**Next earnings report due in late July.**

## Per Share Data ($)

| Yr. End Dec. 31 | 1984 | 1983 | 1982 | 1981 | 1980 | 1979 | 1978 | 1977 | 1976 | 1975 |
|-----------------|------|------|------|------|------|------|------|------|------|------|
| Book Value† | 27.02 | 25.55 | 24.18 | 23.12 | 22.44 | 22.27 | 22.27 | 21.02 | 20.64 | 19.87 |
| Earnings | 4.06 | 3.82 | 3.51 | 3.05 | 2.55 | 2.92 | 3.19 | 2.15 | 2.71 | 2.60 |
| Dividends | 2.56 | 2.40 | 2.28 | 2.12 | 2.04 | 1.94 | 1.84 | 1.76 | 1.66 | 1.53½ |
| Payout Ratio | 63% | 63% | 65% | 70% | 80% | 66% | 58% | 82% | 61% | 59% |
| Prices—High | 30 | 27⅞ | 24⅜ | 19¼ | 19⅞ | 21¼ | 21⅞ | 22⅞ | 21⅜ | 18¾ |
| Low | 23¾ | 23¼ | 17½ | 15 | 14¾ | 18 | 18 | 20¼ | 18¼ | 13⅝ |
| P/E Ratio— | 7-6 | 7-6 | 7-5 | 6-5 | 8-6 | 7-6 | 7-6 | 11-9 | 8-7 | 7-5 |

Data as orig. reptd. 1. As reptd. by co.

**May 30, 1985**

## Exhibit 20-1. (Continued)

# 1518

### Minnesota Power & Light Company

### Income Data (Million $)

| Year Ended Dec. 31 | Oper. Revs. | Depr. | Maint. | Oper. Ratio | [1]Fxd. Chgs. Cover. | Constr. Crs. | Eff. Tax Rate | Net Inc. | % Return On | | |
| | | | | | | | | | Revs. | [2]Invest. Capital | [3]Com. Equity |
|---|---|---|---|---|---|---|---|---|---|---|---|
| 1984 | 417 | 33.9 | 17.4 | 82.9% | 2.28 | 0.2 | 32.6% | 59.3 | 14.2% | 8.9% | 15.4% |
| 1983 | 374 | 31.3 | 16.3 | 81.0% | 2.20 | 0.3 | 43.2% | 54.1 | 14.5% | 8.9% | 15.4% |
| 1982 | 364 | 27.4 | 16.5 | 79.4% | 1.97 | 0.9 | 46.9% | 48.4 | 13.3% | 9.3% | 14.8% |
| 1981 | 369 | 30.5 | 17.0 | 80.0% | 1.86 | 1.1 | 50.5% | 41.6 | 11.3% | 8.9% | 13.4% |
| 1980 | 331 | 22.6 | 14.5 | 81.0% | 1.67 | 7.8 | 44.3% | 34.3 | 10.4% | 8.6% | 11.4% |
| 1979 | 281 | 13.6 | 14.6 | 82.1% | 1.83 | 15.0 | 38.0% | 35.0 | 12.5% | 9.1% | 13.3% |
| 1978 | 252 | 12.2 | 11.1 | 81.7% | 2.02 | 6.8 | 46.7% | 31.6 | 12.5% | 9.7% | 15.1% |
| 1977 | 187 | 10.6 | 11.2 | 84.9% | 1.88 | 4.9 | 45.2% | 17.9 | 9.6% | 7.5% | 10.4% |
| 1976 | 137 | 9.6 | 8.1 | 82.0% | 1.97 | 2.5 | 45.1% | 15.8 | 11.5% | 8.6% | 12.6% |

### Balance Sheet Data (Million $)

| Dec. 31 | Gross Prop. | Capital Expend. | Net Prop. | % Earn. on Net Prop. | Total Invest. Capital | Capitalization | | | | | |
| | | | | | | LT Debt | % LT Debt | Pfd. | % Pfd. | Com. | % Com. |
|---|---|---|---|---|---|---|---|---|---|---|---|
| 1984 | 1,149 | 28 | 888 | 8.3% | 1,115 | 456 | 50.8% | 83.5 | 9.3% | 358 | 39.9% |
| 1983 | 1,049 | 26 | 839 | 8.5% | 1,001 | 403 | 49.6% | 83.5 | 10.3% | 326 | 40.1% |
| 1982 | 1,026 | 32 | 845 | 8.9% | 948 | 403 | 51.5% | 83.5 | 10.7% | 295 | 37.8% |
| 1981 | 1,001 | 39 | 842 | 8.8% | 869 | 379 | 51.7% | 83.5 | 11.4% | 271 | 36.9% |
| 1980 | 965 | 58 | 833 | 7.7% | 833 | 392 | 53.8% | 83.7 | 11.5% | 253 | 34.7% |
| 1979 | 906 | 162 | 793 | 7.0% | 782 | 384 | 54.5% | 83.7 | 11.9% | 237 | 33.6% |
| 1978 | 734 | 207 | 633 | 8.6% | 660 | 326 | 54.7% | 63.7 | 10.7% | 206 | 34.6% |
| 1977 | 529 | 109 | 438 | 7.3% | 469 | 226 | 52.9% | 43.7 | 10.2% | 158 | 36.9% |
| 1976 | 422 | 63 | 340 | 7.9% | 372 | 175 | 50.7% | 43.7 | 12.7% | 126 | 36.6% |

Data as orig. reptd. **1.** Times int. exp. and pfd. divs. covered (aft. taxes). **2.** Based on income bef. interest charges. **3.** As reptd. by co. after 1978. **4.** Utility Plant.

### Operating Revenues (Million $)

| Quarter: | 1985 | 1984 | 1983 | 1982 |
|---|---|---|---|---|
| Mar. | 111.4 | 105.6 | 90.2 | 105.6 |
| Jun. | | 99.4 | 94.0 | 95.6 |
| Sep. | | 98.8 | 95.6 | 81.4 |
| Dec. | | 113.5 | 94.3 | 81.8 |
| | | 417.3 | 374.1 | 364.4 |

Operating revenues for the three months ended March 31, 1985 rose 5.6%, year to year. Operating expenses increased 5.4%, reflecting lower fuel and purchased power expenses; operating income was up 6.3%. With sharply higher other income, net income rose 30%. After preferred dividends, share earnings were $1.52 on 3.9% more shares, compared with $1.20.

### Common Share Earnings ($)

| Quarter: | 1985 | 1984 | 1983 | 1982 |
|---|---|---|---|---|
| Mar. | 1.53 | 1.20 | 1.05 | 0.99 |
| Jun. | | 1.07 | 0.89 | 0.90 |
| Sep. | | 0.89 | 0.98 | 1.00 |
| Dec. | | 0.90 | 0.90 | 0.62 |
| | | 4.06 | 3.82 | 3.51 |

### Dividend Data

Dividends have been paid since 1945. A dividend reinvestment plan is available.

| Amt. of Divd. $ | Date Decl. | Ex-divd. Date | Stock of Record | Payment Date |
|---|---|---|---|---|
| 0.64 | Jul. 25 | Aug. 9 | Aug. 15 | Sep. 1'84 |
| 0.64 | Oct. 24 | Nov. 8 | Nov. 15 | Dec. 1'84 |
| 0.69 | Jan. 30 | Feb. 8 | Feb. 15 | Mar. 1'85 |
| 0.69 | Apr. 24 | May 9 | May 15 | Jun. 1'85 |

Next dividend meeting: late Jul. '85.

### Finances

The company has not filed for a rate increase since mid-1981 and has no plans to seek higher retail rates before 1987. MPL planned only minimal external financing through 1993, much of which was expected to come in 1985 through shareholder and employee stock purchase plans.

### Capitalization

Long Term Debt: $456,299,000.

Red. Cum. Preferred Stock: $40,000,000.

Cum. Preferred Stock: $43,547,000.

Common Stock: 13,255,234 shs. (no par). Institutions hold about 15%. Shareholders of record: 33,000.

Office—30 W. Superior St., Duluth, Minn. 55802. Tel—(218) 722-2641. Chrmn & CEO—J. F. Rowe. Pres—A. J. Sandbulte. Secy—J. R. Habicht. Treas & Investor Contact—D. L. Hollingsworth. Dirs—K. C. Boentje, R. M. Bowman, J. H. Claypool, W. C. Cochrane, D. W. Dunne, R. P. Fox, R. L. Heller, J. H. Lemme, R. S. Mars, Jr., G. A. Rossman, J. F. Rowe, M. E. Ryland, A. J. Sandbulte, F. E. Stout, H. F. Zigmund. Transfer Agents—Company's office; Manufacturers Hanover Trust Co., NYC. Registrars—First Bank, Duluth; Manufacturers Hanover Trust Co., NYC. Incorporated in Minnesota in 1906.

Information has been obtained from sources believed to be reliable, but its accuracy and completeness are not guaranteed.      Michael J. Puleo

### Exhibit 20-2.   Standard & Poor's Evaluation of Middle South Utilities, a Nuclear Powered Electric Utility

# Middle South Utilities                                 1490

NYSE Symbol MSU    Options on CBOE (Mar-Jun-Sep-Dec)    In S&P 500

| Price | Range | P-E Ratio | Dividend | Yield | S&P Ranking |
|---|---|---|---|---|---|
| Sep. 13'85 | 1985 | | | | |
| 9¼ | 15¼-8⅛ | 3 | 4--- | 4--- | NR |

### Summary

This holding company primarily supplies electricity in Arkansas, Louisiana, Mississippi and southeast Missouri. MSU's Grand Gulf 1 nuclear unit began commercial operation in July, 1985, and the Waterford 3 nuclear unit was expected in commercial service in October, 1985. MSU omitted its common dividend in August, 1985 because of liquidity problems associated with the start-up of Grand Gulf 1. Subsequently, two regulatory bodies granted a small amount of emergency rate relief.

### Current Outlook

Earnings for 1985 are tentatively projected at $2.25 a share, down sharply from 1984's $2.76.

Directors omitted the $0.44½ common dividend on August 29, 1985.

Earnings for 1985 will be restricted by increased expenses associated with the commercial operation of Grand Gulf 1 and Waterford 3. Without adequate rate relief to cover operating costs associated with these plants, MSU could face a severe liquidity crisis. While some rate relief has been granted, further increases are necessary; full recovery of costs is not anticipated. Electric kwh sales through 1994 are expected to increase 1.6% a year. Construction spending for 1985-87 is estimated at $2.36 billion.

### Operating Revenues (Million $)

| Quarter: | 1985 | 1984 | 1983 | 1982 |
|---|---|---|---|---|
| Mar. | 754 | 740 | 651 | 643 |
| Jun. | 750 | 729 | 637 | 658 |
| Sep. | --- | 953 | 918 | 888 |
| Dec. | --- | 723 | 703 | 713 |
| | --- | 3,146 | 2,910 | 2,902 |

Operating revenues for the six months ended June 30, 1985 rose 2.4%, year to year. Share earnings rose 3.1%, to $1.34 from $1.30, which excluded a special credit of $0.11.

### Common Share Earnings ($)

| Quarter: | 1985 | 1984 | 1983 | 1982 |
|---|---|---|---|---|
| Mar. | 0.71 | 0.69 | 0.43 | 0.56 |
| Jun. | 0.63 | 0.61 | 0.55 | 0.46 |
| Sep. | E0.60 | 0.96 | 0.97 | 0.95 |
| Dec. | E0.31 | 0.49 | 0.51 | 0.36 |
| | E2.25 | 2.76 | 2.46 | 2.33 |

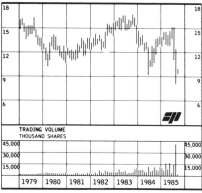

TRADING VOLUME
THOUSAND SHARES

### Important Developments

Sep. '85—The Louisiana PSC refused to grant a $98 million rate increase to Louisiana Power & Light (L P&L). Earlier, the Arkansas PSC approved an $81 million rate hike for Arkansas Power & Light (AP&L), New Orleans regulators granted a $28.3 million 10-month rate increase to New Orleans Public Service (NOPS), and the Mississippi PSC said it would look favorable on a small rate hike for Mississippi Power & Light (MP&L). The regulatory actions followed the omission of MSU's common dividend in August, which was precipitated by liquidity problems resulting from the commercial operation of the Grand Gulf 1 nuclear plant in July. The rate decisions were far below the requests of: MP&L $220 million, LP&L $324 million, AP&L $246 million, and NOPS $118 million.

Next earnings report due in mid-October.

### Per Share Data ($)

| Yr. Ended Dec. 31 | 1984 | 1983 | 1982 | 1981 | 1980 | 1979 | 1978 | 1977 | 1976 | 1975 |
|---|---|---|---|---|---|---|---|---|---|---|
| Book Value[1] | 18.36 | 18.07 | 17.81 | 17.69 | 17.75 | 18.40 | 18.60 | 17.82 | 17.17 | 16.85 |
| Earnings[3] | 2.76 | 2.46 | 2.33 | 2.44 | 2.01 | 2.13 | 2.46 | 2.18 | 1.82 | 1.70 |
| Dividends[2] | 1.75 | 1.71 | 1.67 | 1.63 | 1.59 | 1.53½ | 1.46 | 1.39½ | 1.33½ | 1.27½ |
| Payout Ratio | 63% | 70% | 72% | 67% | 79% | 72% | 59% | 64% | 73% | 75% |
| Prices—High | 14¾ | 16¾ | 15¾ | 13⅞ | 14¼ | 16⅜ | 17⅜ | 17⅞ | 17⅜ | 16⅜ |
| Low | 9¼ | 13⅛ | 12¼ | 11 | 10¼ | 12¼ | 14¼ | 15⅜ | 13⅝ | 12⅜ |
| P/E Ratio— | 5-3 | 7-5 | 7-5 | 6-5 | 7-5 | 8-6 | 7-6 | 8-7 | 10-7 | 10-7 |

Data as orig. reptd. 1. As reptd. by co. prior to 1984. 2. Declared. 3. Bef. spec. item(s) of +0.10 in 1984. 4. Dirs. omitted divd. Aug. 29, 1985. E-Estimated.

September 20, 1985

**Exhibit 20-2. (Continued)**

## 1490                    Middle South Utilities, Inc.

### Income Data (Million $)

| Year Ended Dec. 31 | Oper. Revs. | Depr. | Maint. | Oper. Ratio | [1]Fxd. Chgs. Cover. | Constr. Crs. | Eff. Tax Rate | [2]Net Inc. | % Return On Revs. | [3]Invest. Capital | [4]Com. Equity |
|---|---|---|---|---|---|---|---|---|---|---|---|
| 1984 | 3,146 | 192 | 161 | 82.4% | 1.91 | 537 | 31.7% | 575 | 18.3% | 10.3% | 15.7% |
| 1983 | 2,910 | 183 | 149 | 84.7% | 1.79 | 426 | 29.4% | 458 | 15.7% | 9.9% | 13.8% |
| 1982 | 2,902 | 168 | 143 | 85.0% | 1.67 | 353 | 31.0% | 379 | 13.1% | 10.2% | 13.3% |
| 1981 | 2,772 | 159 | 136 | 85.3% | 1.67 | 301 | 34.8% | 342 | 12.3% | 10.4% | 13.8% |
| 1980 | 2,342 | 142 | 112 | 87.3% | 1.58 | 240 | cr0.5% | 251 | 10.7% | 9.0% | 11.0% |
| 1979 | 1,823 | 119 | 111 | 88.0% | 1.74 | 213 | cr12.9% | 218 | 12.0% | 8.2% | 11.8% |
| 1978 | 1,622 | 113 | 100 | 85.9% | 1.96 | 148 | 14.5% | 211 | 13.0% | 8.5% | 14.2% |
| 1977 | 1,443 | 106 | 73 | 85.9% | 1.90 | 99 | 29.0% | 168 | 11.6% | 7.9% | 13.1% |

### Balance Sheet Data (Million $)

| Dec. 31 | [5]Gross Prop. | [5]Capital Expend. | Net Prop. | % Earn. on Net Prop. | Total Invest. Capital | LT Debt | % LT Debt | Pfd. | % Pfd. | Com. | % Com. |
|---|---|---|---|---|---|---|---|---|---|---|---|
| 1984 | 13,295 | 1,392 | 11,439 | 5.1% | 10,719 | 5,877 | 57.9% | 808 | 8.0% | 3,472 | 34.1% |
| 1983 | 11,942 | 1,513 | 10,248 | 4.6% | 9,275 | 5,032 | 57.2% | 761 | 8.7% | 3,002 | 34.1% |
| 1982 | 10,464 | 1,445 | 8,912 | 5.3% | 8,039 | 4,429 | 58.3% | 686 | 9.0% | 2,482 | 32.7% |
| 1981 | 9,080 | 1,228 | 7,673 | 5.7% | 7,163 | 3,896 | 58.0% | 631 | 9.4% | 2,190 | 32.6% |
| 1980 | 7,894 | 940 | 6,629 | 4.8% | 6,293 | 3,392 | 57.4% | 614 | 10.4% | 1,906 | 32.2% |
| 1979 | 7,002 | 858 | 5,863 | 4.0% | 5,588 | 3,018 | 57.9% | 524 | 10.1% | 1,664 | 32.0% |
| 1978 | 6,052 | 743 | 5,014 | 4.9% | 4,812 | 2,630 | 60.0% | 341 | 7.8% | 1,415 | 32.2% |
| 1977 | 5,183 | 615 | 4,248 | 5.1% | 4,136 | 2,175 | 58.6% | 341 | 9.2% | 1,198 | 32.2% |

Data as orig. reptd. 1. Times int. exp. & pfd. divs. covered (aft. taxes). 2. Bef. pfd. stk. divs. of subs.; bef. spec. item(s) in 1984. 3. Based on income before interest charges. 4. As reptd. by co. 5. Utility Plant. cr-Credit.

### Business Summary

Middle South Utilities is a holding company controlling Arkansas Power & Light, Louisiana Power & Light, Mississippi Power & Light and New Orleans Public Service. Electricity is supplied to a population of 4.6 million in Arkansas, Louisiana, Mississippi and Missouri. Gas service is provided in New Orleans. Revenues in 1984 were 94% electric and 6% gas.

| Electric Revs. | 1984 | 1983 | 1982 | 1981 |
|---|---|---|---|---|
| Residential.......... | 35% | 35% | 35% | 34% |
| Commercial ........ | 22% | 22% | 21% | 21% |
| Industrial.............. | 35% | 34% | 36% | 36% |
| Other ................. | 8% | 9% | 8% | 9% |

The fuel mix in 1984 was 43% gas, 19% nuclear, 15% coal, 1% oil/hydro, and 22% purchased. Peak load in 1984 was 10,456 mw (summer) and system capability at time of peak totaled 13,824 mw, for a reserve margin of 32%.

MSU's 90%-owned Grand Gulf 1 nuclear plant (1,125 mw) began commercial operation on July 1, 1985. Construction of Grand Gulf 2 has proceeded on a limited basis since 1979; at March 31, 1985 Unit 2 was 34%-complete, and MSU's investment in the plant totaled $863 million. The Waterford 3 nuclear unit (1,104 mw) was expected to begin commercial operation in October, 1985.

### Dividend Data

Common dividends were omitted in August, 1985 after having been paid since 1949. Dividends have been maintained on the preferred stock. Common payments in the past 12 months:

| Amt. of Divd. $ | Date Decl. | Ex-divd. Date | Stock of Record | Payment Date |
|---|---|---|---|---|
| 0.44½ | Nov. 30 | Dec. 5 | Dec. 11 | Jan. 2'85 |
| 0.44½ | Feb. 28 | Mar. 5 | Mar. 11 | Apr. 1'85 |
| 0.44½ | May 17 | Jun. 4 | Jun. 10 | Jul. 1'85 |

Directors omitted the dividend Aug. 29, 1985.

### Finances

In May, 1985 MSU filed shelf registrations covering 162,400 common shares. In July, 1985 New Orleans Public Service was allowed to sell $60 million of securities, but could not apply proceeds to Grand Gulf 1. At June 30, 1985 Louisiana Power & Light was unable to issue mortgage bonds or preferred stock. Mississippi Power & Light and Arkansas Power & Light had limited financing ability.

### Capitalization

**Long Term Debt:** $5,915,664,000.

**Subsidiary Preferred Stock:** $799,780,000.

**Common Stock:** 204,345,061 shs. ($5 par).
Institutions hold about 17%.
Shareholders of record: 216,146.

**Office**—225 Baronne St., New Orleans, La. 70112. **Tel**—(504) 529-5262. **Chrmn & Pres**— F. W. Lewis. **VP-Fin**—E. A. Lupberger. **Secy**—D. E. Stapp. **Investor Contact**—Peter Delaney. **Dirs**—J. M. Cain, J. A. Cooper, B. H. Duncan, K. Hodges, Jr., F. W. Lewis, D. C. Lutken, J. L. Maulden, L. P. Percy, R. D. Pugh, H. D. Shackelford, F. G. Smith, Jr., W. S. Smith, W. Washington. **Transfer Agent & Registrar**—Morgan Guaranty Trust Co., NYC. **Incorporated** in Florida in 1949.

Information has been obtained from sources believed to be reliable, but its accuracy and completeness are not guaranteed.      Michael J. Puleo

**Exhibit 20-3.   Moderate Risk: Public Utilities**

**INVESTMENT PROFILE**

| INVESTMENT CHARACTERISTICS | Excellent | Good | Average | Poor | None |
|---|---|---|---|---|---|
| Liquidity | ✓ | | | | |
| Safety of Principal | | ✓ | | | |
| Price Stability | | | ✓ | | |
| Reinvestment Protection | | | ✓ | | |
| Growth of Capital | | ✓ | | | |
| Cash Income | ✓ | | | | |
| Growth of Income | | | ✓ | | |
| Inflation Hedge | | LT | | ST | |
| Tax Advantaged | | | | | ✓* |

**Liquidity**—the ability to quickly realize cash from the sale at fair market value

**Safety of Principal**—the principal is safe from bankruptcy or default

**Price Stability**—the market value of the asset does not change in value

**Reinvestment Protection**—protection against reinvesting cash flow at lower rates as interest rates decline

**Growth of Capital**—the original investment increases over time to create capital gains

**Cash Income**—the cash income relative to treasury bills returns

**Growth of Income**—the ability of the cash income stream to increase over time

**Inflation Hedge**—the ability of total return (cash income plus capital gains) to keep pace with inflation over time

**Tax Advantaged**—the ability to reduce or defer current federal income taxes

*Some utilities have special tax treatment if capital distributions are paid out in dividends. If the IRS continues the $100 deductibility of dividends, the investor can get a small tax benefit.
LT = Long-term holdings of public utilities (5–10 years).
ST = Short-term holdings of public utilities (1–3 years).

# CHAPTER 21

# New Issue Stocks or Initial Public Offerings

## DESCRIPTION

New issues of common stock are often referred to as *initial public offerings*. This is stock that has not previously been owned by the general public.

Initial public offerings are frequently made by companies that have successfully developed a new product or service. Many times these companies are relatively small in terms of total revenues and total assets (less than $10 million). Occasionally, initial public offerings are made for larger and more seasoned companies. This is the exception rather than the rule.

In some instances companies with only a marketing concept or a very raw research and development prototype product raise capital by offering stock to the general public. Typically these companies are involved in a very exciting field. This excitement for a particular industry may make it possible to sell stock in a company that has no earnings, few assets, and perhaps no revenues.

Prior to "going public" most companies are owned by a small group of individuals that founded and continue to manage the company. There may be an ownership position held by venture capital firms in the young company as well.

The stock sold to the general public in an initial public offering may be additional shares issued at the time the company conducts the offering or shares previously owned by the founders. Generally, it is preferable to have all new shares issued. Occasionally, both new shares and some of the founders' shares are issued at the same time. Sometimes founders have all their wealth tied up in one company and they choose to sell a fraction of their shares to increase their portfolio's liquidity and diversification.

Initial public offerings are made by an investment banker through a securities brokerage firm on behalf of the particular company involved. The main investment banking firm involved in the offering is referred to as the *lead underwriter*. This lead underwriter recruits brokerage firms to help sell the new issue of common stock. Together these firms are referred to as the *underwriting group*.

## STRENGTHS

Initial public offerings offer the potential for investors to acquire stock in rapidly growing companies without commission cost.

## WEAKNESSES

Initial public offerings are arbitrarily priced often at a premium to the shares of seasoned companies in the same industry. Prices of the stocks may be very volatile.

## UNIQUE FEATURES

One of the unique features of an initial public offering is the fact that no commissions are charged to investors purchasing the stocks. The selling brokers are paid a fee by the offering company.

Occasionally, an initial public offering may become a "hot issue" and appreciate in price very rapidly. This is discussed more completely later in this chapter.

## TAX CONSEQUENCES

Income from sales of initial public offering stock, like other stock, is taxable the Internal Revenue Service. If investors hold this stock for six months and one day or longer, 60 percent of any gain on sale of the asset above cost basis is excluded from taxation. Only 40 percent of the gain is included in taxable income.

Short-term capital gains are recognized on the profitable sale of initial public offering stock owned less than six months and one day. The entire amount of the gain above the cost basis in the stock is taxable as ordinary income.

Investors that sell initial public offering stock for a long-term capital loss (after a holding period over six months) are subject to long-term tax treatment of their loss. Only 50 percent of the loss can be used as a deduction to offset gross income, while the remaining 50 percent cannot be used at all. This means that one-half of a net long-term capital loss is deductible and the other half is not.

Short-term capital losses for the initial public offering stock investor are more favorable than long-term losses. The entire amount of a short-term capital loss is deductible from gross income up to an annual maximum of $3,000. Amounts in excess of $3,000 can be carried over to future years.

In reality, a special process of combining the gains and losses into a "net capital position" takes place for income tax reporting purposes. Because of this net effect, all of an investor's transactions involving capital gains and losses must be considered as a whole. This can include many transactions in addition to investments in initial public offering stocks.

Investors can best reduce or minimize their taxes for capital gains or losses by following the advice of a qualified tax professional.

## WHERE AND HOW TO BUY

To purchase most initial public offerings, the investor contacts a brokerage firm that is involved in the underwriting syndicate. An investor tells the broker to enter an "indication of interest" for a particular initial public offering. For example, the investor would tell the broker "I wish to enter an indication of interest for 1,000 shares of XYZ Industries." The broker furnishes the investor with a document called a "red herring." Technically this document is a preliminary prospectus that contains information about the initial public offering, including financial information, product information, and a company business plan. Some popular offerings are oversubscribed; investors cannot always be assured of getting all the shares they desire—sometimes they can get no shares at all.

Within a few days the initial public offering is brought to market at a specific price. At this time potential investors accept the shares of the new issue or withdraw their indication of interest. If they accept the stock, they pay for it and take ownership.

## HOW TO SELL

Most initial public offerings are traded in the over-the-counter market. This market system is maintained by the National Association of Securities Dealers (NASD). These stocks trade on a bid-and-offered basis. For example, a new offering in XYZ Industries may be assigned the stock symbol XYZI. XYZI is quoted "8 bid 8.25 offered."

An investor wishing to purchase XYZ Industries would pay $8.25 per share to buy the stock. An investor wishing to sell XYZ Industries would receive $8 per share from a member of the NASD that serves as a market maker in XYZI. The difference between the bid and asked price is the dealer's spread or profit, in this case 25 cents per share.

Generally, several NASD firms offer competing bids and offers for a stock traded over the counter. This tends to ensure a relatively fair and liquid market for the investor who needs to sell a portion of his or her holdings.

Occasionally, recently purchased stock in a new issue may be difficult to liquidate in large blocks. The reason could be that the market may have absorbed all of the stock it could handle at the time of the new issue. Any large blocks of stock being resold quickly could serve to depress the price, as additional new investors need to be found to acquire these outstanding shares of the company.

## TRANSACTION COSTS

As mentioned previously, investors purchasing initial public offerings from a member firm of the underwriting syndicate pay no transaction costs at the time of purchase. The company going public pays the underwriting firm a placement fee for selling the stock to investors. Liquidating the stock acquired in an initial public offering typically cost an investor a sales commission.

Investors should note that not all securities dealers charge the same fees for services performed. *Full-service brokerage firms* provide important services for clients over and above the actual execution of a simple buy or sell order. Other dealers, called *discount brokerage firms,* specialize in offering the lowest possible cost transactions and provide minimal additional services. An individual investor needs to review the level of service he or she requires and select a securities dealer accordingly.

## PORTFOLIO FIT

Initial public offerings are typically considered to be relatively high-risk situations for common stock investors. Many times the company going public for the first time is much smaller than its competitors.

Investors with a well-diversified portfolio of common stocks may wish to include selected new issues as a part of their portfolio. As a general rule, these stocks are considered to be more speculative investments and subject to quick profits or losses on the part of the investor.

Some investors concentrate on initial public offerings as a primary part of an investment strategy. In periods of rising common stock prices (a bull market), new issues tend to perform well. Usually a market can be judged to be at or near a peak by the increases in the number of initial public offerings.

This frenzied speculative activity often marks the end of a "hot market" for initial public offerings. During such a hot market speculators (rather than *investors*) will jump on any new issue. Often these traders work quickly on very small moves in the price of the initial public offering.

An initial public offering made at $8 per share may be up 50 cents or more in just one day. In this case speculators can liquidate their position, pocket the 50 cents per share, and receive a return on investment of 6.25 percent in just one day!

Most initial public offerings are priced based on a good recent track record. This track record is often difficult to match once the company becomes publicly owned.

## SOURCES OF ADDITIONAL INFORMATION

Specialty magazines and newsletters devoted to initial public offerings are advertised regularly in most of the major financial publications.

Most of the major brokerage firms provide a regular calendar type publication that lists all upcoming initial public offerings. Investors that plan to be active in the initial public offering area may wish to find a broker willing to furnish this list on a regular basis.

## COMMENTS

Investors should be very cautious in accessing initial public offerings, due to the arbitrary pricing involved at the time of issue. The price of the issue is determined by the best estimate of the underwriter whenever the issue comes to market. Obviously, it is in the best interest of the underwriter to obtain as much money as possible for the newly public company.

This generally causes new issues to be priced according to what the market will bear, not in accordance with the true or calculated value of the company. Most of the time a speculative premium is involved in initial public offerings. Within a few weeks or months after most new issues become public, interest "whipped up" by the underwriters is lost, and the issue often loses favor with investors.

If an investor has a particular interest in a special company or industry, initial public offerings may offer the opportunity to participate at a nominal cost. The offering documents for most initial public offerings are quite complete and offer a valuable source of information for the investor.

### Exhibit 21-1. Moderate Risk: Initial Public Offerings

### INVESTMENT PROFILE

| INVESTMENT CHARACTERISTICS | Excellent | Good | Average | Poor | None |
|---|---|---|---|---|---|
| Liquidity | | | ✓ | | |
| Safety of Principal | | | * | | |
| Price Stability | | | | ✓ | |
| Reinvestment Protection | | | | ✓ | |
| Growth of Capital | | * | | | |
| Cash Income | | | | ✓ | |
| Growth of Income | | | | ✓ | |
| Inflation Hedge | | ✓ | | | |
| Tax Advantaged | | | | | ✓ |

**Liquidity**—the ability to quickly realize cash from the sale at fair market value

**Safety of Principal**—the principal is safe from bankruptcy or default

**Price Stability**—the market value of the asset does not change in value

**Reinvestment Protection**—protection against reinvesting cash flow at lower rates as interest rates decline

**Growth of Capital**—the original investment increases over time to create capital gains

**Cash Income**—the cash income relative to treasury bills returns

**Growth of Income**—the ability of the cash income stream to increase over time

**Inflation Hedge**—the ability of total return (cash income plus capital gains) to keep pace with inflation over time

**Tax Advantaged**—the ability to reduce or defer current federal income taxes

*This depends on the individual characteristics of the company going public.

# CHAPTER 22

# Variable Annuities

## DESCRIPTION

A *variable annuity* is a special life insurance policy designed for investment purposes. These special life insurance policies qualify for special tax deferred treatment under the Internal Revenue Code. There is a modest amount of pure life insurance associated with the variable annuity product, but generally it is not of significance in the investment decision process.

The primary benefit to investors in variable annuities is its flexibility and diversification, because the variable annuity includes various investments within a single vehicle. Investors are offered a choice of allocating their money into any of several investment options. Typically these portfolios include a growth stock portfolio, a corporate bond (high-income) portfolio, a money market portfolio, and a guaranteed interest rate option. In some variable annuities an investor may find special bond portfolios dedicated to a particular type of bond, for example, only U.S. government bonds.

Each of the various portfolios is professionally managed by the insurance company that underwrites the variable annuity.

An investor is not limited to only one portfolio at a time. Each investor can allocate funds on a percentage basis among the several portfolios. Furthermore, an investor can switch between the portfolios from time to time to achieve an investment strategy that keeps pace with changing economic conditions. All of the various options for investors are detailed in the remainder of this chapter.

## STRENGTHS

Variable annuities are totally tax deferred until money is withdrawn from the contract.

Variable annuities offer a flexible investment program that can change as the economy and individual investor's circumstances change. They incur no sales charges to the investor.

## WEAKNESSES

Variable annuities have a withdrawal penalty similar to that for a certificate of deposit if money is withdrawn shortly after being deposited into the contract. Also, depending on the type of fund the investor selects, the safety of principal is not guaranteed.

## UNIQUE FEATURES

Perhaps foremost of the features of a variable annuity is the flexibility of its investment options.

If investors want to participate in a rising stock market, they can allocate most of their money to the stock portfolio. If inflation is rising and interest rates are headed up, investors can allocate money to a money market portfolio where they earn progressively higher rates of return until the economic situation changes. Later, if the investors need a high rate of income from investments, they simply switch to the professionally managed bond portfolio. A portion of the investment can be withdrawn annually to provide needed income. During periods of declining interest rates, investors can take advantage of capital gains and high interest rates in the bond market by allocating funds to a bond portfolio.

It should be obvious from this example that the number of choices for investment within the variable annuity is almost endless. Even the most rapidly changing economic and personal circumstances can be dealt with within the variable annuity.

In addition to investment flexibility, a major advantage of the variable annuity is tax deferral. Unlike a mutual fund, in which all of the gains and income accumulated annually are taxable to the shareholder, these gains and income are totally tax deferred for owners of a variable annuity.

Variable annuities offer liquidity to investors if it is needed. To summarize, investors can transfer their money among funds whenever they see the need. Variable annuities are offered without sales charges to the investor; however, the insurance company offering the annuity charges fees for the professional portfolio management.

If an investor purchases a $100,000 annuity and designates the investment to be placed into a stock or bond fund, the investor may lose part of the principal. After all, stocks and bonds fluctuate in value.

In the event of the investor's death when the value of the account is lower than the amount originally invested, typically the insurance company will pay the entire original amount invested to the beneficiary designated in the investor's application form.

## TAX CONSEQUENCES

As mentioned previously, all income and capital gains earned within the variable annuity contract are 100 percent tax deferred until the investor withdraws all or a portion of the money.

If the investor makes a partial withdrawal from his or her account, all of the earned income will be considered as being withdrawn first for federal income taxes. This would make the entire amount earned within the contract and subsequently withdrawn taxable as ordinary income.

If an investor withdraws more than the amount earned to date, the portion of the withdrawal that constitutes part of the original investment is not taxed. It is a return of capital.

Thus, if an investor withdraws the entire balance of the annuity, its earnings are taxed as ordinary income, and the original amount invested being returned is treated as a return of capital.

The strategy most variable annuity investors use is simple. Variable annuity investors generally hope to defer taxation until such time as they are no longer in a high tax bracket. The obvious case is an investor (for example, one who is age 50) who can accumulate money in the variable annuity tax deferred and withdraw the money later in life after retirement.

It should be noted that any investor in a variable annuity receives this special tax deferral. It is not necessary to invest within the individual retirement account, Keogh plan, or qualified pension plan to receive the tax deferred status!

## WHERE AND HOW TO BUY

Very few stockbrokers and insurance agents actively market variable annuities. The reasons for this are simple. First, a special license is required in most states from the state insurance commission before an insurance agent, stock broker, investment adviser, or other professional can sell the variable annuity product. Second, variable annuities do not pay sales commissions that are as high as other products offered by life insurance agents and stockbrokers. Variable annuities pay the broker or agent only half as much in commissions as some mutual funds.

An investor completes an application form that requests standard information about the investor's residence, age, social security number, and so on. The form also designates a beneficiary in case of the investor's death. There is an additional space on the form for the initial allocation of funds into the various portfolios offered by the insurance company.

A check made payable to the insurance company is forwarded along with the signed application to the insurance company. The insurance company will open an account in the investor's name and assign the account an identity number. Subsequently the investor receives receipts from the insurance company for any additional contributions to the variable annuity and normally receives quarterly statements of the account's performance.

## HOW TO SELL

Variable annuities are easy to liquidate. Typically an investor need only write a brief letter to the insurance company requesting either full or partial liquidation of an account. The investor may also specify a particular dollar amount to be liquidated. In most cases, an investor should receive a check for the invested funds within five working days.

Another important alternative available to variable annuity investors is the *annuitization* of the contract. In simple terms, an investor can elect to have the insurance company make a series of monthly payments to the investor for a designated period of time, even as long as the investor lives.

Other annuitization plans may be set up to include the spouse of the investor. This ensures income for as long as either spouse lives. One last option for annuitization is payments for life or a certain period, whichever is longer. This guarantees an income stream to a beneficiary should the investor die prior to the guaranteed period's expiration (for example, life or a 20-year period, whichever is longer).

Annuitization of a life insurance contract should be discussed with the investor's financial adviser prior to selecting this conversion option. There are tax considerations, income requirements, and potential health considerations that enter into the decision process.

## TRANSACTION COSTS

Variable annuities have absolutely no sales charges to an investor. If an investor signs a check for $100,000, all of the money goes to work in the annuity immediately.

The insurance company that underwrites the variable annuity product pays the selling agent a placement fee. The investor is not required to pay this placement fee. The insurance company must protect itself from investors who would deposit and withdraw money frequently from the variable annuity (which is intended for long-term accrual). A withdrawal charge similar to the penalty banks attached to certificates of deposit is a part of the product. A typical withdrawal charge would be 5 percent of the value of the contract for a period of 5 years. After the end of the fifth year, the withdrawal charge is eliminated forever.

Simply put, if an investor purchases a variable annuity and leaves the money in the variable annuity for five years, there is no withdrawal penalty. Every time the same investor purchases a certificate of deposit, there is a new withdrawal penalty for the entire length of the certificate's term! Five years does not seem so long compared to duration of a penalty for a long-term certificate of deposit.

There are some good features about this withdrawal charge. Typically, the withdrawal charge does not apply to the first 10 percent of the value of the investor's contributions withdrawn each year. For example, an investor with a $100,000 contribution could withdraw $10,000 each year without any withdrawal charges. This is a very important benefit for those investors that may need a portion of their money in an emergency or those desiring a source of annual income.

In addition to the withdrawal charge that may or may not come into consideration, the insurance company typically receives an annual management fee for services rendered in managing the investment portfolios. The customary fee in this area is 1 to 1-1/2 percent of the assets under management. This fee is typically not charged to those investors selecting the guaranteed interest account investment option.

## PORTFOLIO FIT

Variable annuities are so flexible and offer so many different advantages in one product that it is easiest to describe the people who should not own them.

The only group that realistically should not own a variable annuity is exceptionally high-income investors. Even though a variable annuity offers excellent tax deferral, any income and capital gains that are ultimately withdrawn from the variable annuity are taxable as ordinary income. Because of this, an investor in a very high tax bracket loses the advantage of the favorable long-term capital gains treatment and might be better off investing in a portfolio of capital gains oriented investments. In this way, the high-income investor avoids the ordinary tax treatment on the variable annuity.

Other investors may not find the variable annuity perfect, but in most cases this product has at least some benefits.

One issue to consider for all tax deferred investments is the expected tax bracket during retirement. Often the marginal rates will *not* go down for the retired investor. Tax deferrals work for all investors because they provide the ability to compound returns tax free. However, they work best when a lower marginal tax bracket is expected at retirement.

Young investors can use a variable annuity for small regular contributions to their investment account. Where else can a beginning investor achieve portfolio diversification, professional management, and investment flexibility while retaining liquidity should it be needed suddenly?

Middle-aged investors may appreciate the ability to tax defer the gains and income from their investment portfolio during the highest income years of their lives.

Older investors appreciate the ability to convert the variable annuity contract at any time to a series of income payments guaranteed for life.

## SOURCES OF ADDITIONAL INFORMATION

Additional information can be obtained from licensed stockbrokers and insurance agents. A brochure on a variable annuity is available free of charge by calling collect 617-423-3500 and requesting "The Variable Annuity Brochure."

## COMMENTS

Variable annuities are one of the least discovered investments in our society. It should be obvious to the reader that no investment is perfect. If any one product comes close, it may be the variable annuity.

Variable annuities are tax advantaged; provide flexible investment options; offer diversified, professionally managed investment portfolios; are liquid if money is needed; and guarantee that in the event of death the beneficiary cannot receive less than the amount invested.

With all these advantages, why doesn't everyone own a variable annuity? Most investors are underinformed about variable annuities. The brokerage community does not promote this product, since it is not especially lucrative for salespeople.

**Exhibit 22-1.   Moderate Risk: Variable Annuities**

**INVESTMENT PROFILE**

| INVESTMENT CHARACTERISTICS | Excellent | Good | Average | Poor | None |
|---|---|---|---|---|---|
| Liquidity | | | ✓ | | |
| Safety of Principal | | | * | | |
| Price Stability | | | * | | |
| Reinvestment Protection | | | * | | |
| Growth of Capital | | | * | | |
| Cash Income | | | * | | |
| Growth of Income | | | * | | |
| Inflation Hedge | | | * | | |
| Tax Advantaged | | ✓ | | | |

**Liquidity**—the ability to quickly realize cash from the sale at fair market value

**Safety of Principal**—the principal is safe from bankruptcy or default

**Price Stability**—the market value of the asset does not change in value

**Reinvestment Protection**—protection against reinvesting cash flow at lower rates as interest rates decline

**Growth of Capital**—the original investment increases over time to create capital gains

**Cash Income**—the cash income relative to treasury bills returns

**Growth of Income**—the ability of the cash income stream to increase over time

**Inflation Hedge**—the ability of total return (cash income plus capital gains) to keep pace with inflation over time

**Tax Advantaged**—the ability to reduce or defer current federal income taxes

*Investment profile depends upon the particular allocation of assets among investment types such as bonds, stocks, or money market portfolios.

# CHAPTER 23

# United States Government Bonds

## DESCRIPTION

*United States government bonds* are long-term promissory notes of the U.S. government.

U.S. government bonds are considered to be without credit risk—there is no possibility that an investor will lose principal invested in a U.S. government bond. The government will not default on its legal obligation to pay interest and principal.

U.S. government bonds are issued in units of $1,000. The $1,000 is called the *face value* or *par value* of the bond. This is the amount to be received when the principal is repaid.

The interest payments on the bond are to be made at what is known as the *coupon rate,* or the amount of money the bondholder will receive each year. For example, if the bond has a coupon rate of 10 percent and par value of $1,000 the bondholder will receive $100 of interest each year from that bond. All U.S. government bonds pay interest semiannually.

At the time the bond is issued a maturity date is specified for the bond. This is the date when all of the bonds are to be retired and the investor is to receive the par value ($1,000). The interest rate earned on a U.S. government bond may be referred to in one of three ways.

The first method of calculating the yield of a U.S. government bond is called the *current yield*. The current yield is simply the annual coupon rate of interest paid on the bond divided by the price of the bond. It should be noted that not all bonds remain at par value once they are issued. Bond prices are adjusted by the market in response to changes in interest rates. This yield is calculated as follows:

$$12.5\% \text{ current yield} = \frac{\$100 \text{ annual interest payment}}{\$800 \text{ price paid for bond}}$$

Investors purchasing U.S. government bonds in the open market at some point after the original issue date will be required to pay accrued interest on the bond from the most recent interest payment date.

Investors who would ordinarily receive bond interest payments on January 1st and July 1st of each year may elect to sell their bonds on a business day that falls between the two interest payment dates. Because of this, the new purchaser of the bond will need to pay the former owner of the bond for the interest that is accrued on the U.S. government bonds from the date of the last interest payment until the date that the transaction takes place.

A second form of yield for a U.S. government bond is called the *yield to maturity*. The yield to maturity is the interest rate that equates the present value of the future interest payments and principal repayment on the bond with the current price of the bond. The yield to maturity represents the true rate of return earned on an investor's capital during the holding period for a U.S. government bond.

As an example, a U.S. government bond purchased above par value would have a higher current yield than a yield to maturity. The opposite is also true: a bond purchased below par value has a lower current yield than a yield to maturity. Whether an investor pays a premium or purchases bonds at a discount, the difference must be amortized over the life of the bond issue to calculate the yield to maturity. In reality most brokerage firms precalculate the yield to maturity for the investor at the time the investor contemplates the bond purchase.

For an *approximate* calculation of the yield to maturity, an investor could perform the math operation shown in the following example. A 10-year bond, with a 10 percent coupon rate of interest sells for $900. It is a $1,000 par value bond.

$$\text{YTM} = \frac{\text{Annual Interest} + \dfrac{\text{Face Value} - \text{Bond Value}}{\text{\# Years to Maturity}}}{\dfrac{\text{Face Value} + \text{Bond Price}}{2}}$$

$$\text{YTM} = \frac{\$100.00 + \dfrac{\$1,000.00 - \$900.00}{10}}{\dfrac{\$900.00 + \$1,000.00}{2}}$$

$$\text{YTM} = \frac{\$100.00 + \$10.00}{\$950}$$

$$11.58\% = \frac{\$110}{\$950}$$

As another example, a 10-year bond, with a 10 percent coupon rate of interest sells for $1,100. It is a $1,000 par value bond.

$$\text{YTM} = \frac{\$100.00 + \dfrac{\$1,000.00 - \$1,100.00}{10}}{\dfrac{\$1,100.00 + \$1,000.00}{2}}$$

$$\text{YTM} = \frac{\$100.00 + (\$-10)}{\$1050}$$

$$8.57\% = \frac{\$90}{\$1,050}$$

As a rule the approximation calculation for yield to maturity is not exact. The error increases as the discount or premium gets larger and as the maturity increases. For example, the exact answer determined on an HP12C calculation is 11.72 percent for the first example and 8.496 percent for the second example.

A third type of yield calculation is called the *yield to call date*. This yield is discussed more completely later in this chapter.

Bond yields are often quoted as an interest rate carried to two decimal places. These decimal places are referred to as a *basis point*. A basis point is simply 1/100 of a percentage point.

An example of the returns available for investors is contained Table 23-1.


## STRENGTHS

The principle strengths of U.S. government bonds is the regularity of interest payments to investors and the absolute safety of principal from default risk.

### Table 23-1.   Long-Term U.S. Government Bonds

| Year | Capital Appreciation (Loss) | Yield Returns | Reinvestment Returns | Total Returns |
|------|-----------------------------|---------------|----------------------|---------------|
| 1975 | .73% | 8.41% | .05% | 9.19% |
| 1976 | 8.06 | 8.10 | .59 | 16.75 |
| 1977 | (7.95) | 7.85 | (.57) | (.67) |
| 1978 | (9.08) | 8.64 | (.72) | (1.16) |
| 1979 | (9.79) | 9.42 | (.84) | (1.22) |
| 1980 | (13.77) | 11.24 | (1.43) | (3.95) |
| 1981 | (10.40) | 13.54 | (1.30) | 1.85 |
| 1982 | 23.86 | 13.56 | 2.93 | 40.35 |
| 1983 | (9.92) | 11.56 | (1.06) | .68 |
| 1984 | 2.26 | 12.91 | .27 | 15.43 |
| 1975–1984 | 10-year average annual compound rate of return | | | 7.03% |
| | 10-year Consumer Price Index | | | 7.34% |
| 1980–1984 | 5-year average annual compound rate of return | | | 9.80% |
| | 5-year Consumer Price Index | | | 6.54% |
| 1975–1979 | 5-year average annual compound rate of return | | | 4.34% |
| | 5-year Consumer Price Index | | | 8.15% |

*Source:* Ibbotson and Sinquefield, Exhibit 5, Page 27, 1985 Update. Reprinted with permission.

## WEAKNESSES

The primary weakness of U.S. government bonds is interest rate risk. As interest rates rise, long-term bond prices can fall as much as 15 to 20 percent in one year. Long-term U.S. government bonds are unable to protect the investor against loss of purchasing power over the long run.

## UNIQUE FEATURES

A special feature of U.S. government bonds is a call provision. A call provision enables the government to repay the debt prior to the stated maturity date. The investor has no choice in the matter, since the call provision is stated at the time the bond is issued.

The call provision in U.S. government bonds generally applies only to the last five years prior to maturity of the bond.

This is a much less important call provision than investors may find with corporate bonds.

The government is unlikely to call outstanding bonds unless new bonds can be sold at a lower interest rate to replace the called bonds.

In the event of declining interest rates, the risk of having the bond called away from an investor prevents the bond price from moving as high as it would if it was without a call provision.

The investment community has adapted to the deferred call with the concept of the yield to call date (as compared to the yield to maturity date). The yield to call of a bond is calculated based on the call date becoming the maturity date and amortizing the premium price of a bond in the market place over the time period that remains until the call date.

## TAX CONSEQUENCES

Interest income received from U.S. government bonds is fully taxable for federal income tax purposes. Interest income from U.S. government bonds is not subject to state and local income taxes.

When the investor sells a bond, or when it is held to maturity, capital gain and loss rules generally determine any tax liabilities.

The capital gains rules, original issue discount rule, and nonoriginal issue discount rule are complicated calculations, due to the Tax Reform Act of 1984. Because of these calculations, investors should consult a qualified tax professional to learn the impact of gains, losses, and taxable income on government bonds.

Bonds may be purchased at a premium above face value. When a corporate bond is purchased for an amount above face value, the bondholder may elect to amortize the premium. For the bond holder, this election will result in deductible interest expense from amortizing the premium. This also reduces the bond's cost basis. If the election to amortize is not chosen, then the purchase price will continue to be the cost basis of the bond.

This election is important, because if an investor plans to sell a bond before maturity, it is likely that he or she should elect to amortize the premium, even though the basis is being reduced. The reason for this is that the benefit of offsetting interest income with a dollar-for-dollar interest deduction is probably better than keeping the cost basis high. A higher basis merely reduces a capital gain or loss upon the bonds eventual sale. If the bond is held until maturity for the primary benefit of receiving interest payments, then the election should definitely be made.

In summary, calculation of taxes on bonds at first may seem very straightforward and simple because all interest income received is taxable for federal income tax purposes. In actuality, several special rules may make government bond taxation a relatively tricky area for the typical investor to understand. Once again, investors should seek the advice and council of qualified tax professionals when calculating taxes owed on government bonds.

## WHERE AND HOW TO BUY

United States government bonds may be purchased on any regular business day through virtually all securities brokerage firms or some bank trust departments.

New issues of U.S. government bonds may be purchased directly through the regional offices of the Federal Reserve banking system. Exhibit 23-1 displays an individual application for treasury bonds.

Investors must fill out a purchase order form prior to the issuance of the treasury bonds. Investors indicate the amount of the bond issue that they wish to purchase. These purchase order forms must be submitted prior to 12:00 noon on the date of the issue of the bonds.

The investor who purchases directly from the Federal Reserve bank receives the average yield for the entire bond issue. Investors who purchase directly from the Federal Reserve banking system may pay for bond purchases with a personal check.

All treasury bonds are issued is what is called *book entry form*. Book entry form requires the name and the address of the investor to be recorded by the federal government. These investors then receive interest payments by mail from the federal government. Upon maturity of the bond, the principal is also repaid to the investor by mail. The investor does not actually receive a bond certificate. The book entry method records all the important information on government computers. There are no certificates issued.

When executing a bond purchase from a securities brokerage firm, an investor typically is allowed five business days to pay for the purchase. The brokerage firm will furnish the investor with a written confirmation of the transaction. Once again, book entry form is used to record the purchase information. The investor will receive a regular monthly statement from the brokerage firm which will reflect the ownership position in the U.S. government bonds.

## Exhibit 23-1.   Government Bond Application Form

### INDIVIDUAL APPLICATION FOR TREASURY NOTES/BONDS

Tenders must be received by 12:00 Noon Central Standard Time on the auction date.
(12:00 Noon Central Daylight Savings Time if applicable)

Mail or Deliver Tenders To:  Federal Reserve Bank of Dallas
Attn: Tender For Treasury Offering

| Securities Dept. | Cash/F.A. Dept. | Fiscal Agency Dept. | Cash/F.A. Dept. |
|---|---|---|---|
| Station K | P.O. Box 100 | P.O. Box 2578 | P.O. Box 1471 |
| ☐ Dallas, Texas 75222 | ☐ El Paso, Texas 79999 | ☐ Houston, Texas 77252 | ☐ San Antonio, Texas 78295 |

**PRIVACY STATEMENT**                                                                 **Today's Date** _____

"The individually identifiable information required on this form is necessary to permit the tender to be processed and the securities to be issued. If registered securities are requested, the regulations governing United States securities (Department Circular No. 300) and the offering circular require submission of social security numbers, the numbers and other information are used in inscribing the securities and establishing and servicing the ownership and interest records. The transaction will not be completed unless all required data is furnished."

Pursuant to provisions of the applicable Treas. Dept. Circ., the undersigned hereby subscribes for the following securities:

| DESCRIPTION OF NOTES - BONDS | CUSIP 9128 | DATE OF ISSUE | DUE |
|---|---|---|---|
| | | | |

### TYPE OF BID

**NONCOMPETITIVE TENDER** $ _____ **NOT TO EXCEED $1,000,000**

Noncompetitive tenders for $1,000,000 or less from any one bidder, without stated yield, will be accepted in full at the average price (in three decimals) or accepted competitive tenders.

**COMPETITIVE TENDERS**  $ _____ @ _____  $ _____
                         $ _____ @ _____  $ _____
                         $ _____ @ _____  $ _____

NOTE: THE MANNER IN WHICH COMPETITIVE BIDS MUST BE EXPRESSED IS DETAILED ON THE "HIGHLIGHTS"

### METHOD OF PAYMENT

| | AMOUNT | CK NO. | | AMOUNT |
|---|---|---|---|---|
| ☐ BY CASHIER'S CHECK | _____ | ____ | ☐ BY SECURITIES SUBMITTED | _____ |
| ☐ BY PERSONAL CHECK | _____ | | DESCRIPTION | _____ |
| ☐ BY FEDERAL FUNDS DRAFT | _____ | | CUSIP NUMBER | _____ |

ALL CHECKS MUST BE MADE PAYABLE TO THE FEDERAL RESERVE BANK

### DELIVERY INSTRUCTIONS

TELEPHONE NO. _____

❡ Name(s) to be printed on Security and Address for Mailing Security & Interest Checks ❡

| OWNER NAME/COMPANIES, TRUST, ETC. | PIECES, DENOMINATIONS DESIRED | | |
|---|---|---|---|
| | Pieces | Denom. | Amount |
| | $ | 1,000 | |
| Co-OWNER (FULL NAME REQUIRED) | | 5,000 | |
| OWNER ADDRESS | | 10,000 | |
| STREET | | | |
| CITY, STATE, ZIP | | 100,000 | |
| ADDRESS FOR MAILING IF DIFFERENT FROM ABOVE | | 1,000,000 | |
| | TOTAL | | $ |

### CERTIFICATION OF TAX I.D. NUMBER

**PART I.** — Taxpayer Identification Number (SUBSTITUTE W-9)

SOC. SECURITY NOS.

Enter the taxpayer identification number in the appropriate box. For most individual taxpayers, this is the social security No.    | | | — | | | — | | | | |

OR

Employer identification number

| | | — | | | | | | |

**PART II.** — Backup Withholding On Accounts Opened After 12/31/83

_____

Check the box if you are NOT subject to backup withholding under the provisions of section 3406(a) (1) (C) of the Internal Revenue Code   ► ☐

**Certification.** — Under the penalties of perjury, I certify that the information provided on this form is true, correct, and complete.

Signature ► _____  Date ► _____

### FEDERAL RESERVE BANK ONLY

COST: _____          DEPOSIT: _____

RECEIVED BY: _____ DATE: _____ DUE TO/DUE FROM SUBSCRIBER: _____

SEC-212 A2 NCR            ***THIS FORM MUST BE SIGNED***

## HOW TO SELL

United States government bonds may be sold through virtually all brokerage firms. Investors simply tell the brokerage firm to liquidate the bonds held in their account.

If investors regularly do business with the brokerage firm, their brokers will normally "shop the bonds." This means that the broker will make several phone calls to determine where the best bid for the bonds offered is to be found. This ensures that the client receives the highest possible price for the bonds.

At the time the bonds are sold, an investor receives the proceeds from the transaction within five business days. The investor should remember that accrued interest from the date of the last interest payment is also included in the check for the proceeds.


## TRANSACTION COSTS

Typically, U.S. government bonds have one of the lowest transaction costs for investors of any products sold by the securities industry.

The federal government charges no fees for U.S. government bonds purchased through the Federal Reserve bank. An investor simply needs to fill out the appropriate paperwork.

It is not uncommon for the commission charge on corporate bonds to range between .25 percent and 2 percent. Generally the longer the time until the maturity of the bond, the greater will be the commission charges. Also, the larger the quantity of bonds purchased, the lower the commission charge per bond.

It is not uncommon for investors who frequently purchase government bonds to negotiate the transaction costs in advance with their brokerage firm.

Investors may find that the trust department's purchase of U.S. government bonds is much more convenient than purchased through the federal government directly. Bonds are available every business day from brokerage firms. The federal government only has bonds available on dates when they are originally issued. In addition, the brokerage firms and bank trust departments may provide additional investment advice and service not available through the Federal Reserve banks.

Investors should note that not all securities dealers charge the same fees for services performed. *Full-service brokerage firms* provide important services for clients in addition to actually executing buy or sell orders. On the other hand, *discount brokerage firms* offer no-frills service with the lowest possible cost transactions. An individual investor needs to review the level of service he or she requires and select a securities dealer accordingly.

## PORTFOLIO FIT

United States government bonds are typically used by investors seeking fixed incomes from their investments. Many times these investors are retired citizens.

Other investors who believe interest rates may decline substantially may wish to purchase U.S. government bonds to take advantage of the high yields available at that time and the potential for large capital gains as the interest rates decline. These investors would need to be savvy traders of government bonds in order to capitalize on the price movements that occur when interest rates change.

One benefit of U.S. government bonds for portfolio planning is that many different maturities exist. The investor can choose maturities of between 1 year and 30 years from existing and publicly traded bonds.

## SOURCES OF ADDITIONAL INFORMATION

A brochure titled "United States Government Securities" is available from any Federal Reserve bank. Investors should refer to the list of addresses and phone numbers listed in the appendix to Chapter 13, "Treasury Notes."

## COMMENTS

United States government bonds have proven to be a dependable investment for many years for fixed-income investors. These bonds can be purchased with complete assurance of the safety of the investor's capital.

In recent decades, especially the latter part of the 1970s and early 1980s, many U.S. government bond investors watched the market value of their investments erode as high rates of inflation caused interest rates to climb and the market value of bonds to decline. The lessons of the late

1970s and the early 1980s have taught bond investors to be more careful in selecting the maturity of their bonds. Generally, bond investors have elected to look for more intermediate-term bond maturities (5 to 12 years), thereby reducing the risk of market price fluctuations that have historically occurred in long maturity (20 to 30 years) government bonds.

**Exhibit 23-2.   Moderate Risk: U.S. Government Bonds**

**INVESTMENT PROFILE**

| INVESTMENT CHARACTERISTICS | Excellent | Good | Average | Poor | None |
|---|---|---|---|---|---|
| Liquidity | √ | | | | |
| Safety of Principal | √ | | | | |
| Price Stability | ST | | | LT | |
| Reinvestment Protection | | LT | | ST | |
| Growth of Capital | | | | | √ |
| Cash Income | | √ | | | |
| Growth of Income | | | | | √ |
| Inflation Hedge | | | √ | | |
| Tax Advantaged | | | | √* | |

**Liquidity**—the ability to quickly realize cash from the sale at fair market value

**Safety of Principal**—the principal is safe from bankruptcy or default

**Price Stability**—the market value of the asset does not change in value

**Reinvestment Protection**—protection against reinvesting cash flow at lower rates as interest rates decline

**Growth of Capital**—the original investment increases over time to create capital gains

**Cash Income**—the cash income relative to treasury bills returns

**Growth of Income**—the ability of the cash income stream to increase over time

**Inflation Hedge**—the ability of total return (cash income plus capital gains) to keep pace with inflation over time

**Tax Advantaged**—the ability to reduce or defer current federal income taxes

*Interest is exempt from state and local taxes, so in high tax states there could be a small tax benefit from owning government bonds.
LT = Long-term maturity bond.
ST = Short-term maturity bonds of 1 year or less.

# CHAPTER 24

# Corporate Bonds

## DESCRIPTION

*Corporate bonds* are long-term promissory notes of a corporation. At the time a new bond is issued, an *indenture* agreement, which is a legal document, spells out the obligations and all the terms of the borrowing. Corporate bonds are normally issued in units of $1,000. The $1,000 is called the *face value* or *par value* of the bond. This is the amount to be received when the principal is repaid.

The indenture agreement stipulates the interest payments on the bond are to be made at the coupon rate. The coupon rate states the amount of money the bondholder will receive each year. For example, if the bond has a coupon rate of 10 percent and par value of $1,000, the bondholder will receive $100 of interest each year from that bond. Most corporate bonds pay interest semiannually.

In today's marketplace, virtually all bonds are issued in registered form: the owner's name is recorded, and a check for each interest payment is sent directly to the owner. It is not necessary for the owner of corporate bonds to take delivery of the bond certificates. They may be left on deposit with a bank trust department or brokerage firm.

The indenture agreement also specifies a *maturity date* for the bond. This is the date when all of the bonds are to be retired and the investor is to be paid the par value ($1,000). The indenture agreement also names a *trustee* for each issue of a bond. The trustee is usually a commercial bank and is responsible for enforcement of the bond indenture.

The interest rate earned on a corporate bond may be calculated with three different methods. The first method of calculating the yield of a corporate bond is *current yield*. The current yield is simply the annual coupon rate of interest paid on the bond divided by the price of the bond. Not all bonds remain at par value once they are issued. Bond prices are adjusted by the market in response to changes in interest rates and credit-worthiness of the bond issue.

$$\text{Current yield} = \frac{\$100 \text{ Annual interest payment}}{\$1,000 \text{ Price paid for bond}}$$

Corporate bond purchasers might be surprised to discover that they have to pay more than the market price in order to receive the bond. This additional charge is referred to as *accrued interest*. Investors who would ordinarily receive bond interest payments on January 1st and July 1st of each year may elect to sell their bonds on a business day that falls between the two interest payment dates. Because of this, the new purchaser of the bond must pay the former owner of the bond for the interest accrued on the corporate bond from the date of the last interest payment until the date that the transaction takes place.

The second form of calculating yield for a corporate bond is called the *yield to maturity*. This is the interest rate that equates the present value of the future interest payments and principal repayment on the bond with the current price of the bond. The yield to maturity represents the true rate of return earned on an investor's capital during the holding period for a corporate bond.

As an example, a corporate bond purchased above par value would have a higher current yield than a yield to maturity. The opposite is also true; a bond purchased below par value has a lower current yield than a yield to maturity. Whether an investor pays a premium or purchases bonds at a discount, the difference must be amortized over the life of the bond issue to calculate the yield to maturity. Most brokerage firms precalculate the yield to maturity for the investor at the time of purchase. Yield to maturity calculations are shown in Chapter 23, "United States Government Bonds." A third type of yield calculation is called the *yield to call date,* discussed later in this chapter.

Bond yields are often quoted as an interest rate carried to two decimal places. These decimal places are referred to as *basis points*. A basis point is simply 1/100 of one percentage point.

In the event that the corporation issuing the bonds experiences temporary difficulties, the value of its bonds may not decrease as much as the value of the common stock of the company. This is because bondholders are creditors of the firm, not owners of the company. As creditors of the firm, they would receive preferential treatment during any liquidation of the company.

In an effort to evaluate the riskiness of corporate bonds, two large financial organizations, Moody's and Standard & Poor's Corporation, provide corporate bond ratings for most corporate bonds. These two credit agencies evaluate the corporation's ability to repay the bond based on sophisticated financial analysis techniques. Definitions of bond ratings issued by Standard & Poor's Corporation appear in Table 24-1.

Generally bonds rated triple B or better are considered to be investment grade bonds and can be owned by bank and financial institution trust departments. Bonds rated below triple B are considered to be of higher risk; they are not generally considered to be of investment quality.

Bond ratings are regularly revised for all corporations by the two credit rating agencies. Based on the such information regarding credit ratings, most investors require a slightly higher interest rate to compensate them for slightly higher risks on lower quality bonds. For example, if the best grade corporate bonds currently yield 10.37 percent based on *Barron's* magazine bond index, intermediate grade bonds may currently yield as much as 11.39 percent. The higher the quality, the lower the yield.

The indenture agreement of a corporate bond may require the corporation to make *sinking fund payments*. Sinking fund payments begin prior to the maturity of the bond and are made regularly by the company to the trustee. These payments ensure that full monies will be available to pay off the bond when it matures. Alternatively, sinking fund contributions may be used to retire debt on a systematic basis throughout the life of the obligation.

If a corporate bond has collateral, the bond investors as a group have a claim to the assets described in the indenture agreement if or when the bonds go into default.

A corporate bond issue that offers no collateral is labeled as a *debenture*. A *subordinated debenture* is a corporate bond in which the holder has a claim that is subordinated to the claims of some or all other creditors.

A *mortgage bond* is a bond that is secured by lien on real property owned by the corporation. Many mortgage bonds contain an "after acquired" clause. This clause stipulates that any real property acquired after the bonds have been issued will be collateralized under the original mortgage agreement. This assures the bondholders that they have additional collateral available to secure their bond. *Collateral trust bonds* are corporate bonds backed by stocks and bonds of another corporation. Frequently, these stocks and bonds are the financial securities of one of the firm's subsidiaries. In other cases, these collateral trust bonds may be secured by the financial investments of the firm. *Guaranteed bonds* may be

**Table 24-1.  Standard & Poor's Rating Definitions for Corporate and Municipal Bonds**

| Term | Definition |
|---|---|
| Debt rating | A current assessment of the creditworthiness of an obligor for a specific obligation. This assessment may take into consideration obligors such as guarantors, insurers, or lessees. The ratings are based, in varying degrees, on the following: |
| | I. Likelihood of default-capacity and willingness of the obligor as to the timely payment of interest and repayment of principal in accordance with the terms of the obligation; |
| | II. Nature of and provisions of the obligation; |
| | III. Protection afforded by, and relative position of, the obligation in the event of bankruptcy, reorganization, or other arrangement under the laws of bankruptcy and other laws affecting creditors' rights. |
| AAA | Debt rated AAA has the highest rating assigned by Standard & Poor's. Capacity to pay interest and repay principal is extremely strong. |
| AA | Debt rated AA has a very strong capacity to pay interest and repay principal and differs from the higher rated issues only in small degree. |
| A | Debt rated A has a strong capacity to pay interest and repay principal, although it is somewhat more susceptible to the adverse effects of changes in circumstances and economic conditions than debt in higher rated categories. |
| BBB | Debt rated BBB is regarded as having an adequate capacity to pay interest and repay principal. Whereas it normally exhibits adequate protection parameters, adverse economic conditions or changing circumstances are more likely to lead to a weakened capacity to pay interest and repay principal for debt in this cateogry than in higher rated categories. |
| BB, B, CCC, CC | Debt rated BB, B, CCC, and CC is regarded, on balance, as predominantly speculative with respect to capacity to pay interest and repay principal in accordance with the terms of the obligation. BB indicates the lowest degree of speculation and CC the highest degree of speculation. While such debt will likely have some quality and protective characteristics, these are outweighed by large uncertainties or major risk exposures to adverse conditions. |
| C | The rating C is reserved for income bonds on which no interest is being paid. |
| D | Debt rated D is in default, and payment of interest and/or repayment of principal is in arrears. |

**Table 24-1. (Continued)**

| Term | Definition |
|---|---|
| Plus(+) or Minus(−): | The ratings from "AA" to "B" may be modified by the addition of a plus or minus sign to show relative standing within the major rating categories. |
| L | The letter L indicates that the rating pertains to the principal amount of those bonds where the underlying deposit collateral is fully insured by the Federal Savings & Loan Insurance Corp. or the Federal Deposit Insurance Corp. |
| Bond Investment Quality Standards: | Under present commercial bank regulation issued by the Comptroller of the Currency, bonds rated in the top four categories (AAA, AA, A, BBB, commonly known as "Investment Grade" ratings) are generally regarded as eligible for bank investment. In addition, the Legal Investment Laws of various states may impose certain rating or other standards for obligations eligible for investment by savings banks, trust companies, insurance companies and fiduciaries generally. |

*Source: Standard & Poor's Bond Guide.* Reprinted with permission.

issued by one company with the payment of principal and interest unconditionally guaranteed by another company.

One last form of corporate bond is the *equipment trust certificate.* These bonds are backed by specific pieces of equipment and machinery as collateral. These bonds are generally high-quality securities and are frequently issued by railroads and airlines secured by the equipment of the company.

The total rate of return on corporate bonds is presented in Table 24-2. The total rate of return includes both cash interest payments and actual price changes over the year. Investors should note the wide differences in rates of return from year to year. This change is a result of changes in the market price of the bonds.

Investors should note that it is important to manage a corporate bond portfolio to maximize the total return on investment.

## STRENGTHS

The principal strength of corporate bonds is the regularity of fixed interest payments to investors. Investment grade bonds (rated AAA, AA, A, BBB)

**Table 24-2.   Corporate Bonds Annual Total Return**

| Year | Return | |
|------|--------|---|
| 1975 | 14.64% | |
| 1976 | 18.65 | |
| 1977 | 1.71 | |
| 1978 | (.07) | |
| 1979 | 4.18 | |
| 1980 | (2.62) | |
| 1981 | (.96) | |
| 1982 | 43.79 | |
| 1983 | 4.70 | |
| 1984 | 16.39 | |
| 1975–1984 | 8.39% | 10-year average annual compounded rate of return |
| 1975–1984 | 7.34% | inflation rate |
| 1975–1979 | 5.79% | 5-year average annual compounded rate of return |
| 1975–1979 | 8.15% | 5-year inflation rate |
| 1980–1984 | 11.06% | 5-year average annual compounded rate of return |
| 1980–1984 | 6.54% | 5-year inflation rate |

have a history of default rates of less than .5 percent over the last 40 years. A large variety of maturities is available.

## WEAKNESSES

The primary weaknesses of corporate bonds are the purchasing power risk, the interest rate risk and the credit risk. Purchasing power risks simply reflects the fact that the yield on a bond is a fixed-rate investment. In periods of high inflation, the interest rate earned on a bond may not provide an adequate return to maintain an investor's purchasing power. Interest rate risks reflect the possibility that the price of the bond will go down or up as interest rates change. If interest rates go up, prices of existing bonds will go down, and the opposite is true if interest rates go down. Credit risk involves the chance that a corporation will default on interest or principal payments to the bondholder.

An investor who purchases a bond of a company that experiences financial difficulty may suffer a temporary loss of income or a loss of the entire investment.

One additional weakness of corporate bonds is the inclusion of a call provision in the bond indenture agreement. This provision is discussed in the next section.

## UNIQUE FEATURES

An especially unique feature of corporate bonds is a *call provision*. A corporate bond with a call provision enables the corporation that issues the bond to repay the debt at its own discretion. The investor has no choice in the matter, since the call provision is written into the bond indenture.

The call provision normally requires the corporation to pay a premium over par value if it calls the issue away from investors. The bond indenture will stipulate that this call premium be in the form of an increased price (usually 5 percent to 10 percent over par value) that the firm must pay when calling for the bond. The call premium is usually not constant over the life of the bond; typically it declines as a corporate bond gets closer to maturity.

A corporation is unlikely to call outstanding bonds unless new bonds can be sold at a lower interest rate to replace the called bonds. In the event of declining interest rates, the risk of having the bond called away from an investor prevents the bond price from moving much higher than the call price.

A call provision is generally of great benefit to the corporation and a major disadvantage to the investor. During times of high interest rates, investors frequently insist on what is called a *deferred call provision*. The deferred call is identical to the ordinary call provision, except that the firm is unable to call the bonds for several years after their original date of issue.

The investment community has adapted to the deferred call with the concept of the yield to call date as compared to the yield to maturity date. The interest rate of a bond is calculated based on the call date becoming the maturity date and amortizing the premium price of a bond in the market place over the time period that remains until the call date.

## TAX CONSEQUENCES

Interest income received in cash from corporate bonds is fully taxable for federal income tax purposes. Upon sale of a bond, or when held to maturity, capital gain and loss rules will generally determine any tax liabilities.

The capital gains rules, original issue discount rule, and nonoriginal issue discount rule became complicated calculations when the Tax Reform Act of 1984 became law. Because of these calculations, investors should consult a qualified tax professional for advice about gains, losses, and taxable income on corporate bonds.

Bonds may also be purchased at a premium above face (par) value. When a corporate bond is purchased for an amount above face value, the bondholder may elect to amortize the premium. For the bondholder, this election will result in deductions from amortizing the premium. This also reduces the bond's cost basis. If the election to amortize is not chosen, then the purchase price will continue to be the cost basis of the bond.

If investors plan to sell a bond before maturity, they should elect to amortize the premium even though the basis is being reduced. The benefit of offsetting interest income with a dollar-for-dollar interest deduction is probably better than keeping the cost basis high. An investor is using the amortization of the premium above par value to shelter taxable cash income. If amortization is not elected, the investor could claim a capital loss upon maturity. For most investors tax free cash flow is more desirable than capital losses.

Thus, calculation of taxes on bonds at first may seem very straightforward and simple because all interest income received is taxable. In actuality, several special rules may make corporate bond taxation a relatively tricky area for a typical investor to understand. Once again, corporate bond investors should seek the advice of qualified tax professionals to calculate taxes owed on corporate bonds.


## WHERE AND HOW TO BUY

Corporate bonds may be purchased on any regular business day through virtually all securities brokerage firms in the United States. Corporate bonds may also be purchased through some bank trust departments.

Many large issues of corporate bonds are actively traded on the New York Stock Exchange bond floor. The traders on the bond floor regularly quote bonds on a bid and offered basis with a very narrow spread between the bid price and the offer price. The New York Bond Exchange and the American Bond Exchange are both very efficient at bond trading.

The over-the-counter market trades the bulk of corporate bonds. Your broker or bank officer will need to help you find a bond with an appropriate yield, coupon, and maturity date.

When purchasing bonds, an investor will typically have five business days to pay for the purchase. The brokerage firm will furnish the investor with a written confirmation of the transaction.

## HOW TO SELL

Corporate bonds may be sold by virtually all brokerage firms in the United States. An investor simply needs to take the bond certificates to the brokerage firm and request that the broker bid for them.

If a bond investor regularly does business with the brokerage firm, the broker will normally "shop the bonds." This means that the broker will make several phone calls to determine where the best bid for the bonds offered is to be found. This ensures that the bondholder receives the highest possible price for the bonds.

At the time the bonds are sold, an investor will receive the proceeds from the transaction (minus any commission costs) in five business days. The investor also receives accrued interest from the date of the last interest payment at the time that the bonds are sold.

## TRANSACTION COSTS

Typically, corporate bonds have one of the lowest transaction costs for investors of any products sold by stock brokerage firms.

It is not uncommon for the commission charge on corporate bonds to range between .5 percent and 2 percent. Generally the longer the time until the maturity of the bond, the greater will be the commission charges. Also, the larger the quantity of bonds purchased, the less the commission charge per bond. The minimum charge for one bond will range from $25 to $40. Blocks of 100 bonds may range between $2.50 and $5 per bond.

Investors should note that not all securities dealers charge the same fees for services performed. It is not uncommon for investors that frequently purchase corporate bonds to negotiate the transaction costs in advance with their brokerage firm.

## PORTFOLIO FIT

Corporate bonds are typically used by investors seeking fixed incomes from their investments. Many pension plans and retirement accounts own corporate bonds.

Other investors who believe interest rates may decline substantially may want to purchase corporate bonds to take advantage of the high yields available at that time and the potential for large capital gains as the interest rates decline. These investors would need to be knowledgeable traders of corporate bonds to capitalize on the price movements that occur when interest rates change.

## SOURCES OF ADDITIONAL INFORMATION

An excellent source on additional information on corporate bonds is the *Standard & Poor's Bond Survey,* published monthly by Standard & Poor's Corporation, and *Moody's Bond Survey,* also published monthly. Both of these references are available at local libraries.

## COMMENTS

Corporate bonds have proven to be a dependable investment for many years for fixed-income investors. These bonds can be purchased with high-quality ratings, and the investor can be assured of a sound investment. Investment grade corporate bonds offer better returns than government bonds with very little additional risk.

However, in recent decades, especially the latter part of the 1970s and early 1980s, many corporate bond investors watched the market value of their investments erode as high rates of inflation caused interest rates to climb and the market value of bonds to decline.

The lessons of the late 1970s and the early 1980s have taught bond investors to be more careful in selecting the maturity dates of their bonds. Generally, bond investors have elected to look for more intermediate-term bond maturities (5 to 12 years), thereby reducing the risk of market price fluctuations that have historically occurred in long-maturity (20 to 30 years) corporate bonds.

**Exhibit 24-1.   Moderate Risk: Long-Term Corporate Bonds**

**INVESTMENT PROFILE**

| INVESTMENT CHARACTERISTICS | Excellent | Good | Average | Poor | None |
|---|---|---|---|---|---|
| Liquidity | √ | | | | |
| Safety of Principal | √ * | | | | |
| Price Stability | | | | √ | |
| Reinvestment Protection | | | | √ | |
| Growth of Capital | | | | √ | |
| Cash Income | | √ * | | | |
| Growth of Income | | | | | √ |
| Inflation Hedge | | LT | | ST | |
| Tax Advantaged | | | | | √ |

**Liquidity**—the ability to quickly realize cash from the sale at fair market value

**Safety of Principal**—the principal is safe from bankruptcy or default

**Price Stability**—the market value of the asset does not change in value

**Reinvestment Protection**—protection against reinvesting cash flow at lower rates as interest rates decline

**Growth of Capital**—the original investment increases over time to create capital gains

**Cash Income**—the cash income relative to treasury bills returns

**Growth of Income**—the ability of the cash income stream to increase over time

**Inflation Hedge**—the ability of total return (cash income plus capital gains) to keep pace with inflation over time

**Tax Advantaged**—the ability to reduce or defer current federal income taxes

*Depend on the rating and risk of the particular bond issue. The lower the rating, the lower the safety of principal. Highest rated AAA corporate bonds are extremely safe.
LT = Bonds held over long periods.
ST = Bonds held over short periods.

# CHAPTER 25

# Long-Term Municipal Bonds

## DESCRIPTION

*Long-term municipal bonds* are long-term promissory notes of a state, city, county, town, or other special local taxation district.

Municipal bonds are normally issued in increments of $5,000. The $5,000 is called the *face value* or *par value* of the bond. This is the amount to be received when the principal is repaid.

The *coupon rate* is set at the time the bonds are issued. The coupon rate states, as a percentage, the amount of money the bondholder will receive each year. For example, if the bond has a coupon rate of 8 percent and par value of $5,000, the bondholder will receive $400 of interest each year from that bond. Most municipal bonds pay interest semiannually.

Since January 1984, all bonds are issued in registered form. This means that the owner's name is recorded, and a check for each interest payment is sent directly to the owner. It is not necessary for the owner of municipal bonds to take delivery of the bond certificates. They may be left on deposit with a bank trust department or brokerage firm.

The bonds are issued with a stated maturity date. This is the date when all of the bonds are to be retired and the investor is to receive the par value ($5,000) for the bond.

A municipal bond has three different yield calculations. The first method, *current yield,* is simply the annual coupon rate of interest paid on the bond divided by the market price of the bond. It should be noted that not all bonds remain at par value once they are issued. Bond prices are adjusted by the market in response to changes in interest rates and credit-worthiness of the municipality. The changing price will cause the current yield to fluctuate over time. For example, if the bond price were to fall to $4,800, the current yield would rise to 10.42 percent:

$$\text{Current yield} = \frac{\$400 \text{ annual interest payment}}{\$4,800 \text{ price paid for bond}}$$

Current yield = 8.33%

A second form of yield for a municipal bond is called the *yield to maturity,* which is the rate that equates the present value of the future interest payments and principal repayment on the bond with the current price of the bond. The yield to maturity represents the expected rate of return earned on an investor's capital if the municipal bond is held to maturity.

As an example, a municipal bond purchased above par value would have a higher current yield than a yield to maturity. The opposite is also true; a bond purchased below par value has a lower current yield than a yield to maturity. Whether an investor pays a premium or purchases bonds at a discount, the difference must be spread out over the life of the bond issue to calculate the yield to maturity. An example of an approximate yield to maturity calculation is contained in Chapter 23, "U.S. Government Bonds."

Most brokerage firms precalculate the yield to maturity for the investor at the time of purchase.

A third type of yield calculation is the *yield to call date,* discussed fully later in this chapter.

Bond yields are often quoted as an interest rate carried to two decimal places. These decimal places are referred to as *basis points.* A basis point is simply 1/100 of one percentage point.

In an effort to evaluate the riskiness of municipal bonds, two large financial organizations, Moody's and Standard & Poor's Corporation provide bond ratings for most municipal bonds. These two credit agencies evaluate the municipality's ability to repay the bond based on sophisticated financial analysis techniques. Definitions of bond ratings issued by Standard and Poor's Corporation appears in Table 25-1.

Generally bonds rated triple B or better are considered to be investment grade bonds and can be owned by bank and financial institution trust departments. Bonds rated below triple B are considered to be of higher risk; they are not generally considered to be of investment quality. Bond ratings are regularly revised for all municipalities by the credit rating agencies.

**Table 25-1. Standard & Poor's Rating Definitions for Corporate and Municipal Bonds**

| Term | Definition |
|---|---|
| Debt rating | A current assessment of the creditworthiness of an obligor for a specific obligation. This assessment may take into consideration obligors such as guarantors, insurers, or lessees. The ratings are based, in varying degrees, on the following:<br>I. Likelihood of default-capacity and willingness of the obligor as to the timely payment of interest and repayment of principal in accordance with the terms of the obligation;<br>II. Nature of and provisions of the obligation;<br>III. Protection afforded by, and relative position of, the obligation in the event of bankruptcy, reorganization, or other arrangement under the laws of bankruptcy and other laws affecting creditors' rights. |
| AAA | Debt rated AAA has the highest rating assigned by Standard & Poor's. Capacity to pay interest and repay principal is extremely strong. |
| AA | Debt rated AA has a very strong capacity to pay interest and repay principal and differs from the higher rated issues only in small degree. |
| A | Debt rated A has a strong capacity to pay interest and repay principal, although it is somewhat more susceptible to the adverse effects of changes in circumstances and economic conditions than debt in higher rated categories. |
| BBB | Debt rated BBB is regarded as having an adequate capacity to pay interest and repay principal. Whereas it normally exhibits adequate protection parameters, adverse economic conditions or changing circumstances are more likely to lead to a weakened capacity to pay interest and repay principal for debt in this cateogry than in higher rated categories. |
| BB, B, CCC, CC | Debt rated BB, B, CCC, and CC is regarded, on balance, as predominantly speculative with respect to capacity to pay interest and repay principal in accordance with the terms of the obligation. BB indicates the lowest degree of speculation and CC the highest degree of speculation. While such debt will likely have some quality and protective characteristics, these are outweighed by large uncertainties or major risk exposures to adverse conditions. |
| C | The rating C is reserved for income bonds on which no interest is being paid. |
| D | Debt rated D is in default, and payment of interest and/or repayment of principal is in arrears. |

**Table 25-1.   (Continued)**

| Term | Definition |
| --- | --- |
| Plus(+) or Minus(−): | The ratings from "AA" to "B" may be modified by the addition of a plus or minus sign to show relative standing within the major rating categories. |
| L | The letter L indicates that the rating pertains to the principal amount of those bonds where the underlying deposit collateral is fully insured by the Federal Savings & Loan Insurance Corp. or the Federal Deposit Insurance Corp. |
| Bond Investment Quality Standards: | Under present commercial bank regulation issued by the Comptroller of the Currency, bonds rated in the top four categories (AAA, AA, A, BBB, commonly known as "Investment Grade" ratings) are generally regarded as eligible for bank investment. In addition, the Legal Investment Laws of various states may impose certain rating or other standards for obligations eligible for investment by savings banks, trust companies, insurance companies and fiduciaries generally. |

*Source: Standard & Poor's Bond Guide.* Reprinted with permission.

Based on this information about credit ratings, most investors require a slightly higher interest rate to compensate them for slightly higher risks on lower-quality bonds. For example, best grade 25-year maturity municipal bonds (rated AAA) currently yield a tax-free rate of 9.15 percent based on market yields of October 1985, while intermediate grade bonds (rated BBB) of similar maturity currently yield 10.20 percent. The higher the quality, the lower the yield.

Investors should note that there are two basic types of municipal bonds issued by the various taxing entities.

The first type of bonds are called *general obligation bonds (GOs)*. These bonds have the full faith and credit (and taxing authority) of the issuer to provide repayment of both interest and principal to the holder of the bonds.

This means that the city, county, or other local government entity is pledged to levy enough taxes on property owners in the political subdivision to repay the bonds in full and on time.

A second type of municipal bond is the *revenue* or *project* bond. These bonds have only the revenue generated by a specific project dedicated to repay the bondholders principal and interest. Revenue bonds are issued to finance tollways and turnpike authorities as well as college dormitories, and other public projects.

Revenue bonds generally are higher-risk bonds than general obligation bonds. Many revenue bonds have very good quality ratings, due to the proven success of the projects that back the bonds.

## STRENGTHS

The primary strength of municipal bonds is the totally exempt status that income from the bonds has for *federal* tax returns.

A secondary strength of municipal bonds is the regularity of interest payments to investors.

## WEAKNESSES

Municipal bonds are subject to certain types of risks. The three most important types of risks to municipal bond investors are purchasing power risks, interest rate risks, and credit risks. *Purchasing power risks* simply reflect the fact that the yield on a bond is a fixed rate investment. In periods of high inflation, the interest rate earned on a bond may not provide an adequate return to maintain an investor's purchasing power.

*Interest rate risks* reflect the possibility that the price of the bond will go down or up as interest rates change. If interest rates go up, prices of existing bonds will go down; the opposite is true if interest rates go down.

*Credit risks* involve the chance that a municipality will default on interest or principal payments to the bondholder.

The primary weakness of municipal bonds is interest rate risk. Increases in interest rates may leave a municipal bondholder at a disadvantage if the investor is forced to liquidate the investment prior to maturity. Also, the market value of the bond will decrease as interest rates increase.

An investor who purchases a bond of a municipality that experiences financial difficulty may suffer a temporary loss of income or a total loss of the investment. An investor can compensate for the default risk by buying insured municipal bonds.

One additional weakness of municipal bonds is the inclusion of a *call provision* in the bond indenture agreement, discussed later in this chapter.

## UNIQUE FEATURES

A recently implemented boost for municipal bonds allows the issuer of the bonds to purchase third-party insurance against default of the interest and principal payments on the bond. These issues of bonds are referred to as *insured municipal bonds.*

With insured bonds, a consortium of insurance companies forms a special insurance company to underwrite the risk of default on municipal bonds. Two examples of these insurance consortiums are the Municipal Bond Insurance Association (MBIA) and the Financial Guaranty Insurance Company (FGIC).

These insurance consortiums will guarantee to pay investors full interest payments when they are due and will pay off the principal amount of the bonds if the municipality is unable to do so. This insurance protection virtually eliminates the risk of principal defaults on the insured issues of municipal bonds. However, this insurance cannot eliminate the market risk of the bonds associated with changes in the level of interest rates.

The insurance coverage provided is not without cost. Generally investors can expect to receive a slightly lower interest rate on insured municipal bonds than on regular municipal bond issues. The rate difference on long-term issues of municipal bonds can be from .25 percent up to .50 percent of current yield.

Standard & Poor's Corporation regularly assigns an AAA credit quality rating to insured municipal bonds. Moody's Investor Service does not automatically assign triple A ratings to insured municipal bonds.

An especially unique feature of bonds is a *call provision.* A municipal bond with a call provision enables the municipality that issues the bond to repay the debt before the maturity date at its discretion. The investor has no choice in the matter, because the call provision is written into the bond agreement at the time of issuance.

The call provision normally requires the municipality to pay a premium if it calls the issue away from investors. The bond agreement stipulates that this call premium be in the form of an increased price above par value (usually 5 percent to 10 percent above par) that the local taxing entity must pay when calling for the bond. The call premium may or may not be constant over the life of the bond. Typically the call premium declines as a municipal bond gets closer to maturity.

A municipality is unlikely to call outstanding bonds unless new bonds can be sold at a lower interest rate to replace the called bonds. In the event of declining interest rates, the risk of having the bond called away from an investor prevents the market price of the bond from moving higher, as it would normally without a call provision.

A call provision is generally of great benefit to the municipality and a major disadvantage to the investor. During times of high interest rates, investors frequently insist a *deferred call provision*. The deferred call is identical to the ordinary call provision, except that the municipality is unable to call the bonds for several years after their original date of issue.

The investment community has adapted to the deferred call with the concept of the yield to call date as compared to the yield to maturity date. The yield to call of a bond is a calculation based on the call date becoming the maturity date. The formula for approximate yield to call is given in the following example:

$$\text{YTM} = \frac{\text{Annual Interest} + \dfrac{\text{Face Value} - \text{Bond Value}}{\text{\# Years to Maturity}}}{\dfrac{\text{Face Value} + \text{Bond Price}}{2}}$$

A 10 percent tax free bond, 7 years to call, is priced at 110 ($1,100.00 per 1,000 face value). It is callable at $1,050.

$$\text{YTC} = \frac{\$100.00 + \dfrac{\$1,050.00 - \$1,100.00}{7}}{\dfrac{\$1,100.00 + \$1,050.00}{2}}$$

$$\text{YTC} = \frac{\$100.00 - \$7.14}{\$1,075.00}$$

$$8.64\% = \frac{\$92.86}{\$1,075.00}$$

## TAX CONSEQUENCES

Interest income paid in cash to the holder of a municipal bond is totally free from taxation by the federal government.

When an investor purchases a *zero-coupon municipal bond* (that is, the investor buys the bond on its original issue priced at a discount from par value), it is not subject to federal tax as it appreciates. Only the original issue discount purchased at the time of issue is tax free. Any other discounts on bonds purchased in the secondary market will be treated as a capital gain if that bond was issued before July 19, 1984. For bonds issued after July 18, 1984, any gain upon sale or redemption will be composed of ordinary income and capital gains.

The computations for potential gains or losses on tax free municipal bonds are somewhat complicated. The investors should seek the opinion of a qualified tax professional prior to purchasing the bonds.

## WHERE AND HOW TO BUY

Municipal bonds may be purchased on any regular business day through virtually all securities brokerage firms in the United States. Municipal bonds may also be purchased through some bank trust departments.

A very liquid market exists for municipal bonds in the United States. Many brokerage firms stand ready to bid for an investor's bonds. These same firms offer the bonds for resale to other investors at a slight markup. The broker dealer firms accept the risk of holding the bonds in inventory in order to facilitate this market. While the actual trading does not take place at one central location, the market is supervised by the National Association of Securities Dealers, and very few problems are experienced by investors.

When executing a bond purchase, an investor typically has five business days to pay for the bonds. The brokerage firm will furnish the investor with a written confirmation of the transaction.

A charge is referred to as *accrued interest* will need to be paid at the time the bond is purchased. Accrued interest is the amount of interest the bond has earned since the last interest payment date.

Investors that would ordinarily receive bond interest payments on January 1st and July 1st of each year may elect to sell their bonds on a business day that falls between the two interest payment dates. Because of this, the new purchaser of the bond will need to pay the former owner of the bond for the interest that has accrued on the municipal bond from the date of the last interest payment until the date that the transaction takes place.

## HOW TO SELL

Municipal bonds may be sold by virtually all brokerage firms in the United States. An investor simply needs to take the bond certificates to the brokerage firm (if they are not already being held on account at the firm) and request that the broker bid for them.

If an investor regularly does business with the brokerage firm, the broker normally "shops the bonds," making several phone calls to determine where the best bid for the bonds offered is to be found. This ensures that the client receives the highest possible price for the bonds.

Small issues of municipal bonds (less than $2 million total) are not as liquid as larger issues. The spread between the bid and offered prices of brokerage firms on small issues can be as much as 5 percent of the market value of the bonds.

When bonds are sold, an investor receives the proceeds from the transaction minus commission costs in five business days. The investor will also receive accrued interest from the date of the last interest payment at the time of sale.

## TRANSACTION COSTS

Typically, bonds have one of the lowest transaction costs for investors of any products sold by brokerage firms.

It is not uncommon for the commission charge on municipal bonds to range between .5 percent and 3 percent. Generally, the longer the time until the maturity of the bond, the greater will be the commission charges. Also, the more bonds purchased, the less the commission charge per bond. It is not uncommon for investors who frequently purchase large quantities of municipal bonds to negotiate the transaction costs in advance with their brokerage firm.

## PORTFOLIO FIT

Municipal bonds are ideal for high-income tax bracket investors seeking tax free income. The bonds can be purchased with insurance coverage against default risk, thus insuring a long predictable stream of income.

Table 25-2 illustrates the taxable equivalent yield necessary to equal the after-tax income available to municipal bond investors.

This table shows that the ability to avoid federal income taxes is very important for a municipal bond investor.

**Table 25-2.   Taxable Equivalent Yield Table**

| Federal Tax Bracket | Tax-Exempt Yield Equivalents | | | | | | | | | |
|---|---|---|---|---|---|---|---|---|---|---|
| | 8.75% | 9.00% | 9.25% | 9.50% | 9.75% | 10.00% | 10.25% | 10.50% | 10.75% | 11.00% |
| 28% | 12.15 | 12.50 | 12.85 | 13.19 | 13.54 | 13.89 | 14.24 | 14.58 | 14.93 | 15.28 |
| 30 | 12.50 | 12.86 | 13.21 | 13.57 | 13.93 | 14.29 | 14.64 | 15.00 | 15.36 | 15.71 |
| 33 | 13.06 | 13.43 | 13.81 | 14.18 | 14.55 | 14.93 | 15.30 | 15.67 | 16.04 | 16.42 |
| 34 | 13.26 | 13.64 | 14.02 | 14.39 | 14.77 | 15.15 | 15.53 | 15.91 | 16.29 | 16.67 |
| 38 | 14.11 | 14.52 | 14.92 | 15.32 | 15.73 | 16.13 | 16.53 | 16.94 | 17.34 | 17.74 |
| 42 | 15.09 | 15.52 | 15.95 | 16.38 | 16.81 | 17.24 | 17.67 | 18.10 | 18.53 | 18.97 |
| 45 | 15.91 | 16.36 | 16.82 | 17.27 | 17.73 | 18.18 | 18.64 | 19.09 | 19.55 | 20.00 |
| 48 | 16.83 | 17.31 | 17.79 | 18.27 | 18.75 | 19.23 | 19.71 | 20.19 | 20.67 | 21.15 |
| 49 | 17.16 | 17.65 | 18.14 | 18.63 | 19.12 | 19.61 | 20.10 | 20.59 | 21.08 | 21.57 |
| 50 | 17.50 | 18.00 | 18.50 | 19.00 | 19.50 | 20.00 | 20.50 | 21.00 | 21.50 | 22.00 |

## SOURCES OF ADDITIONAL INFORMATION

An excellent source on additional information on municipal bonds is the *Standard & Poor's Bond Survey,* published monthly.

## COMMENTS

Municipal bonds are long established as an excellent tax free source of income for many millions of Americans. In addition, many investors elect to purchase municipal bonds in the convenient form known as *tax free municipal bond trusts.* Readers should refer to Chapter 23, "U.S. Government Bonds," to learn more about the convenience and safety offered by bond trusts.

In the latter part of the 1970s and early 1980s, many municipal bond investors watched the market value of their investments erode as high inflation rates caused interest rates to climb and the market value of bonds to decline. The lessons of the late 1970s and the early 1980s have taught bond investors to be more careful when selecting the maturity of their bonds. Generally, bond investors have elected to look for intermediate-term bond maturities of 5 to 12 years, thereby reducing the risk of market price fluctuations that have historically occurred in long maturity (20 to 30 years) corporate bonds.

Some investors in higher age brackets opt to purchase the longest possible bonds to increase current income. These investors do not expect to sell the bonds or redeem the bonds at maturity, so the maximization of income becomes virtually the only priority other than default protection.

**Exhibit 25-1.   Moderate Risk: Long-Term Municipal Bonds**

**INVESTMENT PROFILE**

| INVESTMENT CHARACTERISTICS | Excellent | Good | Average | Poor | None |
|---|---|---|---|---|---|
| Liquidity | | ✓ | | | |
| Safety of Principal | Insured | * | | | |
| Price Stability | | ST | | LT | |
| Reinvestment Protection | | | LT | ST | |
| Growth of Capital | | | | ✓ | |
| Cash Income | ✓† | | | | |
| Growth of Income | | | | | ✓ |
| Inflation Hedge | | | ST | LT | |
| Tax Advantaged | ✓ | | | | |

**Liquidity**—the ability to quickly realize cash from the sale at fair market value

**Safety of Principal**—the principal is safe from bankruptcy or default

**Price Stability**—the market value of the asset does not change in value

**Reinvestment Protection**—protection against reinvesting cash flow at lower rates as interest rates decline

**Growth of Capital**—the original investment increases over time to create capital gains

**Cash Income**—the cash income relative to treasury bills returns

**Growth of Income**—the ability of the cash income stream to increase over time

**Inflation Hedge**—the ability of total return (cash income plus capital gains) to keep pace with inflation over time

**Tax Advantaged**—the ability to reduce or defer current federal income taxes

*Depends upon the rating (risk) of the particular bond. The higher the rating the better the safety of principal.
†The aftertax cash income can be very high for investors in high marginal tax brackets.
LT = Municipal bonds with maturities of 5 years or more.
ST = Municipal bonds with maturities up to 5 years.

# CHAPTER 26

# Convertible Securities

## DESCRIPTION

A *convertible security* is a corporate bond or share of preferred stock that can be converted at the option of the holder into common stock.

The owner of a convertible security has a fixed-income security that can be transferred to a common stock interest in the same company if and when the stock price and the affairs of the firm indicate that such a conversion is financially desirable.

Convertible bonds are used for purposes of this discussion. The same principles apply to convertible preferred stocks. A convertible bond is frequently referred to as a *convertible debenture*. A *debenture* is the unsecured debt of a corporation. There is no specific collateral provided for holders of convertible debentures in the event of liquidation or bankruptcy.

When a convertible debenture is initially issued, a conversion ratio is specified. The conversion ratio indicates the number of shares of common stock into which the debenture may be converted. For example, assume that XYZ Company in 1985 issued 10 million dollars face value of a 25 year 6 percent convertible debenture. Each $1,000 bond (at face value) is convertible into 20 shares of common stock. This is a conversion ratio of 20.

The conversion ratio may also be expressed in terms of a conversion price. To calculate the conversion price, simply divide the face value of the bond by the conversion ratio of 20 in this example. The conversion price for the common stock is $50.

$$\frac{\text{Face Value}}{\text{Conversion Ratio}} = \text{Conversion Price} \quad \frac{\$1000}{20 \text{ sh.}} = \$50$$

Investors should be prepared to calculate the value of a convertible debenture in two ways. First, the value of the bond if converted into stock should be calculated. Using the example of XYZ Company, assume that the common stock is selling for $45 per share. The total conversion value is $900 ($45 X 20 shares). At the same time, the convertible bond is selling in the open market for exactly face value or $1,000. This means that there is a $100 *conversion premium,* representing the difference between market value and actual conversion value. The conversion premium results from expectation of future performance of the common stock. If investors are optimistic about the business prospects of the company and the common stock, the conversion premium may be as much as 20 to 25 percent over conversion value.

If the price of the common stock moves upward and trades in the open market for $60 per share, the conversion privilege associated with the bonds becomes quite valuable. The convertible bonds will move up in value to at least $1,200. The bonds may still trade at a slight premium over the common stock value of the bond—perhaps as high as $1,250.

Investors should note that they do not need to convert the holding into common stock immediately upon an increase in the value of the common stock. Investors may enjoy the movement upward in price of the convertible bond in concert with the upward movement of the common stock price while collecting the interest payments from the bond.

Assume that instead of going from $45 to $60 in the first illustration, the common stock of XYZ Company drops from $45 to $25. The common stock value of the XYZ convertible bond is now only $500 ($25 X 20). The owner of the convertible bond will have a debenture worth more than $500 because the convertible debenture still has value as an interest-bearing security. If the going rate of interest in the open market for similar corporate bonds without collateral and of the same maturity is currently at 8 percent, the debenture has a pure bond value of $785.46. The investor can see that a convertible bond does have a floor value (the straight bond value) but no upward limitation.

Investors should also note that convertible bonds like other corporate bonds, can be subject to interest rate risks. This is especially true when the conversion value is very low relative to the market price of the bond. As market interest rates rise above the coupon rate, the bond's value can drop.

The concept of value and pricing of convertible bonds is demonstrated in Exhibit 26-1. The exhibit shows the effect on the convertible bond price as the common stock price (shown along the horizontal axis) is

**Exhibit 26-1.   Price Movement Pattern for a Convertible Bond**

Price movement pattern for a convertible bond

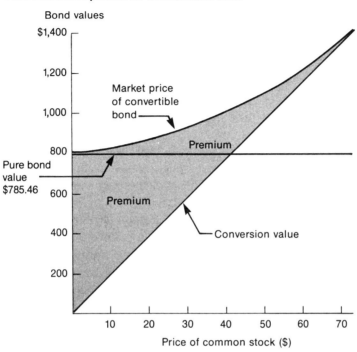

assumed to change. Note that the floor value (pure bond value) for the convertible is well above the conversion value when the common stock price is very low. As the common stock price moves to higher levels, the convertible bond moves in concert with the conversion value.

Market interest rates are 8 percent in the exhibit. The convertible bond pays only 6 percent. This provides a pure bond value of $785.46.

Table 26-1 contains examples of convertible bonds and their pricing patterns.

The NBI Corporation bond has lost virtually all of the conversion premium. It trades like a straight bond, due to a sharp decline in the stock price.

The Merrill Lynch bond trades at a 19.94 percent premium over conversion value.

The Paine Webber bond has a modest premium. Long-term investors are seeking a capital gain along with current income from both the Merrill Lynch and Paine Webber bonds.

**Table 26-1.   Pricing Patterns of Convertible Bonds**

| Issue | Conversion Value | Current Yield | Market Rate for Similar Nonconvertible Bond | Market Value of Bond |
|-------|------------------|---------------|---------------------------------------------|----------------------|
| NBI Corp. 8.25% '07 | 264.24 | 12.55% | 12.7% | $657.50 |
| Merrill Lynch 8.875% '07 | 987.97 | 7.48% | 10.25% | $1185.00 |
| Paine Webber 8.25% '08 | 564.33 | 9.48% | 11.7% | $870.00 |

To summarize, convertible bonds offer investors the ability to earn a fixed rate of return with some limit on downside risk unavailable with common stock ownership. At the same time there is unlimited potential for upside movement.

## STRENGTHS

One strength of convertible bonds is the regular receipt of semiannual interest payments from a corporation. This is the same feature as is included in all other corporate bonds.

A second feature of convertible bonds is the ability for the bonds to be exchanged for common stock. Over a long period of time, this can provide an investor with significant returns above the rate of interest earned on the bond. These returns are received in the form of a capital gain in the value of the bond and can be very valuable to investors willing to be patient and let a company perform over a long period of time.

## WEAKNESSES

Investors are normally expected to accept below-market rates of interest on the bond itself when a conversion privilege is available. The interest rate on convertible bonds is generally 30 to 35 percent less than the same interest rate for bonds of a similar risk class at the time they are issued. For example, if regular corporate bonds are yielding 12 percent, an investor should expect to receive approximately an 8 to 9 percent interest rate on a convertible bond issued by the same company.

## UNIQUE FEATURES

A convertible bond purchase requires a premium payment over the actual conversion value at the time of issue. In this chapter's example, $1,000 invested in the XYZ convertible bonds would have been convertible into 20 shares of common stock at $50 per share. The market price is $45 per share. The conversion value of the bond is $900. This is a $100 conversion premium over the actual market value of the shares of common stock.

Investors should be further cautioned that the downside protection feature of most convertible bonds is virtually meaningless once the bond has appreciated significantly above the $1,000 par value. For example, a convertible bond that has risen in value to $1,200 because the price of the common stock has risen will trade with approximately the same degree of volatility as the common stock itself. The underlying value of the bond as an interest-bearing security becomes less important at this high price.

Convertible bonds always include a call provision that gives the issuing corporation the option of redeeming the bonds at a specified price in the future. It could be an inopportune time for an investor to have the bonds called away should the corporation elect to exercise this privilege.

This call feature is usually exercised by the company when the conversion value is greater than the call price. This forces investors to convert their bonds into the common stock rather than take the lower call price. Investors have the option of liquidating the bonds in the open market and reinvesting the proceeds elsewhere if they do not wish to own the common stock of the corporation.

Investors who carefully study the convertible securities market should be able to minimize the effects of many of these weaknesses by carefully selecting convertible bonds.

One unique feature is that not all bonds are convertible into common stock of the issuing company. Three examples of these unique convertible bonds are shown in Table 26-2.

In each of these cases, the issuing company owns common stock in the conversion company. If the price of the conversion company rises above the conversion price the issuing company may elect to force conversion.

**Table 26-2.   Relation of Conversion Company to Bond Issuing Company**

| Issuer | Interest Rate | Conversion Company | Face Value/CV. Ratio | = | Conversion Price |
|---|---|---|---|---|---|
| CIGNA Corp. | 8% | Paine Webber | $1,000/23.36 shares | = | $42.80 |
| Signal Cos. | 8% | Unitrode Corp | $1,000/25.00 shares | = | $40.00 |
| General Cinema | 10% | R J Reynolds | $1,000/39.84 shares | = | $25.10 |

## TAX CONSEQUENCES

Interest income received by an investor from a convertible bond is fully taxable as interest income.

Any gain or loss experienced by an investor who has owned a convertible bond will be taxable according to the normal capital gains and loss procedures that are in effect for all common stocks. The holding period for long-term capital gains is six months and one day. Any investor that has held the bonds more than six months and one day can treat gains or losses as long-term capital gains/losses.

As with all tax matters, investors should seek the advice of a practicing tax specialist in evaluating the tax obligations of convertible securities.

## WHERE AND HOW TO BUY

Convertible bonds can be purchased on any business day through any securities brokerage firm or those financial institutions offering brokerage services. Many convertible bonds are listed on the New York Bond Exchange and the American Bond Exchange.

Trading in convertible bonds is very similar to trading in other corporate bonds. Bonds may be purchased on the open market at the current price offered by the exchange specialist, or limit orders can be used in an attempt to acquire bonds at a specified price selected by the investor.

The market for convertible bonds is liquid although large blocks are more liquid than small numbers of convertible bonds. Orders for large quantities for bonds are often transacted away from the floor of the bond exchange. In this case these bond orders are treated much like an over-the-counter stock market order. A willing buyer and seller can exchange their bonds via brokerage firms at a predetermined price. The prices are the same price as that for the trading of small quantities of the bonds on the floor of the New York Bond Exchange. An investor purchasing large blocks of convertible bonds is often able to achieve a price approximately .5 to 1 percent lower than the price offered on the floor of the New York Bond Exchange for smaller quantities.

Convertible bond purchases must be paid for in five business days. Convertible bonds are traded with accrued interest. This means that an investor pays the interest that has accrued since the last interest payment date. The same investor will receive a full six-month interest payment on the next regularly scheduled interest payment date.

Investors may take delivery in certificate form of their convertible bonds, or the bonds can be left on deposit with the securities brokerage firm or bank trust department for safekeeping. Most investors find the deposit of the bonds to be more convenient than accepting delivery of the bonds.

## HOW TO SELL

Convertible securities can be liquidated using the same brokerage firms and banks that were used to purchase the convertible bonds. On any regular business day, convertible securities can be sold just like common stock. The investor will receive the proceeds five business days after the sale occurs.

In some instances a corporation may exercise its call privilege and force the investor to either convert the bonds into shares of stock of the corporation or liquidate the bonds in the open market.

This forced liquidation results from the fact that the corporation can call the bonds at a price that is often substantially below the market value of the convertible bond. For example, a convertible bond may be trading on the open market at $1,400 per $1,000 face value of the bond. This is because the common stock has appreciated substantially in price since the time the bond was issued. The company may have the right to call that convertible bond at a price of 105 or $1,050 per bond.

Obviously, an investor wishes to receive the $1,400 market value of the bond, so the bond will be liquidated in the open market, and investor must accept the fact that the bond has been called away. The investor will then need to look for a different investment source for these funds, subjecting the proceeds to reinvestment risk.

The other option available to the investor is to convert from bond ownership to common stock ownership by tendering this bond to the company.

The forced conversion of a convertible security occurs at the option of the corporation. The investor always enjoys the option of converting the securities whenever it is preferable.

A corporation may decide to eliminate the cost of the debt from its balance sheet and force conversion of the bonds into common stock. In the case of a company that pays no dividends on the common stock, a fixed-income investor may elect to seek alternative investment areas for the funds.

## TRANSACTION COSTS

Transaction costs on convertible bonds are generally the same or slightly less than the transaction costs on common stocks. Brokerage firms will charge a commission each time that a convertible bond is purchased or sold. The smaller the quantity of bonds that are purchased or sold, the higher the percentage commission. As an example, the purchase of a single convertible bond may cost $30. An investor purchasing 10 convertible bonds might expect to pay $10 per bond. Ten bonds may have commission cost of $100. If these 10 bonds can be converted into 150 shares of common stock, buying 10 bonds might have a lower commision than buying the 150 shares of stock.

Investors should note that not all securities dealers charge the same fees for services performed. *Full-service brokerage firms* provide important services for clients over and above the actual execution of a simple buy or sell order. *Discount brokerage firms* specialize in offering the lowest cost transactions. An individual investor needs to review the level of service required and select a securities dealer accordingly.

## PORTFOLIO FIT

Convertible bonds are generally used by investors seeking a balance between income and capital gains from their investment portfolio. Most convertible securities investors have as their primary priority the receipt of fixed-income payments. As a secondary investment objective, these investors are seeking capital appreciation subject to limited downside risk of their original principal.

Long-term, income oriented patient investors are likely to be well served by purchasing convertible bonds in carefully selected companies.

## SOURCES OF ADDITIONAL INFORMATION

*Moody's Bond Record* regularly publishes a survey of convertible securities. In addition, Standard & Poor's Corporation publishes a monthly *Bond Guide*. The last section of the bond guide is devoted to convertible bonds. Value Line publishes a weekly advisory service analyzing convertible bonds. These major sources might be available at your library.

## COMMENTS

Convertible securities offer a unique combination of fixed income and capital appreciation potential to investors. Because a convertible security is slightly more difficult to analyze and understand than traditional fixed-income bonds or common stocks, many investors tend to avoid the convertible securities vehicles.

Many market professionals that serve individual investors fail to emphasize the convertible security as an investment. From the standpoint of a stockbroker or a stock brokerage firm, a convertible security combines the purchase of a fixed-income security and the purchase of an equity security. This lowers the total number of transactions for the brokerage firm. In general, brokerage firms receive their revenues based on the number of transactions that they generate. A vehicle like convertible bonds that reduces the number of transactions can reduce the revenue to a brokerage firm. While most large brokerage firms offer special analytical services for convertible investors, they are seldom widely publicized to the general public.

Investors wishing to use convertible securities should be prepared to do the research and analysis necessary on their own. These investors may wish to subscribe to specialty newsletters, to review the Value Line convertible publication, or to review individual convertible securities using the resources available at most public libraries.

**Exhibit 26-2.  Moderate Risk: Convertible Securities**

**INVESTMENT PROFILE**

| INVESTMENT CHARACTERISTICS | Excellent | Good | Average | Poor | None |
|---|---|---|---|---|---|
| Liquidity | | ✓ | | | |
| Safety of Principal | | | * | | |
| Price Stability | | | † | | |
| Reinvestment Protection | | | | ✓ | |
| Growth of Capital | | ✓ | | | |
| Cash Income | | ✓ | | | |
| Growth of Income | | | | | ✓ |
| Inflation Hedge | | LT | | ST | |
| Tax Advantaged | | | | | ✓ |

**Liquidity**—the ability to quickly realize cash from the sale at fair market value

**Safety of Principal**—the principal is safe from bankruptcy or default

**Price Stability**—the market value of the asset does not change in value

**Reinvestment Protection**—protection against reinvesting cash flow at lower rates as interest rates decline

**Growth of Capital**—the original investment increases over time to create capital gains

**Cash Income**—the cash income relative to treasury bills returns

**Growth of Income**—the ability of the cash income stream to increase over time

**Inflation Hedge**—the ability of total return (cash income plus capital gains) to keep pace with inflation over time

**Tax Advantaged**—the ability to reduce or defer current federal income taxes

*Most convertible bonds are rated BBB or less and therefore offer good to poor safety of principal depending on their rating.
†The price stability depends on the relationship of the bonds market price to its conversion value and pure bond value. When the convertible bond price trades close to its pure bond value, price stability will be similar to a nonconvertible bond of equal risk, when the conversion value is much greater than the pure bond value, the price will be about as volatile as the underlying common stock.
LT = Convertible bonds held over long time periods—(5–10 years).
ST = Convertible bonds held over shorter time periods (1–4 years).

# CHAPTER 27

# Zero-Coupon Bonds

## DESCRIPTION

*Zero-coupon bonds* are debt obligations of an issuer that have no cash interest payments. Rather, the bonds are issued at a discount from face value. As time passes, the value of the bonds increases until the bonds are redeemed for full face value at maturity. The total return is received from the internal compounding of interest that is inherent in the bond price.

Zero-coupon bonds are issued by corporations, municipalities, and by far the largest issues are composed of U.S. government bonds. Although the government does issue some bonds as zeros, large investment houses strip the interest coupons from traditional government bonds and package the coupons together to form zeros.

The format for corporate zero-coupon bond quotations is presented in Table 27-1. Zero-coupon bonds are quoted in the regular bond prices section of most major newspapers.

The first zero coupon bond is issued by Allied-Corp. and comes due in 1992. The last price was 50 or 50 percent of face value ($1,000), therefore an investor could purchase one bond for $500 with the promise of receiving the $1,000 face amount in 1992.

This chapter will not attempt to cover all the different aspects of each issuer; rather, this chapter will focus on the uniqueness of debt securities that pay no current interest.

## STRENGTHS

The ability to predict the exact time and amount of return from an investment is often very important to investors. Zero-coupon bonds permit investors to accomplish this objective very efficiently. Because the face value of the bonds and the maturity date are specified, an investor can

**Table 27-1.   Newspaper Format for Zero-Coupon Bond Quotations**

| Bond & Rate | Yld. | Vol. | Last Price | Net Chg. |
|---|---|---|---|---|
| AlldC zr92 | ... | 14 | 50 + | 5/6 |
| AlldC zr91 | ... | 20 | 55-3/4 | ... |
| Bkam zr87A | ... | 11 | 84-7/8 | 1/2 |
| Bkam zr87D | ... | 75 | 82-1/8 − | 3/8 |

purchase just exactly the amount necessary to meet future needs—there is no concern about how to reinvest cash flow from coupon payments.

The investor has no cash flow to reinvest and so during times of declining interest rates, he or she is able to maintain a high yield. Zero coupon bonds are priced so that the yield to maturity at the time of purchase is the effective yield over the life of the bond no matter whether interest rates move up or down.

## WEAKNESSES

The biggest weakness of all fixed-income investments is the effect of inflation on the market value of the original investment. This weakness is exaggerated in the case of zero-coupon bonds, because no interest payments are made to the investor. The only payment made to the investor is the ultimate payoff of the face value of the bond. This lack of cash flow over the life of the bond prevents the owner from reinvesting cash flow at higher rates when inflation is forcing up interest rates.

A second weakness is that these bond prices are extremely sensitive to interest rate changes. As rates rise, zeros can suffer large price drops.

## UNIQUE FEATURES

In the case of zero-coupon bonds issued by the U.S. government, there is no default risk involved in the securities. Default risk may be present in any issue of corporate or municipal zero-coupon bonds. Typically, corporate and municipal issuers of zero-coupon bonds are sound financial entities.

Since no interest is paid prior to maturity with zero-coupon bonds, there is no risk that interest may have to be reinvested at lower rates in the future. Investors lock in the yield to maturity or the "true yield" that they expect when they make the investment.

Zero-coupon bonds are truly an exceptionally flexible investment in terms of scheduling maturity dates. Investors can pick exactly the time they wish to receive a large sum of cash.

An investor who purchases an 11 percent zero and watches interest rates rise to 14 percent one year later will experience a paper loss of 50 percent. Obviously, if the investor holds the position until maturity, he or she will not realize the loss.

The opposite can be true as well. A decline of 3 percent in interest rates to the 8 percent level results in a paper gain after one year of 157 percent in the value of the 30-year zero-coupon bond.

## TAX CONSEQUENCES

The tax treatment of zero-coupon bonds varies depending on the issuer of the bonds. Corporate and U.S. government issues, with their annual internal compounding of interest will build an increasing tax liability in future years. Unless these securities are held in a tax advantaged account, investors will be required to report interest as taxable income annually. This income is accrued but not actually received by the investor. For this reason zeros are not recommended for investors' taxable portfolios.

This means an investor incurs a tax liability for which there is no cash flow from the investment. Often this type of tax liability is referred to as "phantom income." There is no cash to pay the Internal Revenue Service.

Fortunately, this is not the case with municipal zero-coupon bonds. Interest income received by investors from municipalities is tax free. This is true whether the income is actually paid or accrued annually.

Many other circumstances may influence the tax ramifications for zero-coupon bond investors. Investors should seek out professional advice when evaluating the tax ramifications of any investment strategy. Good tax advice is never more important than in the case of zero-coupon bonds.

## WHERE AND HOW TO BUY

All stock brokerage and investment firms offer zero-coupon bonds to clients. A listing of bonds in inventory may be available on a daily basis for review by the investor. The investor should be prepared to provide the brokerage firm with an approximate maturity date and face amount to receive upon maturity. The broker can then shop the market in an effort to secure the highest yield for the client consistent with the client's objectives and timeframe.

## HOW TO SELL

In the event an investor does not wish to hold zero-coupon bonds until maturity, the same brokerage and investment firms that sell these bonds are willing to repurchase zeros every business day.

An investor should receive at least three competitive bids for the bonds in the secondary market from broker dealer firms.

## TRANSACTION COSTS

Investors should note that the price of zero-coupon bonds includes a profit for the brokerage firm. It would be advisable to request offers from several brokerage firms for a particular maturity bond. The sales charges can range from less than 1 percent to as much a 5 percent of the price of a zero-coupon bond.

The actual commissions charged are included in the "net price" paid by the investor. The commission is not disclosed separately.

A small change in the commission earned by the brokerage firm can make a noticeable difference in the interest rate of return earned by the investor. An example is:

**Maturity date of zero-coupon bond**
**5-15-2005**

| Price Quote per $1,000 Face Value | Name of Brokerage Firm | Yield to Maturity |
|---|---|---|
| $133.59 | ABC Securities | 10.65% |
| $136.26 | DEF Securities | 10.49% |
| $138.93 | XYZ Brokerage Inc. | 10.38% |

Investors should shop carefully, as a $5.34 change in price results in a 27 basis-point increase in yield.

Investors purchasing small quantities of zero-coupon bonds (with less than $10,000 invested) cannot expect to receive as competitive an offering as larger purchasers. The brokerage firm has the same transaction costs on an order to buy $2,000 worth of zeros as they do on an order to buy $200,000. Even so, it should pay to shop around for the lowest net offering price when an investor plans to purchase zero-coupon bonds.

## PORTFOLIO FIT

The yield on corporate and U.S. government zero-coupon bonds is taxable as ordinary interest income every year, even though the holder receives no payment until maturity. For this reason, these securities are best suited for tax deferred retirement accounts or low-bracket custodial accounts.

Zero-coupon bonds are well suited for pension and profit sharing plans where the interest is not currently taxable. For example, a professional corporation with four principals purchases $110,000 worth of U.S. government zeros that yield 11 percent and mature in 16 years. These bonds will have a maturity value of over $600,000, which can be used toward pension payments.

Growth and guaranteed safety of principal (by the U.S. government) have made treasury zeros popular investments for IRA and Keogh accounts. $4,000 invested by a married couple today at 11 percent will have an approximate face value of $20,000 at maturity in 15 years.

Often corporate and U.S. government zero-coupon bonds are used in a college education fund for children or grandchildren. As a gift, these securities are tax advantaged when investors purchase them in a custodial account. The tax liability will be calculated based on the child's tax bracket, not that of the custodian.

Investors seeking the advantages of zero-coupon bonds outside of a custodial or retirement account should use zero-coupon municipal securities if the investors' marginal tax bracket is over the 30 percent range. The after-tax return on the municipal zeros will be better than a higher taxable return on corporate or government zeros.

## SOURCES OF ADDITIONAL INFORMATION

Several booklets and brochures are available from the brokerage community that explain in detail zero-coupon bonds. Local brokerage firms will mail them to prospective investors.

## COMMENTS

When used correctly, zero-coupon bonds provide a safe, effective investment planning vehicle.

Investors should make certain they have a balanced portfolio, including some assets in inflation-sensitive investments if a significant portion of the investor's net worth is dedicated to zero-coupon bonds.

**Exhibit 27-1. Moderate Risk: Zero Coupon Bonds**

**INVESTMENT PROFILE**

| INVESTMENT CHARACTERISTICS | Excellent | Good | Average | Poor | None |
|---|---|---|---|---|---|
| Liquidity | | √ | | | |
| Safety of Principal | | √* | | | |
| Price Stability | | | | √ | |
| Reinvestment Protection | √ | | | | |
| Growth of Capital | | √ | | | |
| Cash Income | | | | | √ |
| Growth of Income | | | | | √ |
| Inflation Hedge | | | √ | | |
| Tax Advantaged | | | | | √ |

**Liquidity**—the ability to quickly realize cash from the sale at fair market value

**Safety of Principal**—the principal is safe from bankruptcy or default

**Price Stability**—the market value of the asset does not change in value

**Reinvestment Protection**—protection against reinvesting cash flow at lower rates as interest rates decline

**Growth of Capital**—the original investment increases over time to create capital gains

**Cash Income**—the cash income relative to treasury bills returns

**Growth of Income**—the ability of the cash income stream to increase over time

**Inflation Hedge**—the ability of total return (cash income plus capital gains) to keep pace with inflation over time

**Tax Advantaged**—the ability to reduce or defer current federal income taxes

*Depends on rating of the issuer. U.S. governments would be excellent.

# CHAPTER 28

# Ginnie Maes

## DESCRIPTION

*Ginnie Mae pass-through securities* are fully guaranteed U.S. government securities. A certificate represents a share in a pool of FHA or VA mortgages. An issuer, usually a mortgage banking company, will package a minimum of $1,000,000 worth of FHA/VA single-family home mortgages. The mortgage banker then places the mortgages in the custody of a bank and through the Government National Mortgage Association issues a Ginnie Mae pass-through security collaterized by FHA/VA. The mortgages in the pool must have the same interest rate, term of maturity, and type of dwelling.

The Government National Mortgage Association (GNMA) is a wholly owned corporate instrumentality of the United States within the Department of Housing and Urban Development. It had its origin in the creation of the National Mortgage Association in 1938.

GNMA is authorized by Section 306(g) of Title III of the National Housing Act to guarantee the timely payment of the principal and interest on securities that are based on and backed by a pool composed of mortgages. These mortgages are either insured by the Federal Housing Administration or by the Veterans Administration. Section 306(g) provides that "The full faith and credit of the United States is pledged to the payment of all amounts which may be required to be paid by any guaranty under this subsection."

Ginnie Maes are among the highest-yielding government securities available. Moreover, the faster mortgages in a Ginnie Mae pool are paid off, the higher the yield to the investor.

Investors who own Ginnie Mae certificates receive government guaranteed principal and interest payments each month from the proportionate share of the mortgage pool owned by the investor.

By using Ginnie Maes, an investor no longer has to lock in capital in long-term securities for a high yield. Ginnie Maes are relatively short-term investments offering higher yields than most of today's long-term securities.

## STRENGTHS

Ginnie Maes are guaranteed by the full faith and credit of the U.S. government.

The Ginnie Mae offers liquidity and unusually high cash flow; this enables an investor to be ready to take advantage of alternative investments should the opportunity present itself.

## WEAKNESSES

Ginnie Mae securities are not easily understood. The fact that a portion of the monthly cash flow is a return of capital invested tends to confuse some investors. Rate of return calculations are not simple for Ginnie Maes.

## UNIQUE FEATURES

Ginnie Mae securities contain mortgages that are scheduled to be repaid over a 30-year period. Because many of the mortgages are paid off prior to maturity, the actual average life of the Ginnie Mae is approximately 6 to 7 years.

Each issue of Ginnie Maes will sell either above or below par value to produce a yield that is competitive with both current market conditions and with the highest yielding U.S. government securities.

## TAX CONSEQUENCES

Each certificate holder (GNMA investor) is treated as the owner of an individual interest in the entire pool of mortgages. This means that a GNMA investor will take into account their pro-rata share of the mortgage interest, prepayment penalties, assumption fees, and late-payment charges as ordinary income in the year received.

All certificate holders must report their share of the discount income on the purchase of the mortgages as ordinary income. Service fees incurred for collection and management of the pool are deductible to the certificate owners.

Repayment of principal from the periodic payoff of a mortgage in the pool or from the disposition of a mortgage reduces the investors' adjusted tax basis in the pool.

Investors can experience either a capital gain or capital loss from a Ginnie Mae investment, depending on the cost basis of the pool at the time the investor elects to sell his or her interest in the pool.

Ginnie Maes may be of special interest to investors in the states of Alabama, California, Colorado, and Maryland because these states do not tax income from Ginnie Maes for state income taxes.

Ginnie Mae investors should consult with a qualified tax professional to insure that tax obligations are correctly calculated on GNMA investments.

## WHERE AND HOW TO BUY

Security dealers and some bank trust departments offer Ginnie Mae certificates to investors. Ginnie Maes are traded over-the-counter and quoted just like other bond investments. The price paid by the investor is negotiable between the investor and the firm offering the certificates.

Prices are quoted in points and 32nds. Example, a quote of 85-4/32 is a dollar price of $84.125 per $100 of face value of mortgages remaining in the GNMA pool.

For many investors GNMA purchases are very complicated. An example of the calculations performed at the time a GNMA certificate is purchased is contained in Exhibit 28-1.

Perhaps the most important consideration for GNMA certificate investors is to purchase the certificate from a knowledgeable investment advisor. The assumption of repayment experience is extremely important in calculating the rate of return on a GNMA certificate. An experienced broker or banker will provide accurate, dependable information for the investor.

## HOW TO SELL

Investors can liquidate a GNMA certificate any business day through stock brokerage firms and some banks. An investor should offer the

**Exhibit 28-1.  Sample GNMA Analysis Worksheet**

## GNMA ANALYSIS

Date _12_ / _19_ / _84_

Offered Subject (1) $ _25,000.00_  Pool # (2) _7536_  Interest Rate (3) _8.5_ %

|  | 2 Year | 1 Year | 6 Months | Issue Date |
|---|---|---|---|---|
| FHA Experience | _50_ % | _81_ % | _161_ % | _116_ % |

| | | | |
|---|---|---|---|
| Minimum Face Amount | (4) | $25,000.00 | Servicer (12) _Citicorp Homeowners_ |
| × Current Factor | (5) | _.4914004_ | Location (13) _St. Louis, Mo_ |
| = Balance Remaining | (6) | _12,285.01_ | Dated Date (14) _12/01/75_ |
| × Current Offering Price | (7) | _84.125_ | Due Date (15) _12/15/05_ |
| = Amount of Investment | (8) | _10,334.76_ | Time Elapsed (16) _9 years 0 month_ |
| + Accrued Interest to | (9) | _75.42_ | **Next Month** |
| (10) _12/27/84_ Settlement Date (11) | | | (Minimum) Principal (17) _16.53_ |
| | | | (Minimum) Interest (18) _87.02_ |
| = Total Amount Due | | _10,410.18_ | Total P & I (19) _103.55_ |

At _116_ % FHA Experience  Yield = _11.691_ % Bond Equiv. = _11.979_ %

### CASH FLOW ANALYSIS (20)

(21) **At 50% FHA Experience Yield = _11.192_** % Bond Equiv. = _11.456_ %

| | Next 12 Months | Next 5 Years | Next 10 Years |
|---|---|---|---|
| Principal Pay Down | _525.92_ | _2493.72_ | _5149.59_ |
| + Interest Paid | _1023.73_ | _4696.55_ | _8310.70_ |
| = TOTAL | _1549.65_ | _7190.27_ | _13460.29_ |

### CASH FLOW ANALYSIS

(22) **At 0 % FHA Experience Yield = _10.83_** % Bond Equiv. = _11.077_ %

| | Next 12 Months | Next 5 Years | Next 10 Years |
|---|---|---|---|
| Principal Pay Down | _206.79_ | _1247.01_ | _3199.43_ |
| + Interest Paid | _1036.30_ | _4980.28_ | _9294.25_ |
| = TOTAL | _1243.09_ | _6227.29_ | _12493.78_ |

## Exhibit 28-1. (Continued)

## EXPLANATION OF A GNMA WORKSHEET

(1)  The original face amount we are offering: the minimum purchase is 25,000, multiples of 5,000 thereafter.

(2)  The Identity of the GNMA – all GNMAs are designated by a one to six digit number or as TBA.

(3)  The interest on the GNMA (the interest rate paid by borrower is always ½% greater than the rate of the pool, the ½% being a servicing charge).

(4)  The original fact amount of certificate available 25,000 minimum and multiples of 5,000 thereafter.

(5)  When the pool is originated (brand new) the factor is 1.00000000. As principal is paid off the factor decreases each month i.e. current balance of pool ÷ original balance.

(6)  Original amount × current factor = balance remaining due for the month.

(7)  The suggested offering price to be paid by customer per 100.00 current balance.

(8)  The balance × the offering price = the investment.

(9)  Accrued interest = balance × coupon ÷ 360 days × number of days to settlement less 1 day (i.e. if settlement is 20th you pay 19 days) due the previous owner.

(10) The day the monies are owed from the customer.

(11) Total of investment and accrued interest due on the settlement date.

(12) The name of the servicing entity; i.e. savings & loans, mortgage companies, banks.

(13) The location of the servicing mortgage company.

(14) The date the pool was originated.

(15) The maturity date of the longest mortgage in the pool.

(16) The time elapsed (years & months) from the dated date of the mortgage in the pool.

(17) The minimum principal due with no prepayment expectations.

(18) The interest you will receive is based on the balance (par amount of GNMAs owned) × interest rate of the pool ÷ 12 months. Balance × coupon ÷ 12 = interest.

(19) The minimum principal and interest check you will receive is calculated by the balance × the constant assigned to each interest rate ÷ 12.

Constants

| | | |
|---|---|---|
| | | 11½% = 11.89 |
| 5½% = 6.82 | 8¼% = 9.02 | 12 % = 12.35 |
| 6½% = 7.59 | 8½% = 9.23 | 12½% = 12.81 |
| 7 % = 7.99 | 8¾% = 9.45 | 13 % = 13.28 |
| 7¼% = 8.19 | 9 % = 9.66 | 13½% = 13.75 |
| 7½% = 8.40 | 9½% = 10.10 | 14 % = 14.22 |
| 7¾% = 8.60 | 10 % = 10.54 | 15 % = 15.18 |
| 8 % = 8.81 | 11 % = 11.44 | 16 % = 16.14 |

(20) Although GNMAs can fluctuate in FHA experience from 0% to 100% or even higher, 50% FHA experience has been the national average during the past **5 years.**

(21) Based on a 50% FHA experience a conservative approach is projected for the cash flow to be expected for the next 12 months, 5 years, and 10 years. The owner of the GNMA may now estimate the cash flow of their investment based on the 50% assumed experience.

(22) The minimum yield expected without prepayments during the life of the GNMA pool.

GNMA to several firms and sell the certificate to the firm that bids the highest price for the security. A difference of 2 to 3 percent in the prices bid for a GNMA would not be uncommon.

GNMA certificates are liquid. The existing market for GNMA issues is in excess of $140 Billion dollars. Currently, over $1.5 billion of new GNMAs are created each month.

## TRANSACTION COSTS

Ginnie Maes are offered on a ''net basis'' to investors. Any profit or commission for the brokerage firm or bank is included in the offering price of the securities. It is not uncommon for a firm to charge a 3 percent markup on GNMA securities. By carefully shopping the market, an investor may achieve a better rate of return on investment.

## PORTFOLIO FIT

Purchasers of Ginnie Maes include retirement and pension funds, financial institutions, and individuals. Individuals purchase GNMA certificates because they offer a unique combination of safety, an attractive yield, liquidity, and cash flow.

Even though prepayments of principal may occur at any time, many investors welcome an inflow of funds because they want the additional cash flow to meet pension planning requirements. The monthly cash flow from a Ginnie Mae may permit the investor to hold less liquid assets (such as real estate) for sale at the most opportune time.

As long as an investor realizes that a part of the cash flow from Ginnie Maes represents a return of capital, the GNMA certificate can be an excellent portfolio planning tool.

## SOURCES OF ADDITIONAL INFORMATION

An excellent brochure on Ginnie Mae securities entitled ''Facts about GNMA Mortgage Backed Securities'' is available from the brokerage firm of Butcher and Singer Inc. (305-454-1100). Many other brokerage firms and banks also offer literature on Ginnie Maes.

A most complete source of information on mortgage securities is a book entitled *The Handbook of Mortgage-Backed Securities* by Frank J. Fabozzi (*Probus* Publishing, 1985).

## COMMENTS

Ginnie Maes are available in the form of *unit investment trusts (UITs)*. For most investors the UITs represent a much less complicated form of ownership than direct purchase of Ginnie Maes. A UIT is available in increments of approximately $1,000. UITs also offer better diversification than the purchase of an individual GNMA pool.

With the exception of the wealthiest investors, Ginnie Mae investments may prove to be more trouble to understand than they are worth. The full guarantee of interest and principal makes these securities ideal for use in pension plans.

**Exhibit 28-2.   Moderate Risk: Ginnie Maes**

**INVESTMENT PROFILE**

| INVESTMENT CHARACTERISTICS | Excellent | Good | Average | Poor | None |
|---|---|---|---|---|---|
| Liquidity | | ✓ | | | |
| Safety of Principal | ✓ | | | | |
| Price Stability | | | ✓ | | |
| Reinvestment Protection | | | ✓ | | |
| Growth of Capital | | | | | ✓ |
| Cash Income | ✓ | | | | |
| Growth of Income | | | | | ✓ |
| Inflation Hedge | | | ✓ | | |
| Tax Advantaged | | | | ✓* | |

**Liquidity**—the ability to quickly realize cash from the sale at fair market value

**Safety of Principal**—the principal is safe from bankruptcy or default

**Price Stability**—the market value of the asset does not change in value

**Reinvestment Protection**—protection against reinvesting cash flow at lower rates as interest rates decline

**Growth of Capital**—the original investment increases over time to create capital gains

**Cash Income**—the cash income relative to treasury bills returns

**Growth of Income**—the ability of the cash income stream to increase over time

**Inflation Hedge**—the ability of total return (cash income plus capital gains) to keep pace with inflation over time

**Tax Advantaged**—the ability to reduce or defer current federal income taxes

*Some states (Alabama, California, Colorado, & Maryland) exclude Ginnie Mae interest from state taxes.

# CHAPTER 29

# Unit Investment Trusts

## DESCRIPTION

*Unit investment trusts* (or *bond trusts*) consist of a fixed portfolio of debt securities. Typically the debt securities included in the trust are issued by either municipalities, corporations, or the U.S. government.

Each individual bond is professionally selected by a company that specializes in packaging unit investment trusts for individual investors. These companies are known as the "sponsor" of the trust. The sponsor is a company dedicated to professional bond investing. The employees of the company are specialists in particular types of bonds. These specialists have been educated, trained, and have acquired considerable work experience in a highly specialized segment of the bond market.

For example, the sponsor may employ a municipal bond specialist whose expertise lies, not just in municipal bonds, but in municipal bonds from a small region of the United States, for example, the Pacific Northwest. This specialist is familiar with all of the cities, counties, towns, and special taxation districts that from time to time issue municipal bonds for investors. The specialist is adept at selecting bonds of the highest quality with the highest available yield.

The sponsor companies select a diversified portfolio of bonds to be included in each unit investment trust. An individual investor is able to purchase a small interest in many different bonds with a minimal cash commitment. For as little as $1,000 an investor will directly participate in every bond included in a unit of the unit investment trust.

Once all the bonds have been selected, the bonds are deposited with a large financial institution, typically a large bank that provides custodial services and acts as trustee for the unit investment trust.

**Table 29-1.  Industry Deposits of Tax Exempt Unit
Investment Trusts (UITs)
(Dollars in Millions)**

| Year | UIT Deposit | Year | UIT Deposit |
|------|------------|------|-------------|
| 1961 | $ 20.00 | 1973 | $    725.70 |
| 1962 | 33.00 | 1974 | 999.40 |
| 1963 | 27.00 | 1975 | 2,193.15 |
| 1964 | 68.50 | 1976 | 2,691.55 |
| 1965 | 80.50 | 1977 | 2,343.40 |
| 1966 | 50.50 | 1978 | 2,363.83 |
| 1967 | 50.90 | 1979 | 2,991.71 |
| 1968 | 53.80 | 1980 | 4,376.00 |
| 1969 | 58.50 | 1981 | 5,396.17 |
| 1970 | 216.20 | 1982 | 13,955.70 |
| 1971 | 566.80 | 1983 | 14,808.10 |
| 1972 | 893.30 | 1984 | 14,721.30 |
|      |        | 1985 | 15,339.20 |

*Source:* John Nuveen & Co. Incorporated Investment Bankers. Reprinted with permission.

The trustee is responsible for making regular distributions of interest to the unit holders.

If any of the bonds are repaid early, the trustee will distribute the pro-rata share of the prepayment to each unit holder. When the bonds mature, the principal repayments are returned to the unit holders, just as would be the case on a regular corporate, municipal, or government bond.

The data in Table 29-1 shows the growth in popularity of tax exempt unit investment trusts from 1961 to 1984.

## STRENGTHS

Unit investment trusts have become exceptionally popular in recent years as investors have come to appreciate the convenience of monthly, quarterly, or semiannual income payments by unit investment trusts.

Unit investment trusts offer the additional convenience of safekeeping of the bonds and regular collection of income from the bonds on behalf of the holders.

Unit investment trust owners receive highly competitive yields on their portfolio of bonds, because the sponsor of the unit investment trust is able to purchase in large quantities and receive slightly higher yields at the time of purchase than an individual, small investor can.For example, a unit investment trust may be able to buy $500,000 of bonds with a 10 percent coupon priced at par. This provides a yield of 10 percent to the unit investment trust. An individual investor may have to pay a price of 101 or, in dollar terms, $1,010 for each thousand dollar face value bond. This results in a yield for the individual investor of 9.9 percent.

## WEAKNESSES

The major weakness in unit investment trusts is exactly the same as the main negative feature of all bonds. Long-term bonds when purchased in a unit investment trust are subject to fluctuations in principal value because of changes in the market's interest rates.

When interest rates rise, the market value of a unit of a unit investment trust will decline. When interest rates decline, the market value of a unit investment trust will increase. This is no different than for any other regular bond.

Investors who are well enough informed to correctly interpret economic and interest rate cycles can receive excellent benefits by purchasing unit investment trusts at or near the peak of interest rate levels. These investors then hold the unit investment trusts as rates decline, thereby capturing both a high yield and capital gains during the time they hold the investment.

All investors should know that during the time of rising interest rates the maturity selected by unit investment trust investors should be shortened. By purchasing a short- or intermediate-term maturity, an investor vastly reduces the risk of principal fluctuations as interest rates change.

As many investors will attest, the ability to accurately predict future interest rates is not especially easy. Many investors may be most comfortable purchasing medium-term maturity trusts. These trusts often range in maturity from 5 to 12 years. These trusts offer acceptable rates of return from the interest earned and offer a smaller amount of market value fluctuation than longer term trusts.

## UNIQUE FEATURES

Unit investment trusts offer several unique features for investors. First, unit investment trusts offer what is called the *universal distribution option*. Very simply, this means an investor can receive the income produced by the trust on either a monthly, quarterly, or semiannual basis. This is especially convenient for investors living on fixed incomes.

A second unique feature of unit investment trusts is their immediate liquidity, offered to investors by the sponsor of the trust. At the close of any regular business day, the sponsor of the trust stands prepared to buy the units from the investors at fair market value as of that date.

A third unique feature is the ability of the sponsor of the unit investment trust to execute large quantity purchases of particular groups of municipal bonds as they are offered in the marketplace. These large quantity purchases result in what most people would recognize as a volume discount on the price of the bonds. The net result of these large quantity purchases is a slightly higher effective yield to the individual investor in a unit investment trust.

A fourth unique feature of unit investment trust is optional default insurance coverage. This default insurance coverage provides a third-party guarantee that in the event of default by an issuer of one of the bonds in the trust or by the failure of one issuer to pay interest when due to the trust, the third-party insurance company will guarantee to make timely payments of principal and interest to the unit investment trust.

This special insurance coverage is an optional feature. Not all trusts provide this coverage. Obviously, an insurance premium must be paid to the insurance company by the trust for this insurance service. Because of this premium, insured unit investment trusts provide a slightly lower interest rate to the investor than uninsured unit investment trusts. The yield difference ranges from .25 to .50 percent.

## TAX CONSEQUENCES

The tax status of unit investment trust is determined by the specific type of bonds held in the trust. Municipal bonds are free from federal government taxation and retain this tax free status when packaged in unit investment trusts.

Corporate bonds and U.S. government bonds provide fully taxable income to unit investment trust owners. There is no difference in the tax treatment when these bonds are included in the unit investment trust or purchased separately by individuals. As with all bond investments, gains and losses may result as fluctuations in the market value of the bonds occur over time. Investors should review the capital gains tax treatments and capital loss tax treatments of bonds in each of the separate bond chapters in this book. Capital gains and/or capital losses that occur as a result as a sale of trust units are taxed just as if those units had been individual bonds.

## WHERE AND HOW TO BUY

A sample list of suppliers follows. These suppliers distribute the unit investment trusts through securities dealers.

Kemper Sales Co.
120 S. LaSalle St.
Chicago, IL 60603
312-781-1121

Van Kampen Merritt Inc.
1901 N. Naper Blvd.
Naperville, IL 60566
312-369-8880

Corporate Income Fund
2 World Trade Center
New York, NY 10038
212 791-1000

John Nuveen & Co.
209 LaSalle St.
Chicago, IL 60603
1-800-252-9400

First Trust
Clayton Brown & Assoc.
300 W. Washington
Chicago, IL 60606
312-641-3300

Investors may purchase unit investment trusts from virtually every major securities brokerage firm and most local branches. In recent years, some unit investment trusts have been offered by large financial institutions, insurance companies, and mutual fund salesmen. An individual investor only needs to contact a representative licensed to sell the product, learn the terms of the offering; read, study, and review the prospectus furnished with each trust; and decide an amount to be purchased.

The executing broker or sales agent completes a purchase order form that includes information regarding the distribution option selected, whether or not the securities are to be held at the brokerage firm or shipped out to the client, and other pertinent data.

The purchase of unit investment trust is very easy and a very common occurrence for individual investors. All brokers should be able to assist an investor in the selection of a unit investment trust appropriate for the investor's needs.

## HOW TO SELL

All unit investment trusts may be liquidated on any regular business day by simply contacting the sales organization that provided the trust originally. The investor need only request that the units be disposed of at the close of business on that day. All of the bonds within the unit investment trust are priced according to their actual market value every business day. The individual investor receives the market value of the trust units on the day that they are liquidated. The investor also receives a share of accrued daily interest available to every unit investment holder of the trust.

Virtually every supplier of the trust maintains an active secondary market for the units of the trust. Investors frequently are concerned with their ability to sell the trust. Unit investment trusts are very liquid investment instruments.

## TRANSACTION COSTS

A one-time sales charge that generally ranges between 2.5 percent and 4.5 percent of the amount invested is charged to purchasers of unit investment trusts. This sales charge is included in the price of the units at the time of purchase. The investor will not receive an additional invoice for the amount of the sales charge. The sales charge will not be broken out or separately disclosed on the sales confirmation received by the investor.

All sales charges, fees, and trustee and custodial fees are fully disclosed in the trust prospectus. Investors are always advised to completely review the entire trust prospectus prior to purchasing any units.

Unit investment trust have no liquidation charges or penalties or any kind. An investor has paid all sales charges at the time of purchase and will not be charged in the event of liquidation of the trust.

## PORTFOLIO FIT

The most obvious use of unit investment trusts for a particular investment portfolio is the case of the fixed-income investor. This individual quite often is retired and is seeking a regular, dependable monthly income.

Traditional bonds held by individuals pay interest only every six months. A unit investment trust offers a choice of receiving interest monthly, quarterly, or semiannually. This feature provides a great deal of convenience to a retired individual seeking a regular monthly income.

The unit investment trust may also be used by other fixed-income investors as a regular part of their investment program. These trusts are obvious bond substitutes and offer the additional feature of a diversified portfolio within a purchase as small as one unit ($1,000).

## SOURCES OF ADDITIONAL INFORMATION

Virtually all brokerage firms have brochures available that completely describe unit investment trusts. An investor need only to place a phone call to a local brokerage firm and request one of these brochures for review.

## COMMENTS

To summarize, unit investment trusts have been and will continue to be one of the most popular investment vehicles developed in the last 10 years. The portfolio diversification, universal distribution option, and liquidity have all served to meet many investors' needs.

This product will continue to grow in popularity and has the potential to dominate the market for individual fixed-income investors.

**Exhibit 29-1.   Moderate Risk: Unit Investment Trusts (Bond Trusts)**

**INVESTMENT PROFILE**

| INVESTMENT CHARACTERISTICS | Excellent | Good | Average | Poor | None |
|---|---|---|---|---|---|
| Liquidity | √ | | | | |
| Safety of Principal | | √* | | | |
| Price Stability | | ST | | LT | |
| Reinvestment Protection | | | | √ | |
| Growth of Capital | | | | | √ |
| Cash Income | | √ | | | |
| Growth of Income | | | | | √ |
| Inflation Hedge | | | √ | | |
| Tax Advantaged | MT† | | | | √† |

**Liquidity**—the ability to quickly realize cash from the sale at fair market value

**Safety of Principal**—the principal is safe from bankruptcy or default

**Price Stability**—the market value of the asset does not change in value

**Reinvestment Protection**—protection against reinvesting cash flow at lower rates as interest rates decline

**Growth of Capital**—the original investment increases over time to create capital gains

**Cash Income**—the cash income relative to treasury bills returns

**Growth of Income**—the ability of the cash income stream to increase over time

**Inflation Hedge**—the ability of total return (cash income plus capital gains) to keep pace with inflation over time

**Tax Advantaged**—the ability to reduce or defer current federal income taxes

*Insured unit trusts would provide excellent safety of principal.
†Trusts invested in municipal bonds provide tax free income.
LT = Long term.
ST = Short term.
MT = Municipal trusts.

# CHAPTER 30

# Mutual Funds

## DESCRIPTION

A *mutual fund* is a diversified portfolio of securities that is divided into *shares*. These shares represent ownership of the mutual fund. The shares may be purchased and sold just like other securities on any regular business day.

A *fund manager,* sometimes referred to as the *fund sponsor,* is employed to make investment decisions and provide investment management for the mutual fund.

Typically, the fund manager is a large financial services company, very often one that specializes exclusively in managing mutual funds. The same mutual fund management company may offer many different special purpose mutual funds. For example, Massachusetts Financial Services of Boston offers 16 different mutual funds among which investors can select.

This chapter will focus on the structure and attributes of mutual funds in general, not on one particular dedicated type of mutual fund. Nevertheless, the reader may wish to view the many types of mutual funds that are available as indicated in the following (noncomprehensive) list:

Common Stock Growth Funds
Common Stock Income Funds
Over the Counter Emerging Growth Stock Funds
Oil Stock Funds
Medical Technology Stock Funds
Computer Technology Stock Funds
Foreign Stock Funds
Telecommunications Stock Funds
Aviation Stock Funds
Gold Stock Funds
Corporate Bond Funds
Government Bond Funds

Utility Bond Funds
Tax Free Bond Funds

In addition, balanced funds may invest in combinations of stocks and bonds for a "total return" fund. A very broad variety of special-purpose mutual funds are available.

The reader can examine the results of various mutual funds by referring to Table 30-1. The table gives the performance record of the best mutual funds over various periods of time.

Each year, several investment research firms evaluate the performance of the major mutual funds. Investors can check the latest ratings before they select a new fund.

Exhibit 30-1 compares equity funds and fixed-income funds from 1980 through the third quarter of 1985.

All mutual funds are valued daily. At the end of each business day the total market value of all the securities in the portfolio is totaled then divided by the number of mutual fund shares outstanding. This value per share is called the *net asset value* of the mutual fund. The net asset value is printed in the daily mutual fund quotation section of each major newspaper of the United States.

An example of a newspaper format for Mutual Fund quotations is in Table 30-2.

Mutual funds are available as either load funds or no load funds. *Load mutual funds* include a sales charge at the time the investor purchases the fund shares. A *no load mutual fund* does not involve a front-end sales charge. A more detailed discussion of transaction costs is included later in the chapter.

## STRENGTHS

By far, the largest strength of the mutual fund is the portfolio diversification offered to small investors. The investor purchases a large portfolio of securities and yet only owns one security.

A second strength of mutual funds is professional management of the fund. Mutual funds each employ experienced and educated individuals whose sole responsibility is to professionally select securities for the fund.

Often investors are well versed on investment logic but still lack the time to manage individual securities. Many busy investors find mutual funds to be the answer to their time constraints.

## Table 30-1. Performance Gauge of Mutual Fund Yields

### Performance Gauge

| 3rd QUARTER 6/30/85 to 9/30/85 | | NINE MONTHS 12/31/84 to 9/30/85 | | ONE YEAR 9/30/84 to 9/30/85 | | FIVE YEARS 9/30/80 to 9/30/85 | | TEN YEARS 9/30/75 to 9/30/85 | |
|---|---|---|---|---|---|---|---|---|---|
| Transatlantic Fund | 17.60% | Fidelity Overseas | 45.87% | PaineWebber Atlas | 38.97% | Fidelity Magellan Fund | 230.42% | Fidelity Magellan Fund | 1493.15% |
| Kemper International Fd | 15.51 | Fidelity OTC | 42.36 | Fidelity Sel Leisure | 37.04 | Vanguard Qual Dvd I x | 222.36 | Lindner Fund x | 1075.15 |
| Trustees' Commingled Intl | 15.36 | Hemisphere Fund x | 38.59 | Merrill Lyn Pacific | 36.76 | Quest for Value Fund | 214.24 | Twentieth Century Gro | 1005.09 |
| FT International | 15.34 | PaineWebber Atlas | 37.90 | Hemisphere Fund x | 36.65 | Lindner Dividend x | 213.04 | Evergreen Fund | 983.90 |
| Alliance International | 15.28 | Putnam Intl Equities | 33.75 | Putnam Intl Equities | 36.43 | Hemisphere Fund x | 189.45 | Amer Capital Pace | 936.99 |
| Pru-Bache Global Fd | 14.88 | Fidelity Sel Health | 33.19 | NEL Series Capital Gro | 35.53 | Lindner Fund x | 187.08 | Quasar Associates | 918.50 |
| Fidelity Overseas | 14.67 | Pru-Bache Global Fd | 32.63 | Pru-Bache Global Fd | 34.54 | Loomis-Sayles Capital x | 178.86 | Twentieth Century Select | 890.23 |
| Oppenheimer A I M | 13.32 | Trustees' Commingled Intl | 31.00 | Fidelity Sel Financial | 33.46 | Mutual Qualified Income | 176.98 | Sequoia Fund x | 862.46 |
| Financial Port-Pacific | 13.18 | Alliance International | 30.72 | Alliance International | 32.48 | Sequoia Fund x | 174.50 | Pennsylvania Mutual x | 765.00 |
| T Rowe Price Intl Fund | 12.51 | NEL Series Capital Gro | 30.33 | Fidelity Sel Health | 31.57 | Phoenix Growth | 164.46 | Mutual Shares Corp | 753.40 |
| PaineWebber Atlas | 11.66 | Fidelity Sel Leisure | 30.29 | Vanguard Special-Health | 30.56 | Phoenix Stock | 160.06 | Nicholas Fund | 742.94 |
| GAM International | 11.19 | FT International | 29.28 | Trustees' Commingled Intl | 30.29 | Windsor Fund x | 157.51 | Over-The-Counter Sec | 709.43 |
| IDS International | 11.11 | Twentieth Century Gift | 29.18 | Century Shares Trust | 29.84 | Fidelity Equity-Income | 157.29 | Amer Capital Venture | 696.67 |
| Putnam Intl Equities | 10.55 | Merrill Lyn Pacific | 28.87 | Vanguard Qual Dvd II | 27.45 | Nicholas Fund | 157.22 | Fidelity Destiny | 680.47 |
| Scudder International | 10.26 | Oppenheimer Challenger | 27.15 | Twentieth Century Gift | 27.03 | NEL Growth Fund | 154.11 | Value Line Lvge Growth | 676.36 |
| United Intl Growth | 9.92 | Financial Port-Pacific | 26.49 | Nicholas II | 26.43 | Franklin Utilities | 149.15 | Pioneer II | 663.37 |
| Shearson Global | 8.67 | Transatlantic Fund | 26.20 | Vanguard Qual Dvd I x | 26.42 | Evergreen Total Return | 148.45 | Acorn Fund | 655.80 |
| Europacific Growth | 8.58 | GAM International | 25.91 | FT International | 26.26 | Tudor Fund | 148.04 | Fidelity Equity-Income | 640.11 |
| GIT Special Growth | 8.38 | GIT Special Growth | 25.77 | Northeast Inv Trust | 25.62 | Fidelity Puritan | 146.17 | Amer Capital Comstock | 634.54 |
| Mass Finl Intl Tr-Bond | 7.41 | Kemper International Fd | 24.34 | Sigma Income Shares | 25.06 | Ivy Growth | 145.69 | Security Ultra Fund | 629.77 |
| United Prospector | 7.41 | Scudder International | 24.32 | First Inv Special Bond | 24.87 | FPA Paramount x | 145.66 | Mass Capital Development | 627.72 |
| Dean Witter World Wide | 7.41 | Vanguard Special-Health | 23.58 | Financial High Yield Bnd | 24.39 | Mutual Shares Corp | 142.88 | Weingarten Equity | 626.73 |
| Colonial Adv Str Gold | 7.18 | Quasar Associates | 23.21 | Pilgrim MagnaCap | 24.26 | Amer Capital Pace | 142.34 | Oppenheimer Special | 618.29 |
| Venture Income (+) Plus | 6.89 | T Rowe Price Intl Fund | 22.78 | T Rowe Price Intl Fund | 23.90 | Gemini Fund x | 140.20 | Amev Growth Fd | 590.16 |
| Merrill Lyn Pacific | 6.86 | Babson Enterprise | 22.56 | Fidelity Puritan | 23.79 | Lehman Capital Fund | 139.50 | Sigma Venture Shares | 582.84 |
| GT Pacific Growth Fd | 6.51 | | | | | | | | |

x: Fund closed to new accounts.

Source: *Barron's* and Lipper Analytical Services.

Exhibit 30-1.   General Equity Funds versus Fixed-Income Funds: Total
Reinvested Performance, 1980–1985

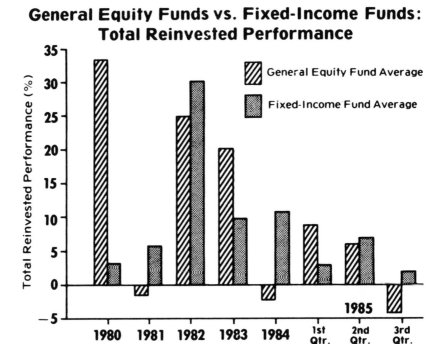

General Equity Funds vs. Fixed-Income Funds:
Total Reinvested Performance

## WEAKNESS

Individual investors exhibit no control over the individual stocks selected for investment for a mutual fund.

It should also be pointed out that mutual funds, in general, have not outperformed the overall market indicators over the last four decades. While mutual funds provide an extremely effective form of diversification, they do not necessarily provide superior returns consistently. A few highly successful mutual funds are, however, an exception to this rule. Investors should not be swayed by one or two years of good performance and automatically project those fund earnings 10 years into the future.

In some cases, mutual funds dedicated to a very narrow investment area can prove to be very risky if selected during the wrong phase of a market cycle. For example, mutual funds dedicated to investments in the

**Table 30-2. Newspaper Format for Mutual Fund Quotations**

| Fund | 1984 %Chg. | 1985 %Chg. | NAV | Offer Price | NAV Chg. |
|---|---|---|---|---|---|
| Pacific Horizon: | | | | | |
| Agresv | ... | + 2 | 20.07 | NL | +.05 |
| Calif | ... | − 0 | 12.90 | NL | −.01 |
| High Yd | ... | + 0 | 15.48 | NL | −.01 |
| Paine Webber | | | | | |
| Atlas | − 1 | +52 | 12.82 | 14.06 | −.02 |
| Fidelity | | | | | |
| Agresv | ... | ... | 10.45 | NL | +.01 |
| Calfr | ... | ... | 9.97 | NL | ... |
| Calmu | ... | ... | 10.59 | NL | −.01 |
| Congrs | + 2 | +20 | 64.32 | NL | +.05 |
| Contfd | −10 | +22 | 11.96 | NL | −.01 |
| CTAR | ... | ... | 10.70 | NL | ... |
| DESTNY | − 0 | +13 | 12.13 | ... | +.03 |

oil and gas industry have not fared well since the 1982 decline in oil and gas prices.

## UNIQUE FEATURES

One of the most unique features of a mutual fund is called a *switch privilege*. With a switch privilege a mutual fund investor, generally by use of a telephone call, may transfer ownership from one special type of fund to a different type of fund managed by the same investment management company. For example, with just a telephone call, an investor would be able to move investment funds from a common stock growth fund to a money market mutual fund in the event the stock market offered too much risk.

In some cases, a small charge is levied to the investor at the time the switch between funds is made. Investors should carefully review each mutual fund to determine whether or not the switch charges apply.

Other restrictions may limit the frequency with which switches can be made. Some mutual fund management companies encourage switching in an effort to attract investors to their particular portfolio of funds.

## TAX CONSEQUENCES

(Note: This tax treatment is quite comprehensive. Many readers may wish to merely glance over it and continue reading the chapter. Those readers with specific tax interests can benefit from reading the material carefully.)

The tax impacts of mutual funds require one of the most complex taxation treatments of any investment product. Investors should pay particular attention to the tax treatments of fund distributions, to the special rules regarding timing involved in mutual fund taxation, and of course to the capital gain and loss rules that apply to all investments.

Various mutual fund distributions are treated differently, depending on the original source of the distribution. Mutual fund distributions may be classified as long-term capital gains, short-term capital gains, interest distributions, tax free distributions, or as stock dividends.

Taxes must be paid on taxable distributions in the year when they were credited to the investor, even if the investor reinvested those distributions, and no cash was actually received. Reinvested distributions are treated for tax purposes as newly issued shares that were purchased by the investor on the date of the reinvestment. It is important to note that for tax purposes the holding period for these new shares begins the day after the date of reinvestment. The cost basis is equal to the amount of the distribution divided by the number shares purchased.

Dividends or interest received and distributed by the mutual fund are classified as ordinary income. These dividends will be reported as dividend income on tax returns. To the extent that the distribution represents dividends from stocks in the funds portfolio, these dividends qualify for the $100 dividend exclusion available on all stocks ($200 on joint returns). It should be noted that money market mutual funds and bond funds generally receive their income as interest from debt securities. Because of this, the distributions from money market mutual funds and bond mutual funds are not eligible for the dividend exclusion.

In the case of capital gain distributions, the holding period is established based on the time the mutual funds has owned the stocks, not the length of time the mutual fund investor has owned shares of the mutual fund. For example, if the mutual fund receives a short-term capital gain and distributes it to its shareholders, it is taxed as short-term capital gains for all shareholders, even if the owner of the mutual fund has held those mutual funds shares in excess of six months. By the same token, all long-term capital gains received by the mutual fund are considered long-term capital gains when they are distributed to shareholders, even if the individual investor has only owned the fund for a very few days. There are several additional important factors in this area of the tax law. First, if mutual fund shares are sold by an investor for a loss within six months after the investor receives a long-term capital gain distribution from the mutual fund, the loss will be considered to be a long-term loss to the extent of the long-term capital gain distribution.

Distribution received from tax exempt money market and tax exempt bond funds are tax free to mutual fund investors. Any gains or losses resulting from the sale of a tax exempt fund are subject to the regular capital gains and loss rules. Once again, any shares sold at a loss within 31 days of receiving a tax exempt distribution have an amount of the loss equal to that distribution disallowed for capital losses.

Many investors are enamored with the idea of receiving dividends from their investments. An investor who attempts to purchase a mutual fund immediately before a dividend is to be paid, may be paying more for the mutual fund than if he or she waited a few days and purchased it immediately after a dividend distribution.

This is because mutual funds that sell at their net asset value will drop in price as soon as the fund goes "ex-dividend." The net asset value will fall by the amount of the distribution. Investors can increase their after tax returns by purchasing shares of the mutual fund after the distribution or selling shares of the mutual fund before the distribution. The distribution is officially recorded on the "ex-dividend date." The ex-dividend date is established for recordkeeping purposes and actually occurs two to three weeks prior to the actual distribution of funds from the mutual fund trustee.

As an example, a mutual fund investor who is considering the purchase of 1,000 shares of brand X mutual fund has called the broker and would like to purchase the fund at the current price of $20 per share. The mutual fund will be going ex-dividend in about one week. The distributions to be made at that time consist of $2 per share of ordinary income and $1 per share of capital gains. If the mutual fund investor purchases the shares prior to the distribution, that investor will pay $20,000 and will receive $3,000 from the distribution. That investor would also have to pay $1,200 in taxes on the distribution assuming a 50 percent tax bracket: (50 percent X $2,000) + (20 percent X $1,000) = $1,200. Immediately after the distribution, that investor would be left with a fund worth only $17 per share. From the mathematical example, the total out-of-pocket expenditure to acquire $1,000 of this fund would be $18,200. If that investor waits and purchases the fund after it goes ex-dividend, he or she will be able to buy the fund at only $17 per share—in other words, at a total out-of-pocket expenditure of $17,000. The result is that the client still has the same 1,000 shares of the mutual fund and has saved $1,200 by purchasing them after the distribution was made.

A similar analysis will make it clear that it is beneficial for an investor of a mutual fund to sell the shares prior to the ex-dividend date rather than receiving the distribution and paying taxes on the distribution and then selling the shares. Although part of the tax is paid on the distribution will be offset by the tax consequences of selling at a higher predividend price, the investor will still come out ahead by selling prior to the ex-dividend date. Selling after the distribution will often replace long-term capital gains with ordinary income.

Investors also should note that certain investment-related expenses of a mutual fund are deductible, and others are not. Annual account maintenance and custodial fees can be deducted as the cost of investment advisory services. Commissions paid to purchase a mutual fund are added to the cost of the shares and are deductible only to the extent that they reduce the amount of taxable profit (or increases the loss) when the shares are eventually sold. Back-end loads and redemption fees are subtracted from the proceeds of the sale.

An additional rule regarding taxation of mutual funds is the *wash sale rule*. The wash sale rule disallows tax benefits for any mutual fund shares that are sold for a loss when shares of the same fund have been purchased 30 days before or after the date of the sale. Investors should note that the wash sale rule applies only to losses. The Internal Revenue Service fully recognizes all gains, even if the shares are repurchased the same day.

This section of the tax code prevents investors from selling their shares, taking a loss for tax purposes only, and immediately reestablishing the same investment. In the case of mutual funds, investors simply should sell shares in which they have a loss (especially a short-term loss) and should repurchase shares of a fund with a similar investment objective and similar portfolio.

One of the best ways to reduce taxes on investment profits is to take advantage of the favorable tax treatment given to long-term capital gains. To qualify for long-term capital gains treatment, mutual fund shares that are being sold at a profit must have been owned for six months and one day. A mutual fund investor with a qualifying sale is entitled to a deduction equal to 60 percent of that gain. After taking this deduction, the mutual fund investor only pays taxes on 40 percent of the profits from the shares that were sold long term. For an investor in a 50 percent tax bracket, the total tax due on a gain of $10,000 would only be $2,000 of the $10,000 profit.

This long-term capital gains treatment works equally well for lower tax-bracket investors.

In the case of mutual fund shares that are held for six months or less, any profit resulting from the sale of those shares is considered a short-term capital gain and is taxed at the investor's regular tax rates.

Any investor that is planning a sale of mutual fund shares should carefully check the length of time the shares have been held. It may be better to wait until those same gains qualify for long-term capital gains treatment.

Capital losses are treated in much the same manner as capital gains. If the amount received from the sale of a fund is less than the initial price paid, there is a capital loss. Any shares of a mutual fund that were held for six months or less are classified as short-term and those held more than six months are considered long-term.

Short-term capital losses are deductible in full from ordinary income and can result in a very substantial tax saving to the investor. Long-term capital losses are less desirable, because only 50 percent of long-term losses qualify as deductions. This means that an investor would deduct $3,000 of short-term losses on a dollar-for-dollar basis from a tax return. The same investor would have to have $6,000 of long-term losses to achieve a $3,000 deduction.

This leads to the fact that only $3,000 of capital losses are deductible each year from an income tax form. Any amount of capital loss deduction in excess of $3,000, whether long- or short-term, is carried over to succeeding years. As an example, an investor with a $5,000 long-term loss would deduct $2,500 from federal taxes. The same investor with a $5,000 short-term loss would deduct only $3,000 in the current tax year and carry forward $2,000 to the next tax year.

In addition to the individual treatment of long-term and short-term gains and losses, all capital gains and losses, regardless of whether they are short-term or long-term, must be netted out against one another. After this is done, the investor will end up with either a net gain or a net loss that may be long-term, short-term, or a combination of both. The investor netting out gains and losses may be able to use beneficial or detrimental tax strategies, depending on when the shares were bought and sold. As an example, a mutual fund investor who has short-term gains can directly offset those short-term gains with long-term losses. Similarly, long-term gains can have their tax advantage destroyed by being offset with short-term losses.

The following example demonstrates this. A mutual fund investor who has a short-term gain of $1,000 and is in the 47 percent tax bracket will have an after-tax return of only $530. At the end of the year, that same mutual fund investor notices that he also has a long-term loss of $1,000 on a different mutual fund. The tax of $470 that will be assessed against the short-term gain can be reduced to zero by taking the long-term loss before the end of the same tax year. If the mutual fund investor waits until the next year to take the loss, he will pay $470 in taxes on the short-term gain. Next year, he will receive a tax benefit of only $235 for the long-term loss. The difference between these two treatments is a knowledge of the tax law that would save $235 in taxes on these two transactions.

Fundamentally, there are two strategies investors should employ when offsetting long-term and short-term gains and losses.

First, investors should always attempt to offset short-term gains with long-term losses whenever that is possible. Investors should remember that while only 50 percent of a long-term capital loss can be used as a deduction from (ordinary) income, 100 percent of long-term losses can be used to offset all capital gains.

Secondly, investors should always try to preserve long-term gains by delaying any type of loss, especially short-term losses, until the next tax year.

## WHERE AND HOW TO BUY

Investors may purchase mutual funds from a variety of different sources. No load mutual funds typically advertise their funds in popular financial publications and local newspapers throughout the United States. Since no load mutual funds do not charge commission, all an investor needs to do is request the offering document for the fund (commonly known as a *pro-spectus*). This prospectus contains all pertinent information regarding the background of the management of the fund, the offering of the fund, and any special types of investments to be made by the fund.

After receiving and reviewing the prospectus and the sales literature, the mutual fund investor simply fills out a subscription form and mails it along with the amount of money to invest in the form of a personal check to the no load mutual fund.

Many discount brokerage firms and banks that provide discount brokers service will transact no load mutual fund shares for a small commission if the investor does not want to so thrust the process.

Investors who typically work with an investment executive, stockbroker, insurance agent, or financial planner may decide to buy a load mutual fund. A load is a sales charge that ranges from a low load of 3 percent to a more usual load of 8 percent of the amount invested. Many load funds have a sliding scale, so that the larger the investment the lower the load. In this case, the investor will be furnished with a prospectus, sales brochure, and other offering documents by the sales representative of the fund.

Typically the sales representative of the fund helps clients complete the mutual fund application form, helps the investor decide whether to select the telephone switch privilege, and discusses whether the investor wishes to receive all distributions in the form of checks mailed out or if those distributions are to be reinvested in additional shares of the mutual fund.

## HOW TO SELL

Mutual funds may be liquidated through the mutual fund management company. An investor writes a letter to the mutual fund company requesting liquidation of shares.

Investors should obtain a signature guarantee before asking the mutual fund manager by letter to liquidate the shares. To obtain a signature guarantee the investor should go to a commercial bank or traditional securities brokerage firm, where a principal of the firm will attach a signature guarantee to the letter. This authenticates the individual's signature and permits redemption of the mutual fund shares as requested. A signature guarantee is not the same as a notary seal.

It is not necessary to totally liquidate an investment in a mutual fund. An individual investor may request a partial liquidation, either a specific dollar amount or a specific number of shares to be liquidated by the fund.

Typically liquidations of mutual funds require approximately 7 to 10 working days to process.

## TRANSACTION COSTS

Transaction costs vary greatly between different mutual funds.

A no load mutual fund does not charge a front-end sales commission.

A load mutual fund will charge a front-end sales commission that ranges between 3 and 8.5 percent of the dollar amount invested. This is a one-time sales charge, not an annual fee.

Investors should carefully compare sales charges among different funds, as well as annual management fees charged by all mutual funds.

A crucial point is that there is no statistical evidence to indicate that load mutual funds outperform no load mutual funds. Therefore, the investor should think very carefully before he or she agrees to pay a heavy front-end commission. To the extent a salesperson for a load fund provides special guidance to the investor, some commission may be justified. On the other hand, because of the unlikelihood of truly superior performance of load funds over no load funds, large commissions should be carefully assessed before the investor decides to buy a load fund in preference to a no load fund. Shares can be purchased in fractional increments.

In recent years some funds have been advertising as no load funds since they charge no front-end sales charge. Many times, however, they charge a commission (end load) on a sale of shares within five years of purchase. Investors should know what they are buying.

## PORTFOLIO FIT

Many different types of investors purchase mutual funds. Large, widely diversified families of mutual funds can be found that will meet the needs of almost any investor. An investor may choose high-growth, high-income, tax free income, or even a gold mutual fund to fulfill portfolio needs.

The convenience offered by mutual funds often provides investors the opportunity to construct an entire investment portfolio and meet almost all of their investment objectives exclusively through the use of mutual funds, should they wish to do so. Mutual funds have become very popular vehicles for IRA and other retirement accounts.

## SOURCES OF ADDITIONAL INFORMATION

All mutual fund companies, stockbrokers, financial planners, and some banks and insurance agents have brochures and a prospectus available for investors.

In addition, several analytical services are available that specialize in mutual funds. Weisenberg Investment Services and Lipper Analytical Service are two. *Barron's* published quarterly mutual fund performance evaluations and *Forbes* magazine presents an annual mutual fund summary each August. Many other magazines specializing in investments publish weekly or monthly columns on mutual funds. A noted book on no-load mutual funds is published annually by the American Association of Individual Investors.

## COMMENTS

Mutual funds have gained tremendous popularity among investors in the United States. Investors have historically purchased more mutual funds near the time when the stock market and bond markets have made new high and record high levels; that is, they have purchased mutual funds during stock and bond price peaks that unfortunately reflect also a peak in the value in the mutual funds themselves.

It is interesting to note that when mutual funds, especially common stock mutual funds, are experiencing a net redemption—that is, they are shrinking in size—many times the stock market is at or near a historically low level.

Investors can very successfully use the switch technique offered by many mutual funds to a great advantage. The ability to switch monies between different types of investments, for example a stock fund and a money market fund, enables an individual investor to attempt to time economic changes simply by changing the type of fund selected for the investment.

## NOTE

The Investment Profile will be a function of the assets managed by the mutual fund. Please see the corresponding chapters for examples.

A growth stock mutual fund will have the same Investment Profile as growth stocks.

# CHAPTER 31

# Public Real Estate Growth Partnerships

## DESCRIPTION

*Real estate growth partnerships* are a specially designed vehicle that allows many individual investors to participate in the ownership of commercial real estate.

Real estate growth partnerships are formed to provide professional property acquisition, operation, and disposition. This professional management uses a structure called a *limited partnership*.

The limited partnership structure provides limited liability for individual investors, moderate tax advantages for investors, and preservation and growth of investors' capital.

As "limited partners," investors agree to pool their investment capital to provide for a "general partner" the funds necessary to purchase a portfolio of commercial real estate properties.

Typically the general partner is a corporation that specializes in the real estate industry. The general partner may employ several hundred people in a variety of geographic locations to provide investors with the full array of services available in real estate growth partnerships.

As can be seen from Exhibit 31-1, real estate growth partnership investors employ the general partner to completely take control of the investment. The limited partners retain no control over what to acquire, how to manage, or when to liquidate the properties.

Limited partners that invest in real estate growth partnerships do

**Exhibit 31-1.**

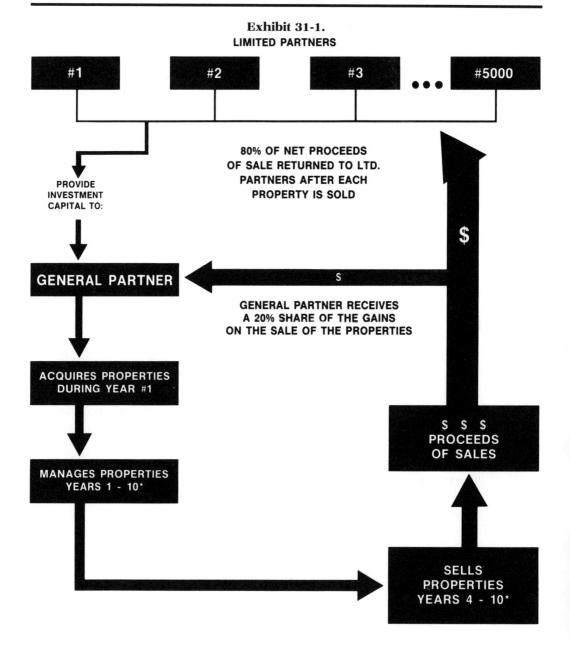

*NORMALLY A 4-8 YR HOLDING PERIOD

*Source: Stanger's Partnership Sponsor Directory.* Reprinted with permission.

receive some safeguards. First, the operations and financial affairs of the partnership are generally audited by an independent certified public accounting firm. Second, most of the real estate growth partnerships are structured with several priority distributions of income and capital to the limited partners in the partnership agreement.

Most real estate growth partnerships offer a sharing arrangement for the financial affairs of the partnership between the limited and the general partners. A typical case is detailed as follows:

| Item | Limited Partners | General Partner |
|---|---|---|
| Capital contributions | 99% | 1% |
| Tax losses from operations | 99% | 1% |
| Cash flow | 99% | 1% |
| Gain on the sale of assets | 80% | 20% |

As is obvious, the general partner has a significant incentive to prudently manage the properties on behalf of all the partners. The bulk of the general partner's earnings come on the back end of the partnership.

Exhibit 31-2 provides 1984 data on the total market of over $8 billion for publicly offered limited partnerships. Almost $2.4 billion was invested in leveraged real estate growth partnerships.

Exhibit 31-3 provides details by type of property sold in public real estate partnerships for 1983 and 1984.

Table 31-1 shows total sales of real estate growth partnerships by year from 1982 through 1985.

## STRENGTHS

Real estate growth partnerships offer individual investors the opportunity to participate in commercial real estate ownership otherwise unavailable to investors of average incomes and net worths.

Real estate growth partnerships provide a complete package of services to investors. Virtually no real estate expertise is needed on the part of a limited partner.

Real estate growth partnerships offer both capital gains potential and some tax deductions that might otherwise not be available to just one investor.

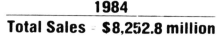

**Exhibit 31-2. Breakdown of Limited Partnership Investments**

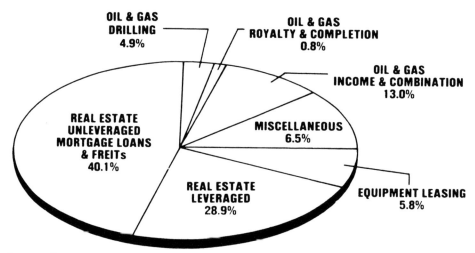

**1984**

**Total Sales - $8,252.8 million**

Source: *Stanger's Partnership Sponsor Directory.* Reprinted with permission.

## WEAKNESSES

By far the biggest weakness of real estate growth partnerships is the total lack of managerial control on the part of the investor. All decisions are made by the general partner for the partnership.

A secondary weakness is the lack of liquidity of the real estate growth partnerships. Typically, investors are unable to liquidate their positions prematurely without substantial financial cost.

## UNIQUE FEATURES

Investors in real estate growth partnerships are called limited partners for a very special reason. The properties purchased by the partnership will typically involve a substantial down payment by the partnership and mortgage financing for the property. These mortgages are called *nonrecourse mortgages,* because the individual limited partner is not liable to pay off the loans. The individual limited partner receives the benefits of this part-

**Exhibit 31-3. Publicly Registered Real Estate Program Sales by Type of Investment**

PARTNERSHIP SALES SUMMARY

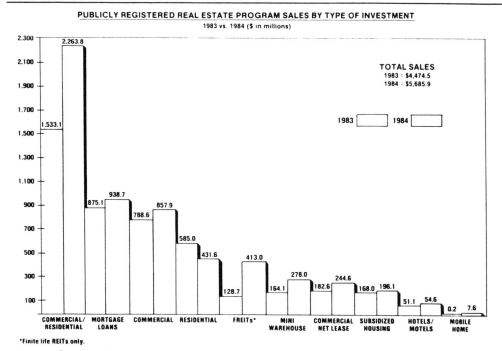

PUBLICLY REGISTERED REAL ESTATE PROGRAM SALES BY TYPE OF INVESTMENT
1983 vs. 1984 ($ in millions)

TOTAL SALES
1983 = $4,474.5
1984 = $5,685.9

*Finite life REITs only.

*Source: Stanger's Partnership Sponsor Directory.* Reprinted with permission.

**Table 31-1. Total Sales of Real Estate Growth Partnerships, 1982–1986**

| Year | Billions of Dollars |
|------|---------------------|
| 1982 | $1,492 |
| 1983 | 2,549 |
| 1984 | 2,380 |
| 1985* | 2,580 |
| 1986** | 2,800 |

\* Preliminary
\*\* Estimated
*Source: Stanger's Partnership Directory.* Reprinted with permission.

nership leverage without making a personal commitment greater than the original investment.

Aside from limited liability, portfolio diversification is a unique opportunity for most individual investors. By purchasing a real estate growth partnership an investor can commit as little as $5,000 and participate in a portfolio of properties diversified in as many as 15 to 20 different locations in the United States.

## TAX CONSEQUENCES

Real estate growth partnerships offer investors several tax advantages. First, because the property is operated as commercial property, depreciation may be calculated and deducted by the partners.

Second, interest expense paid to the holders of the mortgages on the property is tax deductible.

All other operating expenses, including management fees, repairs to the property, and services necessary to maintain the property are deductible expense items.

Records of all these items, as well as the revenues generated by leasing the property, are maintained by the general partner.

The net effect of all these actions are reported to the Internal Revenue Service each year on a partnership tax return. The partnership tax return is then broken down into a special form called schedule K-1. Each limited partner receives a K-1 with information pertaining to his or her proportionate share of ownership in the partnership. In many cases, these public real estate growth partnerships may prepare several thousand K-1s for investors.

All a limited partner needs to do is copy the information onto the federal tax return.

For many real estate growth partnership investors, the tax advantages involved provide a substantial benefit. It is not uncommon to be able to deduct the entire amount invested in a real estate growth partnership from federal taxes. Typically the deductions are spread out over a four- to five-year period. An example illustrates the deductions available to an investor who enters a real estate growth partnership early in calendar year 1986. In this example, the limited partner invests $10,000 in a typical real estate growth partnership.

| Year | 1986 | 1987 | 1988 | 1989 | 1990 |
|------|------|------|------|------|------|
| $ Deducted | $2,500 | $2,500 | $2,500 | $1,500 | $1,000 |

Total Deducted = $10,000.

To an investor in a 40 percent income tax bracket (single person with about $41,000 of taxable income) the actual tax dollars not paid to the Internal Revenue Service break out as follows:

| Year | 1986 | 1987 | 1988 | 1989 | 1990 |
|------|------|------|------|------|------|
| Tax $ Saved | $1,000 | $1,000 | $1,000 | $600 | $400 |

Total Tax Saved = $4,000.

Most investors appreciate the ability to plan future tax obligations by using real estate growth partnerships as a part of their investment portfolios. The tax savings illustrated here should be carefully researched by the investor, as each real estate growth partnership may vary. The biggest variable is the amount of borrowing the programs do to acquire the properties.

## WHERE AND HOW TO BUY

Real estate growth partnerships are typically sold by stockbrokers. In recent years some insurance agents, financial planners, and even financial institutions (banks and insurance companies) have begun to offer the product.

Investors purchase "units" of a real estate growth partnership in multiples of $1,000. Some partnerships may offer other unit sizes.

These units offer a convenient way to purchase just the exact amount of the partnership appropriate for each individual. Most real estate growth partnerships require a minimum commitment of $5,000.

An investor must sign a *subscription document* to participate in the program. The investor's check is typically made payable to the program and is forwarded to the general partner with the subscription document. The subscription document contains basic information about the investor including name, address, telephone, and tax identification number.

Security brokerage firms and the program's general partner are required by law to furnish an investor with a document called a *prospectus*. Typically these documents are very thick and full of difficult and somewhat confusing legal jargon for the average investor. Investors should focus on the performance record of the sponsor in previous real estate growth partnerships.

Additional information of interest will be the exact terms of the offering including all expenses that are to be paid by the limited partners.

## HOW TO SELL

Real estate growth partnerships are *self-liquidating*. These investments begin to produce tax benefits and modest cash flow soon after they are formed. As the properties in a real estate growth partnership grow in value, the general partner may decide to sell selected properties. Typically, the liquidation of the partnership properties occurs between the fifth and ninth years of the partnership. As each property is sold, the limited partners receive their proportionate share of the sale's proceeds.

When all of the properties in a real estate growth partnership are liquidated, the partnership is closed. The general partner does not reinvest the sales proceeds in other properties.

One additional avenue has recently been created for liquidating limited partnership investments. A new exchange called the National Partnership Exchange, Inc. (NAPEX) has been formed to trade existing units of limited partnerships.

NAPEX sells memberships to members of the National Association of Securities Dealers. These NAPEX members can use computer terminals to list units of various partnerships for sale. An investor in an real estate growth partnerships may wish to sell units of the partnership owned for several months or years. A member broker of NAPEX can offer these units to all other members of NAPEX electronically in just minutes!

If a buyer is found and the two parties agree on a price per unit, NAPEX executes the trade for a modest fee. This may well become the primary market for liquidation of real estate growth partnerships in the near future.

## TRANSACTION COSTS

Typically, transaction costs including accounting and legal fees (2 to 6 percent of capital), sales commissions (6 to 9 percent of capital) for the brokerage firm, and an initial management fee (2 to 8 percent of capital) for the general partner are borne by the limited partners.

It should be stressed that these fees vary considerably from one program to the next. Investors should be sure to discuss these fees prior to making the investment.

As a rule of thumb, any program with 87 percent or more of the limited partners' money dedicated to the actual costs purchasing real estate is a fairly good program. This would be a less than 13 percent "front-end load." Front-end loads of greater than 15 percent should generally be avoided in public partnerships.

Investors often lament the costs associated with limited partnerships of all kinds. In most instances, the individual investor could not undertake the proposed investment activity individually. Good real estate growth partnerships offer a proven track record and considerable management expertise for the fees received.

## PORTFOLIO FIT

Because of the moderate size commitment necessary real estate growth partnerships find very broad portfolio applications.

Investors aged 30 to 60 find real estate growth partnerships offer tax benefits that help shelter earned income. As these investors near retirement the returns from sale of the properties may offer investment capital that can be converted to income during the retirement years.

Capital gains oriented investors use real estate growth partnerships as a diversification tool to balance an equities portfolio.

Investors seeking high cash flows and investors who require a great deal of liquidity should avoid real estate growth partnerships.

A classic application of real estate growth partnerships is the purchase by investors who have owned a home for a good period of time, have finished raising a family, and still have 5 to 15 years of relatively high earned income ahead of them. These investors can make excellent use of the tax deductions, usually have low liquidity requirements, and will appreciate the capital gains and inflation protection afforded by real estate growth partnerships.

**Table 31-2. Real Estate: All
Limited Partnership Sales**

| Year | Sales (in $ millions) |
|---|---|
| 1970 | $ 13.574 |
| 1971 | 66.846 |
| 1972 | 104.884 |
| 1973 | 176.040 |
| 1974 | 131.700 |
| 1975 | 81.578 |
| 1976 | 158.226 |
| 1977 | 342.356 |
| 1978 | 849.699 |
| 1979 | 769.714 |
| 1980 | 1,468.626 |
| 1981 | 2,043.085 |
| 1982 | 2,882.700 |
| 1983 | 4,711.400 |
| 1984 | 6,000.000 |
| 1985* | 3,600.000 |

*First six months.
*Source: Questor Real Estate Syndication Yearbook,* 1984 edition, Stephen Rolack & Co., San Francisco, California. Reprinted with permission. Information supplied courtesy of Fox Capital, a major supplier of Real Estate Public Partnerships.

## SOURCES OF ADDITIONAL INFORMATION

Complete information about a particular partnership and the sponsor of the partnership must be furnished to an investor in a prospectus. The prospectus should be immediately available from any sales representative of the partnership.

An excellent outside source of information about real estate growth partnerships is the Robert Stanger Company. The Stanger Company publishes a variety of data on partnership investments. Investors who wish to subscribe to any of the Stanger Company publications should write the company at 1129 Broad Street, Shrewsbury, NJ 07701.

**Table 31-3. Returns of Leading Real Estate Partnership Sponsors**

| Sponsor | Years in Business | Capital Raised ($ millions) | Properties Bought | Properties Sold |
|---|---|---|---|---|
| Fox Group 40.40% | 16 | 879.0 | 270 | 70 |
| Angeles/ Quinoco 18.00% | 14 | 210.0 | 122 | 36 |
| Dain Bosworth 36.80% | 12 | 73.6 | 20 | 2 |
| Diversified 39.00% | 10 | 48.4 | 26 | 1 |
| Equitec 24.90% | 12 | 537.5 | 56 | 20 |
| First Capital Investment 21.00% | 10 | 535.0 | 78 | 34 |
| JMB (Carlyle) 30.00% | 16 | 1,800.0 | 229 | 46 |
| Mc Neil 34.80% | 19 | 550.0 | 177 | 33 |
| Southmark Capital 34.00% | 20 | 262.0 | 93 | 30 |

*Source: Robert Stanger Co. Register*, January 1985 edition. Reprinted with permission.

## COMMENTS

Investments in all real estate partnerships have gained substantially popularity over the last 15 years. Table 31-2 illustrates the growth of dollars invested in these vehicles.

As more investors evaluate real estate growth partnerships, the growth trend is likely to continue.

In a modest inflation environment of 4 to 5 percent, returns of 12 to 15 percent per year after taxes should not be unrealistic to expect from real estate growth partnerships. Table 31-3 details rates of return for selected real estate growth program sponsors. This data is for completely liquidated partnerships. The percentage returns are simple (noncompounded) annual rates of return.

Investors should be more comfortable with real estate growth partnerships as the general partners acquire more experience. Generally, investors should look for managing general partners with at least a 10-year track record in the business and a low turnover of key management personnel.

**Exhibit 31-4. Moderate Risk: Real Estate Growth Partnership**

**INVESTMENT PROFILE**

| INVESTMENT CHARACTERISTICS | Excellent | Good | Average | Poor | None |
|---|---|---|---|---|---|
| Liquidity | | | √* | | |
| Safety of Principal | | | √ | | |
| Price Stability | | | √ | | |
| Reinvestment Protection | | | √ | | |
| Growth of Capital | | √ | | | |
| Cash Income | | | | √ | |
| Growth of Income | | √ | | | |
| Inflation Hedge | √ | | | | |
| Tax Advantaged | √ | | | | |

**Liquidity**—the ability to quickly realize cash from the sale at fair market value

**Safety of Principal**—the principal is safe from bankruptcy or default

**Price Stability**—the market value of the asset does not change in value

**Reinvestment Protection**—protection against reinvesting cash flow at lower rates as interest rates decline

**Growth of Capital**—the original investment increases over time to create capital gains

**Cash Income**—the cash income relative to treasury bills returns

**Growth of Income**—the ability of the cash income stream to increase over time

**Inflation Hedge**—the ability of total return (cash income plus capital gains) to keep pace with inflation over time

**Tax Advantaged**—the ability to reduce or defer current federal income taxes

*If the partnership units are not traded over the counter, liquidity could be poor.

# CHAPTER 32

# Public Real Estate Income Partnerships

## DESCRIPTION

Real estate income partnerships are a specially designed vehicle that allows many individual investors to participate in the ownership of commercial real estate.

Real estate income partnerships are formed to provide professional property acquisition, operation, and disposition. This professional management uses a structure called a *limited partnership.*

The limited partnership structure provides limited liability on the part of individual investors, moderate tax advantages for investors, and preservation and growth of investors' capital.

As "limited partners," investors agree to pool their investment capital to provide a "general partner" the funds necessary to purchase a portfolio of commercial real estate properties and to make selected mortgage loans to quality borrowers.

Typically the general partner is a corporation that specializes in the real estate industry. The general partner may employ several hundred people in a variety of geographic locations to provide investors with the full array of services available in real estate income partnerships.

The properties owned in income partnerships are typically purchased for 100 percent cash. There is normally no debt involved in the ownership of the properties. The properties provide immediate cash flow to the limited partners.

**Exhibit 32-1.**

LIMITED PARTNERS

| #1 | #2 | #3 | ••• | #5000 |

80% OF NET PROCEEDS
OF SALE RETURNED TO LTD.
PARTNERS AFTER EACH
PROPERTY IS SOLD

PROVIDE
INVESTMENT
CAPITAL TO:

$

**GENERAL PARTNER**

S

GENERAL PARTNER RECEIVES
A 20% SHARE OF THE GAINS
ON THE SALE OF THE PROPERTIES

ACQUIRES PROPERTIES
DURING YEAR #1

$ $ $
PROCEEDS
OF SALES

MANAGES PROPERTIES
YEARS 1 - 10*

SELLS
PROPERTIES
YEARS 4 - 10*

*NORMALLY A 4-8 YR HOLDING PERIOD

Source: Stanger's Partnership Sponsor Directory. Reprinted with permission.

Some partnerships may use a balanced approach: they not only purchase all cash properties, they also invest part of the money in high-quality mortgages on commercial property. These mortgages provided very high immediate cash flow to the individual partners.

Many times these are *participating mortgages*. Participating mortgages will share in any future rent increases in the property and may share in any capital gains on the sale of the property. Over time this feature serves to increase cash flow and hedge the limited partner against inflationary price increases in the economy.

Both all-cash ownership and participating mortgages provide inflation protection to the owner of a real estate limited partnership. To the extent that the properties are purchased in growing economic areas, some growth of capital may result as well.

An illustration of the partnership relationships appear in Exhibit 32-1.

Limited partners that invest in real estate income partnerships do receive some safeguards. First, the operations and financial affairs of the partnership are generally audited by an independent certified public accounting firm. Second, most of the real estate income partnerships are structured with several priority distributions of income and capital to the limited partners in the partnership agreement.

Most real estate income partnerships offer shared gains and losses between the limited and the general partners. A typical case is detailed as follows:

| Item | Limited Partner | General Partner |
|---|---|---|
| Capital contributions | 99% | 1% |
| Tax losses from operations | 99% | 1% |
| Cash flow until preferred return % is achieved | 99% | 1% |
| Cash flow above preferred return % | 80% | 20% |
| Gain on the sale of assets | 80% | 20% |

Obviously, the general partner has a significant incentive to prudently manage the properties on behalf of all the partners. The bulk of the general partner's earnings come on the back end of the partnership.

In addition, many real estate income partnerships offer investors a preferred rate of return on investment. An investor may receive a cumulative rate of return of 10 percent per year for the entire duration of the partnership before the general partner is entitled to receive any distribution of funds.

**Table 32-1.   Real Estate Income Partnership
Sales (millions), 1982–1985**

| Year | 1982 | 1983 | 1984 | 1985* | 1986** |
|------|------|------|------|-------|--------|
| Sales | $456 | $920 | $1953 | $2600 | $3200 |

*Preliminary
**Estimated

Table 32-1 contains the sales volume in million of dollars for real estate income partnerships from 1982 to 1985.

## STRENGTHS

Real estate income partnerships offer individual investors the opportunity to participate in commercial real estate properties otherwise unavailable to investors of average incomes and net worths. They comprise over 40 percent of all public limited partnerships sold in 1984. Table 32-2 illustrates the increasing popularity of real estate limited partnerships.

Real estate income partnerships provide a complete package of services to investors. Virtually no real estate expertise is needed on the part of a limited partner.

Real estate income partnerships offer modest capital gains potential and good tax sheltered cash flow that might otherwise not be available to just one investor. Total expected rates of return in a 3 to 4 percent inflation situation should be 12 to 16 percent.

Real estate income partnerships offer investors a preferred return on invested capital prior to any sharing of partnership earnings with the general partner. That is, the general partner will subordinate its corporate interest to the limited partners until the limited partners have received a stated rate of return.

## WEAKNESSES

The main weakness of real estate income partnerships is the total lack of managerial control by the investor. All decisions are made by the general partner for the partnership.

**Table 32-2.   Real Estate: All
Limited Partnership Sales**

| Year | Sales (in $ millions) |
|------|----------------------|
| 1970 | $    13.574 |
| 1971 | 66.846 |
| 1972 | 104.884 |
| 1973 | 176.040 |
| 1974 | 131.700 |
| 1975 | 81.578 |
| 1976 | 158.226 |
| 1977 | 342.356 |
| 1978 | 849.699 |
| 1979 | 769.714 |
| 1980 | 1,468.626 |
| 1981 | 2,043.085 |
| 1982 | 2,882.700 |
| 1983 | 4,711.400 |
| 1984 | 6,000.000 |
| 1985* | 3,600.000 |

*First six months
*Source: Questor Real Estate Syndication Yearbook,* 1984 edition, Stephen Roulac & Co., San Francisco, California. Reprinted with permission. Information supplied courtesy of Fox Capital, a major supplier of Real Estate Public Partnerships.

A secondary weakness is the lack of liquidity of real estate income partnerships. Typically, investors are unable to liquidate their positions prematurely without substantial costs.

## UNIQUE FEATURES

The preferred return offered to real estate income partnership investors is truly a unique feature. An example that illustrates the preferred return concept follows.

Stated rate of preferred return on investment: 10 percent simple annual interest. Investment amount = $10,000.

|  | 1986 | 1987 | 1988 | 1989 | 1990 | 1991 |
|---|---|---|---|---|---|---|
| Actual | | | | | | |
| Cash Flow | $ 700 | $ 850 | $1,000 | $1,100 | $1,200 | $1,300 |
| Preferred | | | | | | |
| Amount Due | 1,000 | 1,000 | 1,000 | 1,000 | 1,000 | 1,000 |
| Deficit | | | | | | |
| or surplus | −300 | −150 | 0 | 100 | 200 | 300 |
| Cumulative | | | | | | |
| deficit | −300 | −450 | −450 | −350 | −150 | +150 |

The general partner in this example would receive none of the cash flow from the partnership until the year 1991. At that time, as long as cash flow remained above the 10 percent level, the general partner would receive the portion of cash provided for in the partnership agreement. Typically this would be a split of 80 percent to the limited partners and 20 percent to the general partner.

Portfolio diversification is a unique opportunity for most individual investors. By purchasing a real estate income partnership, an investor can commit as little as $5,000 and participate in a portfolio of properties diversified in as many as 15 to 20 different locations in the United States.

## TAX CONSEQUENCES

Real estate income partnerships offer investors several tax advantages.

First, because the property is operated as commercial property depreciation will be calculated and deducted by the partners.

All other operating expenses, including management fees, repairs to the property, and services necessary to maintain the property are deductible expense items.

Records of all these items as well as the revenues generated by leasing the property are maintained by the general partner.

Much of the cash flow generated by a real estate income partnership will be available to the individual investor on a tax sheltered basis. The depreciation expense from owning the buildings and the operating expenses serve to shelter at least a part of the cash flow.

Example of a $10,000 investment follows.

As the rentals received from the properties and participating mortgages increases the depreciation is not sufficient to cover the additional income. Investors generally prefer the increased income stream as the partnership progresses.

| Year | 1986 | 1987 | 1988 | 1989 | 1990 | 1991 |
|---|---|---|---|---|---|---|
| Actual | | | | | | |
| Cash Flow | $700 | $850 | $1,000 | $1,100 | $1,200 | $1,300 |
| Shelter | | | | | | |
| Available | 700 | 700 | 700 | 700 | 700 | 700 |
| Taxable | | | | | | |
| Income | 0 | 150 | 300 | 400 | 500 | 600 |

The net effect of all these actions are reported to the Internal Revenue Service each year on a partnership tax return. The partnership tax return is then broken down into special forms called schedule *K-1s*. Each limited partner receives a K-1 with information pertaining to his or her proportionate share of ownership in the partnership. In many cases, these public real estate income partnerships may prepare several thousand K-1s for investors.

All a limited partner needs to do is copy the information onto the tax return.

## WHERE AND HOW TO BUY

Real estate income partnerships are typically sold by stockbrokers. In recent years some insurance agents, financial planners, and even financial institutions (banks and insurance companies) have begun to offer the product.

Investors purchase "units" of a real estate income partnership in multiples of $1,000. Some partnerships may offer other unit sizes. These units offer a convenient way to purchase just the exact amount of the partnership appropriate for each individual.

Most real estate income partnerships require a minimum commitment of $5,000.

An investor must sign a form called a *subscription document* to participate in the program. The investors check is typically made payable to the program and is forwarded to the general partner with the subscription document.

The subscription document contains basic information about the investor including name, address, telephone, and tax identification number.

Security brokerage firms and the program general partner are required by law to furnish an investor with a document called a *prospectus*, which is usually very thick and full of difficult and somewhat confusing legal jargon to the average investor. Investors usually focus on the performance record of the sponsor in previous real estate income partnerships.

Additional information of interest will be the exact terms of the offering including all expenses that are to be paid by the limited partners.

## HOW TO SELL

Real estate income partnerships are *self-liquidating*. These investments begin to produce tax sheltered cash flow soon after they are formed.

As the properties in a real estate income partnership grow modestly in value, the general partner may decide to sell selected properties. Typically, the liquidation of the partnership properties and mortgages occurs between the 7th and 10th years of the partnership. As each property is sold, the limited partners receive their proportionate share of the sales and liquidation proceeds.

When all of the properties in a real estate income partnership are liquidated, the partnership is closed. The general partner does not reinvest the sales proceeds in other properties.

One additional avenue has recently been created for liquidating limited partnership investments. A new exchange called the National Partnership Exchange, Inc. (NAPEX) has been formed to trade existing units of limited partnerships.

NAPEX sells memberships to members of the National Association of Securities Dealers. NAPEX members use computer terminals to list units of various partnerships for sale. An investor in an real estate income partnerships may wish to sell units of the partnership that he has owned for several months or years. A member broker of NAPEX can offer these units to all other members of NAPEX electronically in just minutes!

If a buyer is found, and the two parties agree on a price per unit, NAPEX will execute the trade for a modest fee. This may well become the primary market for liquidation of real estate income partnerships in the near future.

## TRANSACTION COSTS

Typically, transaction costs include the following:

| | |
|---|---|
| Accounting and legal fees | 2-5% |
| Sales commissions | 8-9% |
| Front-end management fees | 3-8% |

It should be stressed that these fees vary considerably from one program to the next. Investors should discuss these fees prior to making the investment.

As a rule of thumb, any program with 87 percent or more of the limited partners money dedicated to the actual costs ofpurchasing real estate, is a fairly good program. This would be a less than 13 percent "front-end load." Front-end loads of greater than 15 percent should generally be avoided in public partnerships.

Investors often lament the costs of limited partnerships of all kinds. In most instances, the individual investor could not undertake the proposed investment activity independently. Good real estate income partnerships offer a proven track record and considerable management expertise for the fees received.

## PORTFOLIO FIT

Because of the moderate size dollar commitment necessary, real estate income partnerships find very broad portfolio applications.

Investors seeking high cash flows should purchase real estate income partnerships as a portion of a balanced income oriented portfolio. Real estate income partnerships serve as an excellent companion investment to tax free municipal bonds.

A classic application of real estate income partnerships is the purchase by investors that have retired and have established a very safe, high-yielding portfolio of bonds, certificates of deposit, utility stocks, and other high-yielding investments. These investors can make excellent use of the tax sheltered cash flow and the inflation protection afforded by real estate income partnerships.

## SOURCES OF ADDITIONAL INFORMATION

Complete information about a particular partnership and the sponsor of the partnership must be furnished to an investor in a prospectus. The prospectus should be immediately available from any sales representative of the partnership.

An excellent outside source of information about real estate income partnerships is the Robert Stanger Company. The Stanger Company publishes a variety of data on partnership investments. Investors that wish to subscribe to any of the Stanger Company publications should write the company at 1129 Broad Street, Shrewsbury, NJ 07701.

## COMMENTS

Investments in real estate income partnerships have gained substantial popularity over the last decade. Table 32-2 illustrates the dollars invested in these real estate partnerships since 1970.

As more investors evaluate real estate income partnerships the trend is likely to continue. In a modest inflation environment of 4 to 5 percent returns of 10 to 12 percent per year on an after tax basis should not be unrealistic to expect from real estate income partnerships. These returns will escalate if the inflation rate moves higher.

Investors should be more comfortable with real estate income partnerships as the general partners acquire more experience. Generally investors should look for managing general partners with at least a 10-year track record in the business and a low turnover of key management personnel.

**Exhibit 32-2.  Moderate Risk: Real Estate Income Partnership**

**INVESTMENT PROFILE**

| INVESTMENT CHARACTERISTICS | Excellent | Good | Average | Poor | None |
|---|---|---|---|---|---|
| Liquidity | | | | √ | |
| Safety of Principal | | | √ | | |
| Price Stability | | | | | N.A.* |
| Reinvestment Protection | | | √ | | |
| Growth of Capital | | √ | | | |
| Cash Income | | √ | | | |
| Growth of Income | | √ | | | |
| Inflation Hedge | √ | | | | |
| Tax Advantaged | | √ | | | |

**Liquidity**—the ability to quickly realize cash from the sale at fair market value

**Safety of Principal**—the principal is safe from bankruptcy or default

**Price Stability**—the market value of the asset does not change in value

**Reinvestment Protection**—protection against reinvesting cash flow at lower rates as interest rates decline

**Growth of Capital**—the original investment increases over time to create capital gains

**Cash Income**—the cash income relative to treasury bills returns

**Growth of Income**—the ability of the cash income stream to increase over time

**Inflation Hedge**—the ability of total return (cash income plus capital gains) to keep pace with inflation over time

**Tax Advantaged**—the ability to reduce or defer current federal income taxes

*Not applicable unless listed on NAPX.

# CHAPTER 33

# Real Estate Investment Trusts

## DESCRIPTION

Real estate investment trusts function as financial intermediaries that allow investors to pool funds together to either own or finance real estate.

The real estate investment trust vehicle was initially designed to allow small investors that are otherwise unable to participate in large commercial real estate projects the opportunity to do so. These commercial real estate projects include lending funds for the development of commercial, industrial, retail, and residential properties. Real estate investment trusts also purchase these properties for direct ownership participation.

By adhering to a specified set of tax code regulations, real estate investment trusts are untaxed at the business trust level. Real estate investment trusts can therefore payout very substantial dividends to shareholders of the trust.

Without analyzing all of the details, a real estate investment trust will qualify as a nontaxable entity if, (a) it distributes at least 95 percent of its taxable net income to its shareholders, (b) it has at least 75 percent of its assets invested in real estate and real estate related ventures, and (c) it derives at least 75 percent of its gross income from real estate and real estate-related ventures.

Real estate investment trusts are generally seeking income and long-term capital gains from ownership and investment in real estate. Most real estate investment trusts employ independent parties to manage the real estate portfolio. A direct comparison can be made between a real estate investment trust and a mutual fund that invests in common stocks, bonds, or other financial instruments. The key difference is that a real estate investment trust will distribute virtually all of its income to its shareholders, retaining very little income for reinvestment in the trust.

In some cases, real estate investment trusts can pay out dividends in excess of their net operating income. These dividends arise when net cash flow exceeds net income due to noncash expenses, such as depreciation or amortization of debt discounts. Distributions of this nature are treated as a return of capital by the Internal Revenue Service and are not taxed. Finally, any dividends paid to shareholders that result from a gain on the sale of the property in the form of a capital gain are taxed at capital gains rates.

There are various types of real estate investment trusts. The two most common types are equity trusts and mortgage trusts.

An *equity real estate investment trust* owns all of its properties directly. A *mortgage real estate investment trust* owns a portfolio of mortgages and real estate loans. The real estate equity investment trust derives income primarily from the rents on its buildings, while the mortgage oriented real estate investment trust derives its income from interest received on loans.

Some real estate investment trusts combine these two types of asset ownership. A combination real estate investment trust owns some properties directly and makes loans to other real estate concerns with a portion of its funds.

Historically, real estate investment trusts have not had a defined life. Because there is uncertainty as to when the properties involved in the trust may be sold, most real estate investment trusts have traditionally carried market values lower than the actual value of the property that backs each share of the trust. For example, a real estate investment trust may have a liquidation value of $20 per share; however, in the open market the shares trade for only $15. This is because investors cannot be certain when they will receive proceeds from sale of the trust assets.

Exhibit 33-1 shows the boom and bust cycle of real estate investment trusts during the 1970s. It shows the total market value of real estate investment trusts from 1960 to 1985 in billions of dollars. (1960 = .1; 1968 = 1.0; 1974 = 20.0; 1980 = 7.0; 1985 = 10.0)

The real estate investment trust vehicle became very popular with investors at the peak of economic activity in 1974. The deep recession that followed nearly halted real estate investment trusts.

**Exhibit 33-1. Boom and Bust Cycle of Real Estate Investment Trusts**

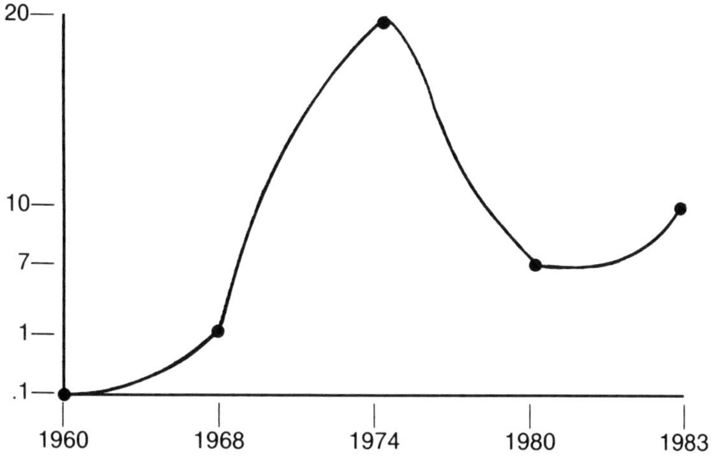

Source: Drexel Burnham Lambert, "Real Estate Investment Trusts." Reprinted with permission.

## STRENGTHS

Perhaps the largest strength of a real estate investment trust is the liquidity of the investment itself. Most real estate investment trusts are listed on either the New York Stock Exchange or the American Stock Exchange. Investors can buy and sell shares of these trusts on any regular business day. This type of liquidity is rarely associated with real estate investments.

A second strength of real estate investment trusts is the professional management of the trust assets by experienced professionals. The directors of the trust are obligated to select real estate industry experts to manage the affairs and the assets of the trust.

## WEAKNESSES

Real estate investment trusts are unable to provide the historic benefit of real estate ownership of excess tax deductions. Many investors, whether they purchase a simple rent house or participate in public partnerships that invest in real estate, are accustomed to receiving tax deductions that offset earned and other investment income of the individual investor.

Real estate investment trusts provide cash flow and in some cases, tax advantaged cash flow to investors. However, they do not provide excess deductions that many real estate investors have come to appreciate.


## UNIQUE FEATURES

Real estate investment trusts offer investors seeking high income from real estate the added advantage of a liquidity of their investment. Shares of a real estate investment trust can be bought and sold on any business day.

Real estate investment trusts provide a vehicle that permits many small investors an opportunity to own commercial real estate projects that would otherwise be unable to own using their own capital.

It is very important that an investor carefully review the portfolio of properties owned in a real estate investment trust before deciding to purchase the trust. Frequently an individual real estate investment trust will pay out a very large distribution to its shareholders. This distribution is normally nonrecurring, as it is a result of a sale of a parcel of property and the return of capital and capital gains to shareholders.

Real estate investment trust shareholders must carefully evaluate the ongoing operations of the real estate investment trust so that they thoroughly understand the expected level of operating income that the trust will distribute. It is very important that distributions of capital gains not be confused with regular operating income.


## TAX CONSEQUENCES

Regular dividends declared by real estate investment trusts are fully taxable income to the individual investor.

Real estate investment trusts may declare special dividends as a result of capital gains from the sale of properties. These capital gains dividends flow through to the individual investor's tax form and are treated as long-term capital gains by each individual investor.

In certain limited circumstances, additional cash flow produced by the real estate investment trust over and above net income may be distributed to the shareholders as a return of capital. These returns of capital are not taxed by the Internal Revenue Service. Most of the income produced by real estate investment trusts is fully taxable to the shareholder.

Individual investors should carefully review the tax status of distributions from a particular trust prior to investing in that trust.

## WHERE AND HOW TO BUY

Most real estate investment trusts are traded on one of the two listed stock exchanges. Some smaller real estate investment trusts are traded in the over-the-counter market.

All real estate investment trusts may be bought and sold through regular securities brokerage firms on any regular business day.

Unlike real estate partnerships, information that is contained in a legal document called a *prospectus* is not required for sale and ownership of a real estate investment trust. Investors do not need to fill out subscription documents to participate in the ownership of a real estate investment trust. The only requirement is that the investor open an account at a brokerage firm and direct that firm to purchase shares of the trust.

Real estate investment trusts trade on the same basis as common stocks.

## HOW TO SELL

Real estate investment trusts are generally liquidated by brokerage firms. An investor simply instructs the brokerage firm to sell the shares of the trust. On normal settlement conditions, the investor receives the proceeds from the sale five business days after the sale is transacted.

## TRANSACTION COSTS

Real estate investment trusts are purchased and sold through brokerage firms. These brokerage firms charge a commission on each transaction initiated by the investor.

Investors should note that not all securities dealers charge the same fees for services performed. *Full-service brokerage firms* provide important services for clients over and above the actual execution of a simple buy or sell order. *Discount brokerage firms* specialize in offering the lowest possible cost transactions. An individual investor needs to review the level of service he or she requires and select a securities dealer accordingly.

## PORTFOLIO FIT

Real estate investment trusts are generally purchased by income oriented investors. Because the trusts provide high rates of dividends, many retired investors use real estate investment trusts as a portion of their investment portfolios.

These same retired investors often appreciate the immediate liquidity available of a real estate investment trust. In an emergency, an investor can liquidate a real estate investment trust position very quickly.

Many investors are beginning to purchase and hold real estate investment trust shares in their IRA, Keogh, and other retirement plan accounts. Because most of the income distributed by a real estate investment trust is fully taxable and these accounts provide a tax deferred investment vehicle, investors can avoid paying taxes on the income distributed by the real estate investment trust as long as it is owned in an IRA or other retirement plan.

Because most retirement plans are long-term investment situations, these investors seek not only income but an inflation hedge and the potential for capital gains. The real estate investment trust achieves the primary objective of high income and provides a secondary objective of an inflation hedge due to the ownership of real estate properties and the potential for long-term capital gains if the properties are in well-selected, high-growth areas of the United States.

## SOURCES OF ADDITIONAL INFORMATION

Virtually all brokerage firms have research reports available that completely describe real estate investment trusts. An investor need only to place a phone call to a local brokerage firm and request one of these research reports.

## COMMENTS

Real estate investment trusts are an excellent vehicle for income investors willing to do extensive research and to thoroughly understand the true value of the assets owned by the trust.

It is easy for shareholders of a real estate investment trust to be deceived by unusually large irregular distributions by the trust. Real estate investment trusts require thorough financial analysis prior to investment.

Once an investor is comfortable in understanding the value of the assets of the trust, knows the regular operating income that should be achieved by the trust, and has become familiar with the particular type of trust, that investor is in a position to participate in a high-income oriented investment. A real estate investment trust offers the secondary benefit of an inflation hedge and a tertiary benefit of the potential for long-term capital gains.

**Exhibit 33-2.   Moderate Risk: Real Estate Investment Trusts**

**INVESTMENT PROFILE**

| INVESTMENT CHARACTERISTICS | Excellent | Good | Average | Poor | None |
|---|---|---|---|---|---|
| Liquidity | | √ | | | |
| Safety of Principal | | | √ | | |
| Price Stability | | | √ | | |
| Reinvestment Protection | | | | √ | |
| Growth of Capital | | | √ | | |
| Cash Income | | √ | | | |
| Growth of Income | | √ | | | |
| Inflation Hedge | | √ | | | |
| Tax Advantaged | | | | √* | |

**Liquidity**—the ability to quickly realize cash from the sale at fair market value

**Safety of Principal**—the principal is safe from bankruptcy or default

**Price Stability**—the market value of the asset does not change in value

**Reinvestment Protection**—protection against reinvesting cash flow at lower rates as interest rates decline

**Growth of Capital**—the original investment increases over time to create capital gains

**Cash Income**—the cash income relative to treasury bills returns

**Growth of Income**—the ability of the cash income stream to increase over time

**Inflation Hedge**—the ability of total return (cash income plus capital gains) to keep pace with inflation over time

**Tax Advantaged**—the ability to reduce or defer current federal income taxes

*Only to the extent that the REIT is able to pass on long-term capital gains and occasionally some tax sheltered distributions.

# PART 5

# High-Risk Investments

# CHAPTER 34

# Over-the-
# Counter Stocks

## DESCRIPTION

There are hundreds of different types of companies whose stock is traded in the National Association of Securities Dealers' *over-the-counter* market. This chapter defines and discusses three groups of these stocks: local bank stocks, mining stocks, and penny stocks. The groups selected in this chapter are the smaller OTC companies. Many very large companies' common stock is also traded over-the-counter.

Generally, the very large companies do not experience as many problems with liquidity, transaction costs, and dissemination of investment information as the groups of stocks highlighted in this chapter.

Many fast-growing industrial and service companies are traded in the over-the-counter market as well. They share many of the characteristics covered in this chapter but also offer investors qualities discussed in Chapter 19 on growth stocks.

*Local Bank Stocks*—the common stock of thousands of small banks and bank holding companies is traded in the over-the-counter market. Many times bank stocks are very infrequently traded. Investors in a given locality can often find buyers for local bank stocks. Sellers are not as readily available. Information on local banks is generally available by requesting annual and quarterly reports from the bank's chief financial officer.

For exmple, see Zions Utah Bancorporation in Table 34-1. The ticker symbol is ZION. The stock is bid 50-2/4 offered 51-1/4. Many National Association of Securities Dealers firms serve as market makers.

*Mining Stocks*—small mining companies are often traded in the over-

**Table 34-1.   Over-the-Counter Stock Listing**

*National Daily Quotation Service*
*February 11, 1986*

| Stock | Ticker Symbol | Broker Dealers | Phone | Bid | Offered |
|---|---|---|---|---|---|
| ZAMBIA CONS CPPR | | Carl Marks & Co. Inc. | 800 221-7420 | 5/8 | 1 |
| ZMN ORD B | | Merrill Lynch PFS Inc. NY | 800 221-8505 | | |
| | | Arnhold Bleich-roeder NY | 212 943-7518 | 5/8 | 7/8 |
| Zeus Energy Inc. Com | | Main Street Secs Inc. SLC | 800 453-9460 | .005 | .02 |
| | | Troster Sgr STVN RTH CY | 800 222-0890 | | |
| | | Norbay Secs Inc. Bayside NY | 718 423-2604 | | |
| Zions Utah Bancorporation | ZION | Dean Witter, EF Hutton, Paine Webber, Merrill Lynch | | 50-3/4 | 51-1/4 |

the-counter market. These companies may be located in foreign countries (especially Canada). Information about mining concerns is very difficult to analyze due to the fact that assumptions must be made about the quality of ore reserves the company owns. It is common for these small mining companies to be the subject of rumors among investors. A large strike of a precious metal can significantly increase the value of a small mining company.

For example, see Zambia Consolidated Copper Mining ordinary class B stock in Table 34-1. It is abbreviated as ZAMBIA CONS CPPR MN ORD B. The bid is 5/8 and the offer price is 7/8. This company has three market making firms.

*Penny Stocks*—these stocks can be found in any industry. Among investors they are recognized by one common trait, an exceptionally low price. These companies may be in bankruptcy proceedings, involved in exotic research and development projects, or be left over from an exceptionally strong new issues market that has gone sour. As an example, hundreds of small oil and gas exploration companies were sold to investors at the peak of the 1981 oil boom. Most of these stocks are now traded in the over-the-counter market at exceptionally low prices.

One last example from Table 34-1 is appropriate. Zeus Energy is bid 1/2 cent offered 2 cents. An investor would have to more than quadruple this value to break even after brokerage commissions.

## STRENGTHS

From an investor's viewpoint, over-the-counter stocks may offer good values due to the lack of publicity, infrequent trading, and general lack of attention paid to the over-the-counter market by brokerage industry analysts.

The ability to thoroughly analyze the financial statements of small over-the-counter stocks often reveals undervalued assets. In particular, tax loss carryforwards, unused investment tax credits, and undervalued real estate assets may be available at very low cost.

## WEAKNESSES

Small over-the-counter stocks are relatively illiquid when compared to other equity investments. Very high transaction costs can be encountered by over-the-counter stock investors. It is very difficult to find complete financial information on many of these companies.

## UNIQUE FEATURES

Small over-the-counter stocks are often very low priced. Many individual investors are excited about the ability to own many thousands of shares of a particular stock. These stocks are high risk, have very volatile prices, and often trade on rumors rather than fact. Few small over-the-counter stocks have stable financial statements.

## TAX CONSEQUENCES

Small over-the-counter stocks are treated like all other equities for tax purposes. Dividends (if any) from these stocks are fully taxable.

Over-the-counter stocks are a qualified asset according to the Internal Revenue Service for capital gains treatment. If an investor has held the stock for six months and one day or longer, 60 percent of any gain on sale of the asset above cost basis is excluded from taxation. Only 40 percent of the gain is included in taxable income. Since tax laws change often, always check current laws on capital gains.

Short-term capital gains are recognized on the profitable sale of over-the-counter stock owned less than six months and one day. The entire amount of the gain above the cost basis in the stock is taxable as ordinary income.

A special process of combining all gains and losses into a "net capital position" occurs for income tax reporting. Because of this net effect, all of an investors transactions involving capital gains and losses must be considered as a whole. This can include many transactions in addition to investments in over-the-counter stocks.

Investors should obtain advice from a qualified tax professional to set strategies for tax reduction or minimization.

## WHERE AND HOW TO BUY

Investors may contact any member firm of the National Association of Securities Dealers to buy over-the-counter stocks. Each member firm receives a weekly list of all the stocks, price quotes for the stocks, and a list of phone numbers of all the broker dealer firms that are willing to buy and sell over-the-counter stock to and from investors.

Investors must make certain they receive a current price quote for a over-the-counter stock. Because the market may be small and illiquid for over-the-counter stocks, prices tend to be very volatile. A relatively small order may change the price of an over-the-counter stock quickly.

## HOW TO SELL

Sales of over-the-counter stocks may be arranged through any stock brokerage firm. Investors will sell over-the-counter stocks to a member of the National Association of Securities Dealers that regularly makes a public market in the stock they wish to sell.

## TRANSACTION COSTS

Over-the-counter stocks incur abnormally high transaction costs. These high transaction costs stem from two sources.

Over-the-counter stocks are quoted on a bid and offered basis. The example in Table 34-1 illustrates how this works. The reader should find the line for Zeus Energy Company.

The reader can see that four broker dealers make a market in Zeus Energy Company. The bid and offer price, where available, is listed to the right of the dealers phone number.

In the case of Zeus Energy Company, the most money a dealer is willing to pay for a share of stock is $.005. If investors wish to buy shares of Zeus Energy Company they will have to pay $.02. The difference between the purchase price of $.005 and the sale price of $.02 is known as the "spread." In this case the spread is $.0150 or 400 percent of the purchase price. This is the profit the broker dealer firm makes by providing the market making service.

In addition to the spread that must be overcome by the owner of a over-the-counter stock, the brokerage firm that executes the order for the investor will add a regular brokerage commission to the purchase price for serving as the agent of the investor.

Investors should note that not all securities dealers charge the same fees for services performed. *Full-service retail stockbrokers* provide important services for clients over and above the actual execution of a simple buy or sell order. *Discount brokerage firms* specialize in offering the lowest possible cost transactions. An individual investor needs to review the level of service required and select a securities dealer accordingly.

## PORTFOLIO FIT

Over-the-counter stocks represent unusual investment opportunities for an individual investor. Most institutional investors will consider only the largest over-the-counter stocks for inclusion in an equities portfolio.

An individual investor that is prepared to spend considerable time and effort to carefully research the financial and operating condition of an over-the-counter stock may reap rich rewards. Generally these stocks will need to be held in a portfolio for a long period of time to achieve substantial appreciation.

Within an investment portfolio, over-the-counter stocks would need to be considered high risk capital gains type investments. Few if any income oriented investors and safety of principle investors would be interested in owning most over-the-counter stocks.

## SOURCES OF ADDITIONAL INFORMATION

For additional information on over-the-counter stocks, call a securities investment firm and request a research report. Standard & Poor's Corporation publishes a report called a *Stock Guide* on hundreds of over-the-counter companies. Moody's Investor's Services *Over-The-Counter Industrial Manual* also contains research reports on hundreds of over-the-counter stocks. Both Standard & Poor's and Moody's reports are available in most public libraries.

Several specialty publications dedicated to over-the-counter and low-priced stocks also are available. Two that may be found in libraries and on newsstands are the *The Over the Counter Journal* and *Penny Stock News*.

## COMMENTS

Over-the-counter stocks are often the subject of rumors that circulate among investors. Very often these rumors are untrue. Investors should be careful to select over-the-counter stocks only after a complete research study of the company.

Because transaction costs are very high, over-the-counter stock investors face a steep handicap prior to entering the investment arena. Special care should be taken in placing over-the-counter stock orders to specify a maximum price that will be paid to purchase the stock, and a minimum price that will be accepted when investors sell an over-the-counter stock.

**Exhibit 34-1.   High Risk: Over-the-Counter Stocks (Small Companies)**

**INVESTMENT PROFILE**

| INVESTMENT CHARACTERISTICS | Excellent | Good | Average | Poor | None |
|---|---|---|---|---|---|
| Liquidity | | | √ * | | |
| Safety of Principal | | | | √ | |
| Price Stability | | | | √ | |
| Reinvestment Protection | | | | | √ |
| Growth of Capital | Potential | | | | |
| Cash Income | | | | | √ |
| Growth of Income | | | | | √ |
| Inflation Hedge | Potential | | | | |
| Tax Advantaged | | | | | √ |

**Liquidity**—the ability to quickly realize cash from the sale at fair market value

**Safety of Principal**—the principal is safe from bankruptcy or default

**Price Stability**—the market value of the asset does not change in value

**Reinvestment Protection**—protection against reinvesting cash flow at lower rates as interest rates decline

**Growth of Capital**—the original investment increases over time to create capital gains

**Cash Income**—the cash income relative to treasury bills returns

**Growth of Income**—the ability of the cash income stream to increase over time

**Inflation Hedge**—the ability of total return (cash income plus capital gains) to keep pace with inflation over time

**Tax Advantaged**—the ability to reduce or defer current federal income taxes

*Can range from good to poor depending on the size of the company, number of market makers and shares publicly traded.

# CHAPTER 35

# Options

## DESCRIPTION

The word *option* has many different meanings, but most of them include the ability or right to choose a certain alternative. One definition provided by Webster's dictionary is "the right, acquired for a consideration, to buy or sell something at a fixed price within a specified period of time." This definition is very general and applies to puts, calls, warrants, real estate options, or any other contracts entered into between two parties in which a choice of action or decision can be put off for a limited time at a cost. The person acquiring the option pays an agreed upon amount of money providing the option. The seller of the option has committed to deliver a particular parcel of land or other good and valuable consideration for a specified time period at a specified price.

The seller of the option has given up the ability to sell that property to another buyer for the specified period of time.

*Put options* and *call options* pertain to the sale or purchase of common stock, respectively. A put is an option to sell 100 shares of common stock at a specified price at a given period of time for which the option buyer pays the writer or seller of the option a premium. This premium is also referred to as the *price* of the option. Call options are the opposite of put options and allow the owner the right to buy 100 shares of common stock from the seller of the call option. The seller of an option contract, either a put or a call, is often referred to as the "writer" of the option contract.

Before investors can understand various option strategies, they must be able to comprehend what creates option prices. Investors should look at the Ford Motor example in Table 35-1. Ford Motor common stock closed at 54.125 per share on the New York Stock Exchange on this day and the puts and calls are available at strike prices $40, $45, $50, $55. The

**Table 35-1.   Newspaper Format for Options Quotations**

| Options & N Y Close | Strike Price | Vol. | Last Price —Dec— | Vol. | Last Price —Mar— | Vol. | Last Price —Jun— |
|---|---|---|---|---|---|---|---|
| Ford | 40 | 131 | 14-3/8 | 56 | 14-1/2 | | no trade |
| 54-1/8 | Put 40 | | no trade | 15 | 1/16 | | no trade |
| 54-1/8 | 45 | 1016 | 9-3/8 | 48 | 9-7/8 | 2 | 10-3/8 |
| 54-1/8 | Put 45 | | no trade | 29 | 1/4 | 5 | 1/2 |
| 54-1/8 | 50 | 2701 | 4-3/8 | 127 | 5-3/8 | 101 | 6-1/8 |
| 54-1/8 | Put 50 | 586 | 1/8 | 100 | 1 | 7 | 1-7/8 |
| 54-1/8 | 55 | 550 | 13/16 | 248 | 2-1/4 | 49 | 3 |
| 54-1/8 | Put 55 | 111 | 1-1/8 | 32 | 3 | 3 | 3-1/2 |
| 54-1/8 | 60 | 60 | 1/8 | 82 | 11/16 | 61 | 1-1/4 |

December 50 call closed at 4-3/8 ($437.50 for one call on 100 shares), while the December 55 call closed at 13/16. The $50 call is said to be "in-the-money" because of the market price $54.125 is above the strike price of $50. The $55 call is "out of-the-money" since the strike price is above the market price.

"In-the-money" options have an intrinsic value equal to the market price minus the strike price. In the case of Ford Motor, December 50 call, the intrinsic value is $4.125, as indicated by the following formula:

$$\text{Market} - \text{Strike} = \text{Intrinsic Value}$$
$$\$54.125 - \$50.000 = \$4.125$$

Options that are "out-of-the money" have no tangible intrinsic value. The Ford Motor December 55 call would have a negative $.875 intrinsic value derived from the same formula. When the market price minus the strike price is negative, the negative value represents the amount the stock price must increase to have the option "at-the-money," where the strike price and market price are equal. Returning to the Ford Motor $50 December call, we see the total premium is 4-3/8, while the intrinsic value is 4-1/8. This call option has an additional premium of $1/4 due to other factors. The total premium (option price) is a combination of the intrinsic value plus the speculative premium (which is a function of the common stock volatility and risk), time remaining until expiration of the option contract, dividend yield on the underlying common stock, potential leverage of the option contract, and market expectations of price changes in the common stock.

Generally speaking, the higher the volatility of a common stock, the greater will be the speculative premium in the options contracts. The longer the time remaining until expiration of the contract, the higher the speculative premium. The deeper the option is in the money, the smaller leverage potential, and therefore the smaller the speculative premium for that option contract.

The speculative premium for any given company's option contracts may vary a great deal. Ford Motor speculative premiums are not very high, due to a relatively low volatility in the price of the common stock. Option premiums for companies that traditionally have had larger price changes in the market place, will be higher than Ford Motor's.

## STRENGTHS

One of the strengths of an options contract is the ability to control 100 shares of common stock at a vastly reduced price. The leverage involved in an options contract can be very large. A very small percent change in the price of a common stock can cause a very large percentage change in the price of options contracts for the same company.

A second strength of an options contract is the ability to use either put or call options as a form of insurance for stocks already owned in an investor's portfolio. An investor may wish to purchase a put option contract should he or she feel the value of a particular stock in the portfolio may be subject to a substantial decline. The put option contract would give that investor the right to sell 100 shares of stock for a specified price for a set period of time.

## WEAKNESSES

Weaknesses of options contracts include very volatile price movements, relatively high transaction costs, and a relatively short period of ownership.

## UNIQUE FEATURES

One of the most unique features for options investing is the ability to write a call option contract against an existing stock portfolio as a means of substantially enhancing the total income received from that portfolio. An investor who owns 100 shares of Exxon Corporation may elect to sell (or write) an option contract against the 100 shares of Exxon. For selling this contract the investor will receive the option price, sometimes referred to as "the premium," offered by the market place at a particular point in time. This premium that is received by the owner of Exxon is retained no matter what future events follow. If the price of Exxon goes down and the time period expires for the call option, the call writer retains the entire amount of the call premium. If the price of the stock goes up above the strike price of the option contract the call writer may have the stock called away but retains the premium originally paid for that option.

## TAX CONSEQUENCES

Any option transaction of six months or less is taxed as a short-term gain or loss. Any option transaction of six months and one day or longer is taxed as a long-term capital gain.

Investors should consult a qualified tax professional before entering into complex option transactions. In some cases, the use of options by an investor can affect the holding period for a stock already owned by the investor.

## WHERE AND HOW TO BUY

The Chicago Board Options Exchange (CBOE) was established in 1973 as the first exchange for option contracts. The response from the investment community was overwhelming, and within three years the American, Pacific, and Philadelphia stock exchanges were also trading options contracts. By 1985 the list of stocks with available option contracts increased from the original list of 20 companies to over 390 companies.

Table 35-2 displays a list of all companies with listed options traded on the Chicago Board Options Exchange. Other options exchanges trade equity options on additional stocks. All stock options are quoted daily in national business newspapers such as *Investor's Daily* or *The Wall Street Journal*.

The options contracts on individual common stocks are designed with a standardized three-, six-, and nine-month expiration dates. These expiration dates operate on three calendar cycles.

## Table 35-2. Companies with Options Traded on the Chicago Board Options Exchange

| | |
|---|---|
| Alcoa | Intern'l. Min. & Chem. |
| Amdahl | Intern'l. Paper |
| Amer. Electric Power | ITT |
| American Express | Jim Walter Corp. |
| Amer. Hosp. Supply | Johnson & Johnson |
| AMP | K Mart |
| Apache | Kerr McGee |
| AT&T | Lifemark |
| Atlantic Richfield | Litton Industries |
| Avon | Loral |
| Bally Mfg. | Mary Kay Cosmetics |
| BankAmerica | McDonald's |
| Baxter Labs | Medtronics |
| Bethlehem Steel | Merck |
| Black & Decker | Merrill Lynch |
| Boeing | Middle South Utilities |
| Boise Cascade | MMM |
| Bristol-Myers | Mobil |
| Brunswick | Monsanto |
| Burlington Northern | NCR |
| Burroughs | Nat'l. Semiconductor |
| Capital Cities Comm. | Norfolk Southern |
| CBS | Northern Telecom |
| Celanese | Northrop |
| Cessna | Northwest Airlines |
| Champion Intern'l. | Northwest Industries |
| CIGNA | Occidental Petroleum |
| Citicorp | Owens-Illinois |
| Coastal | Paine Webber |
| Coca-Cola | Paradyne |
| Colgate-Palmolive | Pennzoil |
| Commonwealth Ed. | PepsiCo |
| Computer Sciences | Polaroid |
| Continental Illinois | Ralston Purina |
| Control Data | Raytheon |
| Corning Glass | RCA |
| Datapoint | Revlon |
| Delta Air Lines | R.J. Reynolds |
| Diebold | Rockwell Intern'l. |
| Digital Equipment | ROLM |
| Disney | Sabine |
| Dow Chemical | Safeway Stores |

**Table 35-2.   (Continued)**

| | |
|---|---|
| du Pont | Schlumberger |
| Eastman Kodak | Sears Roebuck |
| Eckerd (Jack) | Skyline |
| Edwards (A.G.) | Southern |
| Engelhard | Southern Pacific |
| Esmark | Southwest Airlines |
| Exxon | Sperry |
| Federal Express | Squibb |
| First Boston | Standard Oil (Ind.) |
| Fluor | Storage Technology |
| Ford | Superior Oil |
| Freeport McMoRan | Syntex |
| General Dynamics | Tandy |
| General Electric | Tektronix |
| General Foods | Teledyne |
| General Motors | Texas Instruments |
| Great Western Fin. | Tidewater |
| Gulf & Western | Toys "R" Us |
| Halliburton | UAL |
| Harris | United Technologies |
| Hewlett-Packard | Upjohn |
| Hitachi | Viacom Intern'l. |
| Holiday Inns | Wal-Mart Stores |
| Homestake Mining | Warner Comm. |
| Honeywell | Weyerhaeuser |
| Hughes Tool | Williams |
| Humana | Xerox |
| IBM | |
| Intern'l. Flavors & Fragrances | |

Companies may be added or deleted from this list at any time because of mergers, acquisitions, or other reasons. There are other options that may be trading on other options exchanges.

Some stocks trade during cycle one with expiration dates in January, April, July, and October. Cycle two is February, May, August, and November. Cycle three is March, June, September, and December.

As one month's expiration date comes up, another month in the cycle is added. For example, as the January option expires, the October nine-month option is added, and the cycle is continued. The use of three cycles spreads out the expiration dates for the options so that not all contracts come due on the same day. Any options positions approaching expiration must be closed out no later than the third Friday following the third Thursday of the month when the option is scheduled to expire.

The exercise price of an option contract is often referred to as the striking price of the contract. This is the fixed price at which the contract is specified for either sales or purchase. For all stocks priced under $100 per share the striking price changes by $5 intervals, and for stocks selling over $100 per share the strike price changes by $10 per share.

As the underlying stocks change price in the open market, options with new striking prices are added. For example, a stock selling at $30 per share when the January option is added, will have a striking price of $30, but if the stock gets to $32.50 per share, which is halfway to the next striking price, the options exchange may add another option with a $35 strike price.

This standardization of expiration dates and strike prices creates more certainty when buying and selling options in a changing market and allows more efficient trading strategies because of better coordination between stock prices, striking prices, and expiration dates. Dividend payments by the companies involved do not affect the option contract. Transactions in option contracts occur at arm's length between buyer and seller without any matchmaking needed on the part of an individual stock broker.

All options transactions are governed by the Options Clearing Corporation. Much of the liquidity and ease of operation of all of the options exchanges is due to the role of the Options Clearing Corporation. The Options Clearing Corporation functions as the issuer of all option contracts listed on the major option exchanges. Investors who want to trade puts and calls need to have an approved account with a brokerage firm. Upon opening the account, the investor will receive a prospectus from the Options Clearing Corporation detailing all aspects of options trading.

Options are bought and sold through member brokerage firms just like other securities. The exchanges allow special orders such as price limit orders, market orders, and stop orders for option buyers and sellers. The order process originates with the broker and is transacted on the floor of an options exchange. For every order there must be both a buyer and a seller or a buyer and a writer so that the orders can be "matched." Once the orders are matched, they are filed with the Options Clearing Corporation. The Options Clearing Corporation then issues the necessary options to the investors. There are four basic transactions handled by the Options Clearing Corporation.

1. Opening Purchase Transaction—a transaction in which an investor intends to become the holder of an option.
2. Opening Sale Transaction—a transaction in which an investor intends to become the seller or writer of an option.
3. Closing Purchase Transaction—a transaction in which an investor who is obligated as a writer of an option intends to terminate his or her obligation as a writer. This is accomplished by purchasing and option identical in maturity and strike price to the option that he originally wrote. Such a transaction has the effect, upon acceptance by the Options Clearing Corporation, of canceling the investor's preexisting position as a writer.
4. Closing Sale Transaction—a transaction in which an investor, who is the holder of an outstanding option, intends to liquidate his or her position as a holder. This is accomplished by selling an option of identical strike price and maturity date as the option previously purchased. Such a transaction has the effect upon acceptance by the Options Clearing Corporation of liquidating the investor's preexisting position as holder of the option.

What occurs in any of these transactions is that the holders and writers of options are not contractually linked together, but are committed to the Options Clearing Corporation.

There are no certificates issued for options. A customer must maintain a brokerage account as long as he or she holds an option position and must liquidate the option through the broker originating the transaction in most cases.

If holders of options contracts wish to exercise their option, they must do so through the Options Clearing Corporation. The Options Clearing Corporation will randomly select a writer from all those persons that have written that serious of options. This would be true whether the holder chooses to exercise prior to the expiration date or on the expiration date of the option contract. Upon notice of the Options Clearing Corporation, a call writer must sell 100 shares of the underlying common stock at the exercise price, while the put writer must buy 100 shares from the holder exercising the put.

All option contracts are adjusted for stock splits, stock dividends, or other stock distributions. To summarize where and how to buy options contracts, an investor will initiate all paperwork and transactions with the securities broker. This broker will supply the investor with the Options Clearing Corporation prospectus and will generally be prepared to provide price quotes and other investment advice about the particular option positions of interest to the investor.

## HOW TO SELL

As with purchases of options, the investor negotiates the sale of options with the securities broker.

## TRANSACTION COSTS

Investors should note that not all securities dealers charge the same fees for services performed. Some firms provide important services for clients over and above the actual execution of a simple buy or sell order. Other firms specialize in offering the lowest possible cost transactions. An individual investor needs to review the level of service he or she requires and select a securities dealer accordingly.

It is not uncommon for small investors to encounter commission charges as high 10 percent or more of the total amount of money invested in option contracts. There is usually a minimum transaction cost of $25 per trade. As an investor increases the quantities of the contracts traded, substantial discounts may be available from all brokerage firms based on the volume of contracts executed in any one order.

## PORTFOLIO FIT

The use of options by investors can be very aggressive and risky, or they can be quite conservative and used as a means of reducing risk. Option buyers and writers both attempt to take advantage of the option premium discussed in the preceding section.

Aggressive investors may wish to purchase call options as a means of increasing the leverage in their investment portfolio. Leverage is a very common reason for buying call options when the market is expected to rise during the exercise period of the option contract. The call options are priced much lower than the common stock and the leverage is derived from the small percentage change in the price of the common stock that

**Table 35-3.   Federal Express $40 October Call Option**

| Date | Option Price | Stock Price |
|------|-------------|-------------|
| 7/5/84 | 1.00 | 34.375 |
| 9/5/84 | 4.25 | 42.875 |
| Percentage Change in Value | +325% | +24% |

can cause a very large percentage change in the price of the call option. Table 35-3 gives the example of a Federal Express call option.

The options price increase was more than 13 times greater than the stock price increase.

In this same example, as long as the common stock closes under $40, the buyer of the call option loses the entire investment. At a price of $41, the call buyer would break even, as the option is worth an intrinsic value of $1. As the stock price rises past $41, the profit starts accumulating for the call option buyer. If the option contract is sold prior to expiration, the speculative premium may alter the profit potential for the call buyer.

An investor striving for maximum leverage will generally buy options that are "out-of-the-money" or slightly "in-the-money." Buying high-priced options for $10 or $15 that are well "in the money" definitely limits the potential for leverage. An investor may have to commit almost as much in the options contracts as he would to purchase the stocks.

Investors can see from this example that leverage works in both directions. In purchasing call options, if the price of the common stock does not rise, an investor may lose all the invested funds.

A second portfolio use of options contracts is the ownership of call options instead of owning common stock. Consider an investor who wishes to own 100 shares of Exxon Corporation with the common stock trading for $50 per share. The investor will receive a tax refund check from the federal government in approximately 90 days for approximately $5,000. However, the investor wants to buy Exxon today because she expects that during the next 90 days Exxon will appreciate in price. The investor could purchase a call option contract for 100 shares of Exxon and receive any benefits of that price appreciation during that 90-day period until she had time to pay for the stock itself. This is referred to as *guaranteeing a price* for purchase of the stock at a later date.

An additional use of options within an investment portfolio is *covered call writing*. The writers of call options take the opposite side of the market from the buyers of call options. The writer is similar to a short seller in that he or she expects the stock to stay at the same price or decline. An option writer who writes covered call options owns the underlying shares of common stock. An option writer that writes "naked" call options does not own the underlying common stock.

Writing covered call options is often considered a hedged position because if the stock price declines, the writer's loss on the stock is partially offset by the option premium. Before writing a covered call option the writer must decide if he or she is willing to sell the underlying stock if it closes above the strike price and the option is exercised.

The use of put options in investment portfolios generally falls in one of three categories. The first category involves the buyer of a put option contract who simply is seeking insurance from price declines in common stocks that he already owns. For example, an investor may have purchased 100 shares of Exxon at $30 several years ago. The market price today has risen to $50. The investor does not wish to sell her Exxon shares because she wants the dividend income received from Exxon shares. This investor may purchase a put option contract to hedge any price decline in Exxon common stock. The put contract gives the investor the right to sell her Exxon holdings for a strike price of $50 per share for a specified period of time in the future.

A second strategy employed by buyers of put option contracts is simply to profit from a bear market or a decline in a particular common stock price. For example, investors may believe that due to price declines in crude oil during the mid-1980s most oil stock prices would decline. An investor seeking to profit from that particular strategy would purchase put contracts without having any ownership position in the common stock. If the price of the stock does decline, the put option contract purchaser should be able to close out this position at a profit.

A third strategy for put option investors is the sale of a put option contract or the writing of a put option contract. This may be done either while the investor owns the underlying common stock or without having the common stock in the portfolio at all. Put writers believe that the price of the common stock will increase over time, thereby causing the put option contract to be worth less money or perhaps to be worth nothing at all upon expiration. For example, the seller of an Exxon 50 put option that expires in April may believe the price of Exxon will rise to $55. If in fact a price rise does occur, the 50 Exxon put would be worthless and the investor would pocket the entire amount of the option premium as a profit from the transaction.

Obviously there are many diversified uses within an investment portfolio for stock options. Investors should thoroughly review the fundamentals of investing in stock options prior to actually using them in their portfolio.

## SOURCES OF ADDITIONAL INFORMATION

Most stock brokerage firms and the options exchanges—American Stock Exchange, Chicago Board of Options Exchange, Philadelphia Stock Exchange, and the Pacific Stock Exchange—offer extensive brochures that describe the use of option contracts. Some of these brochures are available for specific uses (for example, covered option writing strategies).

Many books have been written on the use of option contracts and are available from most public libraries and at most commercial book stores.

## COMMENTS

Since the introduction of equity options contracts in 1973, investors have responded to them with overwhelming favor. The ability to use option contracts to either reduce risk or increase the leverage of an investment portfolio has not gone unnoticed by the investment community.

It is expected that these contracts will not only remain a significant portion of many investment portfolios, but will grow and expand over the coming years.

**Exhibit 35-1.   Moderate Risk: Options**

**INVESTMENT PROFILE**

| INVESTMENT CHARACTERISTICS | Excellent | Good | Average | Poor | None |
|---|---|---|---|---|---|
| Liquidity | √ | | | | |
| Safety of Principal | | | | √ | |
| Price Stability | | | | | √ |
| Reinvestment Protection | | | | | N.A. |
| Growth of Capital | Potential | | | | |
| Cash Income | | | | | N.A. |
| Growth of Income | | | | | N.A. |
| Inflation Hedge | | | | | N.A. |
| Tax Advantaged | | | | | |

**Liquidity**—the ability to quickly realize cash from the sale at fair market value

**Safety of Principal**—the principal is safe from bankruptcy or default

**Price Stability**—the market value of the asset does not change in value

**Reinvestment Protection**—protection against reinvesting cash flow at lower rates as interest rates decline

**Growth of Capital**—the original investment increases over time to create capital gains

**Cash Income**—the cash income relative to treasury bills returns

**Growth of Income**—the ability of the cash income stream to increase over time

**Inflation Hedge**—the ability of total return (cash income plus capital gains) to keep pace with inflation over time

**Tax Advantaged**—the ability to reduce or defer current federal income taxes

# CHAPTER 36

# Stock
# Index Options

## DESCRIPTION

*Stock index options* allow the investor to speculate on or hedge against major stock market price movements. Stock index options are similar in many respects to the standard call and put options on individual stocks discussed in Chapter 35.

A stock index is a mathematic model (such as the Dow Jones Industrial Average or the Standard & Poor's Index) that calculates an average price for a large group of stocks. Stock indexes are designed to indicate the magnitude of price changes of stocks as a broad group. For example, the Standard & Poor's 500 Stock Index calculates the price movement for 500 large companies. The Dow Jones Industrial Average accomplishes the same task for 30 major industrial firms.

Call options and put options are available based on stock index prices. A *call option* is an option to buy units of the stock index at a specified price over a specified period of time. The buyer of a call option pays the writer of the call option a premium for that privilege. *Put options* on stock index futures are the opposite of call options. Put options allow the owner of the option the right to sell a specified number of units of the index to the buyer at a specified price. The seller of a stock index option contract, whether it is a call or a put, is often referred to as the *writer* of the stock index option contract.

The major option contracts are the Standard & Poor's 100 Index and the Standard & Poor's 500 Index. By far, the most popular index option traded by individual investors is the option on the Standard & Poor's 100 Index. Additional index options include the American Exchange Major

**Table 36-1.   Price Quotations: S&P 100 Index Stock Options
(Chicago Board Options Exchange) (April 19, 1984 prices)**

| Strike Price | Calls | | | Puts | | |
|---|---|---|---|---|---|---|
| | *April* | *May* | *June* | *April* | *May* | *June* |
| 140 | — | — | 1/4 | — | 1/16 | — |
| 145 | 10 | 10-1/2 | 10-7/8 | — | 3/16 | 5/8 |
| 150 | 5-3/4 | 6-5/8 | 7-3/8 | 1/16 | 7/8 | 1-1/2 |
| 155 | 3/4 | 3-1/4 | 4-1/2 | 1/16 | 2-3/8 | 3-1/8 |
| 160 | 1/16 | 1-1/8 | 2-1/4 | 4-1/8 | 5-3/8 | 6 |
| 165 | 1/16 | 1/4 | 3/4 | 10 | 10-1/2 | 10-3/4 |
| 170 | — | 1/16 | 1/4 | 15 | 15-1/4 | — |
| 175 | — | 1/16 | 1/8 | 20-1/2 | — | — |

The multiplier times the premium is 100.
Value of the S&P 100 Index (April 19, 1984) = 155.78.
*Source:* Standard & Poor's Corp. Reprinted with permission.

Market Index, the American Exchange Market Value Index, and the New York Stock Exchange Options Index (based on the New York Stock Exchange Composite Index).

The Standard & Poor's 100 Index represents a market value weighted index of 100 of the stocks currently listed for option trading on the Chicago Board of Options Exchange (CBOE). The movement of the Standard & Poor's 100 Index closely parallels that of the Standard & Poor's 500 Index and of the stock market as a whole.

As an example of stock index options trading, review the CBOE Standard & Poor's 100 Index quotations in Table 36-1.

At the bottom of the table, the index closed on April 19, 1984 at 155.78. With this value in mind, we can examine the strike price and the option premiums for the various contracts. The premium in each case is multiplied by 100 to determine the total cash involved. Looking down to the 150 strike price and across to the June call option. (the third monthly column), the premium is 7-3/8 (7.375).

Assuming an investor bought a June 150 contract for a $7.375 premium on April 19, 1984, when the June contract expired the Standard & Poor's 100 index was 165. This is an optimistic assumption. We could further assume, as a pessimistic assumption, that the index was at 145. At a value of 165, the option value is 15 (165 − 150). The ending price is 15 points higher than the strike price. The option costs $7.375. The profit, if the contract is closed at the time of expiration, is shown to be $762.50. If

**Table 36-2.   Differences between Optimistic and Pessimistic Assumptions about a Stock Index**

|  | 165 Optimistic Assumption | 145 Pessimistic Assumption |
|---|---|---|
| Final value (100 × 15) = | $1,500.00 | $0 |
| Purchase price (100 × 7.375) = | 737.50 | 737.50 |
| Profit or loss = | +$762.50 | −$737.50 |

on the other hand the pessimistic assumption is correct, the ending value of 145 for the stock index would render the option worthless. The investor would lose his entire investment of $737.50. These results are shown in Table 36-2.

These examples have used call options. Put options operate on a similar basis. If a 150 June put option (the option to sell at an index price of 150) had been purchased on April 19, 1984 we can see in the last monthly column of Table 36-1 that the initial price of the June put option would have been 1-1/2 (1.50). We could assume that when the June put contract expired the Standard & Poor's 100 Index was 165, under what is now the pessimistic assumption since a loss would be incurred on the put. If the put closed at 145 it would now be the optimistic assumption since a gain would arise.

At a final value of 165, there is no value associated with a put option that allows you to sell at 150. Since the put option costs the investor $1.50, there is a loss of $150. $150 results because the index and the price are multiplied by 100 to determine the contract value and the option value respectively. At a final value of 145 on the index, the put option to sell at 150 has a value of 5. With a cost of 1-1/2, or $150, a $350 profit takes place. The profits and losses are illustrated in Table 36-3.

**Table 36-3.   Profits and Losses from Put Options**

|  | 165 Pessimistic Assumption | | 145 Optimistic Assumption | |
|---|---|---|---|---|
| Final Value (0) = | $ 0 | (100 × 5) = | | $500 |
| Purchase price (100 × 1-1/2) = | 150 | (100 × 1-1/2) = | | 150 |
| Profit or loss = | −$150 | | | +$350 |

**Table 36-4.   Newspaper Format for Index Option Quotes and Graphs**

| Strike Price | NASDAQ | | | | | |
| | Calls—Last | | | Puts—Last | | |
| | Dec | Jan | Feb | Dec | Jan | Feb |
| | NASDAQ 100 INDEX | | | | | |
| 225 | ... | 29-1/8 | ... | ... | 3/16 | ... |
| 230 | 19-7/8 | 23-7/8 | ... | ... | ... | ... |
| 235 | 15 | 19 | ... | 1/4 | 3/4 | ... |
| 240 | 13-7/8 | 15-1/4 | 16-1/2 | 9/16 | 1-1/8 | ... |
| 245 | 8-1/2 | 11-1/8 | 10-1/2 | 1-7/16 | 3-1/2 | 4-11/16 |
| 250 | 5-1/2 | 7-3/4 | 10 | 2-5/8 | 4-1/4 | 7-1/4 |
| 255 | 2-3/4 | 4 | 7-3/8 | 5 | ... | ... |

There are also index option contracts designed for specific industry groups. Investors who want to speculate on the performance of a particular industry or to hedge their portfolio because they own many stocks in that industry can use industry index options. These industry index options are similar to the previously discussed stock index options in that put and call contracts are available at various strike prices. The industry index options trade a value equal to 100 times the premium for each contract.

Table 36-4 illustrates the investment newspaper format for index quotes.

## STRENGTHS

Stock index options' primary strength is the ability to hedge a stock portfolio from declines without having to liquidate the individual securities.

Many long-term investors, fearing a temporary market decline, may protect their portfolios by utilizing stock index options.

A second strength of stock index options is the ability for speculative investors to make transactions based on the entire stock market rather than just one individual company. A small percentage change in the overall market index could generate a large percentage gain in the index option.

## WEAKNESSES

Weaknesses of stock index options contracts include very volatile price movements, relatively high transaction costs, and a relatively short period of ownership.

Many investors expecting large gains, lose their entire investment in this volatile market. Statistics demonstrate that approximately 60 percent of the investors in this market lose money.

## UNIQUE FEATURES

The most unique feature of stock index option contracts is the ability to participate in one particular industry or in a broad spectrum of stocks using the option contract as a vehicle. The investor is not limited to speculating or hedging a position in a specific equity. The investor can participate in price movements of a broad market without the transaction costs associated with building and maintaining a large stock portfolio.

## TAX CONSEQUENCES

Any option transaction in stock index options of six months or less is taxed as a short-term gain or loss. Any stock index option transaction of six month and one day or longer is taxed as a long-term capital gain.

## WHERE AND HOW TO BUY

Investors may purchase and sell stock index option contracts through any securities brokerage firm. The investor will need to provide the securities brokerage firm with information regarding financial status, address, social security number, and so on. Investors also sign options trading agreements in which they acknowledge that they have received disclosure of information regarding options contracts. Investors receive a prospectus detailing the particulars of stock index option trading at the time they open accounts.

Stock index options trade on monthly cycles. This means that stock index options have expiration dates once each month.

As one month's expiration date comes up another month is added as a tradable stock index option contract. Any stock index options positions approaching expiration must be closed out no later than the third Friday following the third Thursday of the month when the option is scheduled to expire.

An essential difference between stock index options and options on individual securities is that stock index options may be settled only via a cash settlement. Options on individual securities may be settled by delivery of the particular securities involved in the options contract.

The exercise price of a stock index option contract is referred to as the *strike price* of the contract. This is the fixed price at which the contract is specified for either sale or purchase. For all indexes the strike prices trade in increments of $5.

This standardization of expiration dates and strike prices creates more certainty for investors when they are buying and selling stock index options in a changing market. This standardization also allows more efficient trading strategies because of better coordination between stock prices, striking prices, and expiration dates.

There are no certificates issued for stock index options, a customer must maintain a brokerage account as long as he or she holds an option position and must liquidate the option through the broker that originated the transaction in most cases.

All stock index options, as well as the underlying indexes, are adjusted for stock splits, stock dividends, or other distributions that occur on any particular stock contained in that index.

To summarize, a stock index option investor will initiate all the paperwork and transactions with a securities broker of his or her choice. This broker and brokerage firm will supply the investor with the appropriate information and prospectus that will apply to the trades. The same securities brokerage firm is prepared to provide price quotes and enter orders on behalf of the investor in stock index option.

## HOW TO SELL

(Purchase and sale of stock index options are opposite but identical transactions. Investors should use the same techniques described for purchasing the options when the holders wish to sell them.)

## TRANSACTION COSTS

Investors should note that not all securities dealers charge the same fees for services performed. *Full-service brokerage firms* provide important services for clients over and above the actual execution of a simple buy or sell order. *Discount brokerage firms* specialize in offering the lowest possible cost transactions. An individual investor needs to review the level of service he or she requires and select a securities dealer accordingly.

It is not uncommon for small investors to encounter commission charges as high as 10 percent or more of the total amount of money invested in options contracts. As an investor purchases and sells larger quantities of the contracts, substantial discounts may be available from all brokerage firms based on the volume of contracts executed in any one order.

## PORTFOLIO FIT

The use of stock index options by investors can be very aggressive and risky or they could be quite conservative and used as a means of reducing risk in a stock portfolio. Aggressive stock index investors may wish to purchase call options as a means of increasing the leverage in their investment portfolio. Leverage is a very common reason for buying stock index call options when the general stock market is expected to rise during the exercise period of the option contract. Stock index options are priced much lower than the comparable common stocks that an investor would purchase to build a similar portfolio. A small percentage change in the price of the stock index can cause a very large percentage change in the price of the stock index call option.

An investor striving for maximum leverage generally buys options that are "out-of-the-money" or slightly "in-the-money." Out-of-the-money options have strike prices just above the current value of the index. A slightly in-the-money option has a strike price just below the current price of the index but still affords considerable upside leverage. Buying high-priced options that are well "in-the-money" definitely limits the potential for leverage. An investor may have to commit almost as much in the options contracts as would be needed to purchase a portfolio of stock to represent the same stock index.

It should be obvious to investors that like all other option contracts, stock index options may provide the potential for gains and also the ability to lose the entire amount of an investor's capital. An additional use of stock index options involves investors hedging a large portfolio of securities. If these investors believe that the stock market may decline substantially, the investor may wish to purchase put options on indexes to protect the portfolio in the event prices decline.

In this case, the put option works as an insurance policy against a broad and general decline in stock prices. The investor is not forced to liquidate the portfolio and assume significant transactions costs and tax ramifications of such trading. The put options may appreciate in value and substantially offset any paper losses incurred in the regular stock portfolio.

As an alternative strategy to protecting against the impact of market declines, the investor may also write call options against a major market index.

## SOURCES OF ADDITIONAL INFORMATION

Most stock brokerage firms offer extensive brochures that describe the use of option contracts. Some of these brochures are available for specific uses, for example, how to hedge a stock portfolio with the use of stock index option.

In addition to the brokerage firms, the Chicago Board of Options Exchange and the other options markets have brochures available for investors. Titles of two very helpful CBOE booklets are *The Index Edge* and *Industry Index Options*. Most brokerage firms distribute these brochures free of charge.

## COMMENTS

Investors have responded with overwhelming favor to the introduction of stock index options. The ability to use stock index option contracts to either reduce the risk in a stock portfolio or to increase the speculative returns to an individual investor has not gone unnoticed by the investment community.

It is expected that these stock index option contracts will not only remain a significant portion of many investment portfolios, but will grow and expand in the coming years. The volume in the S & P 100 index surpassed the total value of all the individual calls listed on the CBOE during 1985.

**Exhibit 36-1. High Risk: Stock Index Options**

**INVESTMENT PROFILE**

| INVESTMENT CHARACTERISTICS | Excellent | Good | Average | Poor | None |
|---|---|---|---|---|---|
| Liquidity | ✓ | | | | |
| Safety of Principal | | | | ✓ | |
| Price Stability | | | | ✓ | |
| Reinvestment Protection | | | | | N.A. |
| Growth of Capital | Potential | | | | |
| Cash Income | | | | | ✓ |
| Growth of Income | | | | | ✓ |
| Inflation Hedge | | | | | ✓ |
| Tax Advantaged | | | | | ✓ |

**Liquidity**—the ability to quickly realize cash from the sale at fair market value

**Safety of Principal**—the principal is safe from bankruptcy or default

**Price Stability**—the market value of the asset does not change in value

**Reinvestment Protection**—protection against reinvesting cash flow at lower rates as interest rates decline

**Growth of Capital**—the original investment increases over time to create capital gains

**Cash Income**—the cash income relative to treasury bills returns

**Growth of Income**—the ability of the cash income stream to increase over time

**Inflation Hedge**—the ability of total return (cash income plus capital gains) to keep pace with inflation over time

**Tax Advantaged**—the ability to reduce or defer current federal income taxes

# CHAPTER 37

# Futures Contracts

## DESCRIPTION

A *futures contract* is an agreement that provides for the delivery of a specific amount of a product, at a designated time in the future, at a specified price.

As an example, a contract to deliver 5,000 bushels of corn in September 1986 may be specified at a price of XXXX per bushel. The person who sells the contract does not need to have actual possession of the corn, nor does the purchaser of the contract need to plan on taking delivery of the 5,000 bushels of corn.

The initial buyer and the initial seller of a futures contract can reverse their initial position to terminate their investment. Over 97 percent of all contracts are terminated in the open market rather than by taking actual delivery of the product.

Futures markets were originally established to permit agricultural commodity producers to hedge their position in a particular commodity. For example, a soybean producer might have a five-month lead time between the planting of the crop and the actual harvesting of the crop and delivery to the market. While the current price of soybeans is $5 per bushel, there is a tremendous amount of risk for the producer that the price might change before the producer is able to deliver the soybeans to the market. The soybean producer realizes that if today's price could be secured five months from now, the producer could make a profit on the growing of the soybeans. The soybean producer then would enter the futures markets and hedge the position by offering to sell futures contracts for delivery of the soybeans at $5 per bushel. If the price of soybeans goes down, the producer will have to sell the crop for less money than the producer anticipated at planting time, but the producer can make up the difference with the profit from the sale of a soybeans futures contract. This is because the producer will be able to buy back the contract for less money than it sold for.

The exact opposite is also true. If the price of soybeans goes up, the extra profit the producer makes on the actual sale of the soybeans crop will be lost on the futures transaction that took place. The net effect is that the producer of the soybeans has "locked in" a price for selling the soybeans. Doing so insures a profit from raising the soybeans and eliminates the risk of price changes for a specified period of time in the future.

This example involves the producer of a commodity wishing to hedge the production position. Futures contracts also involve high-risk investors who take purely speculative positions without any intent to hedge actual ownership of a commodity. There are speculators in the soybean market who believe that the next major price move can be predicted to such an extent that a substantial profit can be made by trading soybean futures contracts.

Because commodities are purchased on the basis of a small invest-ment in the form of margin, there is substantial leverage on a speculator's investment. The percentage return to a speculator on the gains and losses will be greatly magnified by the use of a margin account.

A margin account requires a deposit, usually between 5 and 10 per-cent of the actual value of the futures contract, to be placed with a broker-age firm executing the transaction for the speculator. As price changes occur, the speculator may watch very large profits occur relative to the size of the deposit into the brokerage account. The typical commodities speculator often suffers many losses with the anticipation of making very substantial gains from only a small percentage of the transactions into which he enters. Futures contract speculation represents a very high-risk investment.

Futures contracts can be broken down into a number of categories based on their essential characteristics. As indicated in Table 37-1, there are six primary categories. In each case the table lists representative items.

The first five categories represent traditional commodities, but cate-gory six came into prominence in the 1970s with foreign exchange futures trading originating in 1972 and interest rate futures trading beginning in 1975.

Financial futures contracts also have tremendous implications for fi-nancial managers. In essence, many investment managers now have the

**Table 37-1.   Categories of Commodities and Financial Futures**

| (1)<br>Grains and oilseeds: | (2)<br>Livestock and meat: | (3)<br>Food and fiber: |
|---|---|---|
| Corn | Cattle—feeder | Cocoa |
| Oats | Cattle—live | Coffee |
| Soybeans | Hogs—live | Cotton |
| Wheat | Pork bellies | Orange juice |
| Barley | Turkeys | Potatoes |
| Rye | Broilers | Sugar |
| | | Rice |
| | | Butter |

| (4)<br>Metals and petroleum: | (5)<br>Wood: | (6)<br>Financial futures: |
|---|---|---|
| Copper | Lumber | a. Foreign exchange |
| Gold | Plywood | (pound, yen, franc, |
| Platinum | | and so on) |
| Silver | | b. Interest rate futures |
| Mercury | | GNMA certificates |
| Heating oil no. 2 | | Treasury bonds |
| | | Treasury bills |
| | | Certificates of |
| | | deposit |
| | | Commercial paper |
| | | Eurodollars |
| | | c. Stock index futures |
| | | S&P 500 |
| | | Value Line |

opportunity to hedge their investment positions in the same manner that the soybean farmer has been able to hedge the crop positions for many years.

Contract specifications for futures contracts are provided in Table 37-2.

As can be seen from the table, all futures contracts are specified in terms of the units involved per contract. A further specification will indicate the month in which the contract ends. Futures contracts typically run up to one year into the future; however, some interest rate futures contracts extend over two years.

### Table 37-2. Size of Commodity Contracts

| Contract | Trading Units | Size of Contract Based on Mid-1984 Prices |
|---|---|---|
| Corn | 5,000 bushels | $ 16,200 |
| Oats | 5,000 bushels | 9,500 |
| Wheat | 5,000 bushels | 20,000 |
| Pork bellies | 38,000 pounds | 26,500 |
| Coffee | 37,500 pounds | 53,250 |
| Cotton | 50,000 pounds | 42,500 |
| Sugar | 112,000 pounds | 6,720 |
| Copper | 25,000 pounds | 17,500 |
| Gold | 100 troy ounces | 35,000 |
| Silver | 5,000 troy ounces | 40,000 |
| Treasury bonds | $100,000 | 59,150 |
| Treasury bills | $1,000,000 | 878,200 |

## STRENGTHS

For individual investors the primary strength of a futures contract is the highly leveraged position the investment offers. This leverage can magnify by several times, the actual return to the investor.

A second strength of a futures contract is the very high liquidity transactions in futures contracts have. If a large gain is available to the investor from the initial position, it can be recognized very quickly.

A third strength of futures contracts is the somewhat favorable tax treatment accorded under the rules of the Internal Revenue Service.

## WEAKNESS

The single most devastating weakness of futures contracts is the magnification of any loss from a change in the price of the underlying commodity. These losses can occur very rapidly and often result in a loss to the investor of significantly more money than was originally deposited with the brokerage firm to initiate the transaction.

Futures contracts represent extremely high-risk investment positions. Occasionally prices may move "limit up" and no new buying can take place at that price. If prices move "limit down" no selling is possible and a speculator could be locked into a losing position for days with no escape.

## UNIQUE FEATURES

The most unique feature of a futures contract is the use of margin rather than actual cash dollars. Margin requirements are typically 5 to 10 percent of the value of a contract and may vary from one exchange to another for a particular commodity.

In an effort to examine a potential gain or loss in a futures contract, an example follows. Assume an investor is considering the purchase of a December wheat contract. (It is now May 1.) The price on a futures contract is $4 per bushel. Since wheat trades in units of 5,000 bushels, the total price is $20,000. This example will examine many important features associated with commodity trading, especially the margin requirements.

The margin requirement on the wheat futures contract is $1,500. This represents 7.5 percent of the actual value of the contract ($20,000). Margin requirements on commodities contracts are much lower than margin requirements on stock transactions, in which 50 percent of the purchase price is the margin requirement.

In the case of a futures contract, the margin payment to the brokerage firm is considered to be a good faith deposit against losses that might be incurred by the investor. There is no actual borrowing or interest to be paid on this deposit.

In addition to the initial margin requirements, there are also margin maintenance requirements that may run as high as 70 to 80 percent of the value of the initial margin. In the case described previously, the margin maintenance requirement might be $1,200. If the initial margin of $1,500 is reduced by $300 due to losses on the contract, the investor will be required to replace the $300 to cover the margin position. If the investor does not do so, the brokerage firm may close out the contract and realize the actual losses to date. Margin requirements are determined every business day based on the closing price of the margin contract on that day.

Margin requirements on financial futures contracts are even smaller than margin requirements on commodity futures contracts. As an example, a $1,000,000 treasury bill contract may require an initial margin of as little as $1,500.

An investor may be required to put up additional margin deposits the same day he or she initiates a futures contract position, if the price of the commodity has moved against the investor.

As noted previously, gains and losses on futures contracts can be quite spectacular. For example, on the wheat futures contract purchased at $4 per bushel, a price change from $4 to $4.35 or 35 cent increase per

**Table 37-3.   Maximum Daily Price Changes for Commodities**

| Commodity | Exchange | Normal Price Range | Maximum Daily Price Change (from previous close)* |
|---|---|---|---|
| Corn | CBT | $2.30–$4.00 | $.10 per bushel |
| Oats | CBT | $1.25–$2.40 | $.06 per bushel |
| Wheat | CBT | $3.00–$5.50 | $.20 per bushel |
| Pork bellies | CBT | $ .40–$ .80 | $.02 per pound |
| Copper | CME | $ .60–$1.50 | $.03 per pound |
| Silver | CMX | $6.00–$50.00 | $.50 per ounce |
| Treasury bills | IMM or CME | 85% of par and up | 50 basis points |

*These values may change slightly from exchange to exchange and are often temporarily altered in response to rampant speculation.

bushel establishes an actual gain for the investor of $1,750. This results because the investor controlled 5,000 bushels of wheat and made a profit of 35 cents per bushel. Because the initial margin requirement was only $1,500 the investor has made a profit of 116.7 percent.

If this transaction took place over a one-month time period, the annualized gain would be 1,400 percent—all accomplished by a 35 cent change in the price of a bushel of wheat!

Lest this sound too good to be true, investors should be aware that futures contracts are a double-edged sword. Had the price of wheat had declined, a substantial loss even in excess of the amount of the initial margin deposited by the investor would have occurred. Investors can recognize and calculate from this wheat example the effects of a modest decline in the price of wheat per bushel.

An important feature of commodities contracts involves price movement limitations. Because of the enormous opportunities for gains and losses in the commodities markets, the commodity exchanges do place some broad limitations on maximum daily price movements in a commodity. Some examples are shown in Table 37-3.

These daily trading limits obviously must affect the efficiency of the market somewhat. If market conditions indicate the price of wheat should decline by 30 cents and the daily limit is 20 cents, then obviously the price of wheat is not in equilibrium as it opens the following morning. However, the desire to stop market panics tends to override the desire for total market efficiency in the commodity markets. Nevertheless, the potential intraday trading range is still large. Recall, for example, that a 20-cent change in the price of wheat, which is the daily limit, is more than enough to place tremendous pressure on the investor to repeatedly increase the margin position. On the typical 5,000-bushel contract, this would represent a daily loss of $1,000.

This potential for open ended losses prevents many investors from entering the futures markets.


## TAX CONSEQUENCES

Tax treatment of commodity contracts is very simple. In an effort to prevent abuses of our income tax system, all commodity contracts are "marked to the market" on December 31 of each year.

As an example, investor A purchases a corn futures contract in June and resells the contract in September of a particular tax year. This investor has opened and closed the transaction and for tax purposes has established both the cost basis and the sales price of the property. Investor B purchases a corn futures contract on December 1. This investor does not resell the contract by yearend. For tax purposes on December 31 the value of the corn futures contract is noted. Any taxable gain or taxable loss that results between December 1 and December 31 will be a taxable event to investor B for that particular year.

One additional tax treatment that is favorable for commodity futures is the fact that 60 percent of all commodity gains are treated as long-term capital gains whether or not the contract was held for at least six months. This means that an investor can purchase a commodities contract and resell it as often as desired still have 60 percent of the gains treated as long-term capital gains and 40 percent of the gains treated as short-term gains.

The marked to the market system applies to all commodity contracts entered into by investors. A different set of rules will apply to investors wishing to hedge commodity futures contracts. Investors who enter into commodity contracts for hedging purposes should consult with a qualified tax professional to determine their tax obligations from the transactions.


## WHERE AND HOW TO BUY

All investor orders for futures contracts are executed by a securities brokerage firm. The firm carries the individual investor's account on its books. The firm maintains a record of each customer's open positions, margin deposits, money balances, and completed transactions. The investment firm also provides facilities and personnel necessary to execute customer orders.

In addition to these services, many of the larger securities brokerage firms maintain research staffs that evaluate market situations and offer trading recommendations to investors.

The individual investor generally establishes a relationship with a registered representative (broker) who is licensed to execute commodities orders. These account executives supply required documents to open new accounts and make sure that these documents are properly executed for futures contract investors. The account executive explains trading rules and procedures to the investor and keeps the clients informed of price changes and market conditions. The account executive enters customer orders and reports the execution of orders to the client. This professional acts as a link between the investor and the brokerage firm's research department.

In addition, it is the account executive's and brokerage firm's responsibility to ensure that an investor's financial suitability is substantial enough to trade futures contracts.

## HOW TO SELL

The liquidation of futures contracts is accomplished through the same securities firms and account executives as the purchase of futures contracts. Orders to buy and to sell are regularly executed by the brokerage firm.

Trading volume is reported in the standard futures contract section on most major newspapers each day, as shown in Table 37-4. This trading volume is reported for each individual futures contract for a particular commodity at a particular future expiration date. This volume is defined as the total number of contracts traded during an individual trading session.

Investors will note a column that specifies the open interest for a particular futures contract. Open interest represents those contracts that have not yet been liquidated by an offsetting futures transaction. This gives an investor an idea of the number of contracts currently in existence for that particular commodity.

Many different types of orders may be entered to buy and sell futures

**Table 37-4. Newspaper Format for Futures Price Quotations**

| Season | | Open | | | | | |
|---|---|---|---|---|---|---|---|
| High | Low | Interest | Open | High | Low | Close | Chg. |

**OATS (CBOT)—5,000 bu minimum—dollars per bushel**
**Vol. Mon 807, open int 4,184—73**

| Season High | Low | | Open Interest | Open | High | Low | Close | Chg. |
|---|---|---|---|---|---|---|---|---|
| 1.82-1/2 | 1.15 | Dec | 1,217 | 1.22 | 1.22-3/4 | 1.21-1/8 | 1.22-3/4 | +.00-3/4 |
| 1.67-3/4 | 1.24-1/2 | Mar | 1,904 | 1.32 | 1.32-3/4 | 1.31-1/2 | 1.32-3/4 | +.01 |
| 1.63 | 1.27-1/2 | May | 875 | 1.35-3/4 | 1.36-1/2 | 1.35-3/4 | 1.36-1/4 | +.00-1/4 |

contracts. Investors should be thoroughly briefed on the different types of orders by their account executive prior to beginning futures trading.

Each order entered by an investor should contain the following items of information: whether the order is a buy or a sell order; the number of contracts to be bought or sold; the specific futures contract involved indicating both delivery month and year; and the order will specify whether it is a market order that is immediately executable or a contingent order. A *market order* is executed at the best price available at the time the order is received at the commodity exchange. A *contingent order* will be based on some future change in the price of that particular commodities contract. A change in the price may trigger execution of the investor's order.

Once again it is emphasized that investors thoroughly review and consult with their account executives prior to entering orders for futures contracts.

## TRANSACTION COSTS

Transaction costs in commodities futures trading are generally expressed as dollars per "round trip." This is simply both a buy and a sell transaction in the same commodities contract. Commissions of $35 to $60 per round trip are common.

Investors should note that not all securities dealers charge the same fees for services performed. *Full-service brokerage firms* provide important services for clients over and above the actual execution of a simple buy or sell order. *Discount brokerage firms* specialize in offering the lowest possible cost transactions. An individual investor needs to review the level of service he or she requires and select a securities dealer accordingly.

## PORTFOLIO FIT

Use of futures contracts by individual investors is generally reserved for those investors of substantial means who are willing to accept an especially large loss on their initial investment positions.

These investors take extremely high speculative risks in the hope of making very high profits from their transactions. These investors often stand to lose substantially more than the original amount that they invest in a futures contract.

An exception to this high-risk idea would be the use of futures as a hedging device to actually reduce the risk exposure from the ownership of a given commodity or security. In this case, commodity futures represent a risk reduction mechanism.

## SOURCES OF ADDITIONAL INFORMATION

Several excellent brochures and publications are available that discuss futures contracts. One of the best brochures available for investors wishing to examine futures contracts is available from the Futures Industry Association Inc. and is entitled "An Introduction to the Futures Markets." It may be obtained from many securities firms that trade futures contracts or by writing the Futures Industry Association at 1919 Pennsylvania Avenue NW, Suite 204, Washington DC 20006.

## COMMENTS

Speculators seeking to obtain extremely high profits from very modest investments frequently use futures contracts.

It is very difficult for most individual investors to realize a consistent profit from the trading of futures contracts.

**Exhibit 37-1.   High Risk: Futures Contracts**

**INVESTMENT PROFILE**

| INVESTMENT CHARACTERISTICS | Excellent | Good | Average | Poor | None |
|---|---|---|---|---|---|
| Liquidity | √* | | | | |
| Safety of Principal | | | | | √ |
| Price Stability | | | | √ | |
| Reinvestment Protection | | | | | N.A. |
| Growth of Capital | Potential | | | | Potential |
| Cash Income | | | | | √ |
| Growth of Income | | | | | √ |
| Inflation Hedge | | √ | | | |
| Tax Advantaged | | | √† | | |

**Liquidity**—the ability to quickly realize cash from the sale at fair market value

**Safety of Principal**—the principal is safe from bankruptcy or default

**Price Stability**—the market value of the asset does not change in value

**Reinvestment Protection**—protection against reinvesting cash flow at lower rates as interest rates decline

**Growth of Capital**—the original investment increases over time to create capital gains

**Cash Income**—the cash income relative to treasury bills returns

**Growth of Income**—the ability of the cash income stream to increase over time

**Inflation Hedge**—the ability of total return (cash income plus capital gains) to keep pace with inflation over time

**Tax Advantaged**—the ability to reduce or defer current federal income taxes

*Except when prices are ''limit up'' or ''limit down.''
†Special tax treatment on gains & losses.

# CHAPTER 38

# Gold and Other Precious Metals

## DESCRIPTION

Gold and other *precious metals* (such as silver and platinum) can be considered as a group for investment portfolio purposes.

When investors think of gold, they have traditionally thought of the refined bullion product. This refined bullion is generally available in increments of one ounce or more for investment purposes. The actual bullion is stamped with a metal stamp to authenticate its purity. Most investment grade gold has a .999 purity. This process is referred to as *assaying* the gold.

In addition to gold bullion, gold and other precious metals are available in the form of coins, commodities futures contracts, options on commodities futures contracts, and gold mutual funds.

Generally speaking, each of these investment vehicles provides the same strengths and some of the same weaknesses as ownership of gold bullion proper.

Coins may retain additional value over and above their actual bullion content as a collector value to numismatists. This numismatic value is very difficult to predict from one type of coin to the next. The one constant factor the underlies the numismatic value of the coin is the actual value of the bullion contained within that coin. The presumption is that the coin could be melted down and reformulated into the pure bullion.

Futures contracts and options on futures contracts offer a highly leveraged, extremely speculative way for investors to participate in price changes on gold and other precious metals. Most investors do not wish to assume the high risk involved in these contracts. Because futures contracts and options on futures contracts for bullion are very highly leveraged and somewhat shorter in duration than is generally acceptable to the average investor, professional speculators tend to use these contracts for their precious metals investments.

Mutual funds that are dedicated to the precious metals investment area specifically own shares of gold mining and production companies. These funds specialize in research and knowledge of the ore reserves, productive capacities, and other factors that are important to the ownership of shares of a gold mine or a gold mining company. Mutual funds offer some other advantages over direct ownership of bullion, coins, and futures contracts. Liquidity is enhanced in a mutual fund versus owning bullion and to a lessor extent coins. Safekeeping and transportation are not as difficult with a mutual fund as they are with bullion and coins, and mutual funds are generally not nearly as speculative as futures contracts in the commodity markets.

## STRENGTHS

Very simply, whether an investor elects to participate in the futures markets, mutual funds, coins, or in gold bullion itself, gold has historically been held in investment portfolios as a hedge against inflation. Gold also serves for some investors as an ultimate disaster hedge. These investors believe that in a case of economic breakdown and chaos gold will prove to be an acceptable medium of exchange in a barter economy.

## WEAKNESSES

Investors who wish to have gold exposure in their portfolio find several weaknesses of direct ownership of the bullion and coins. Gold bullion is not always immediately transferable, due to the fact that the bullion itself must be authenticated or tested for purity before it can be bought and sold. This tends to slightly reduce the liquidity of ownership of gold bullion.

An additional weakness is associated with futures contracts and options on futures contracts that being the very high-risk and short-term nature of these investment.

Bullion and coins are generally nonincome-producing assets. These assets do not produce anything of economic value to society. They must be held strictly for price appreciation resulting from high rates of inflation.

## UNIQUE FEATURES

Perhaps the biggest unique feature of an investment in gold, especially that of bullion or gold coins, is the psychological return received by an investor who knows that he or she owns the ultimate disaster hedge or inflation hedge.

Most rational investment objectives can be met by using investments other than that of bullion and coin ownership. Even inflation protection can be accomplished by the ownership of more productive assets, for example real estate, oil and gas investments, or investment in other mineral extraction industries.

## WHERE AND HOW TO BUY

Gold coin dealers and gold and silver exchanges provide a convenient avenue in most cities for investors to purchase gold coins and/or gold bullion. Securities brokerage firms generally provide a bullion-purchasing service to their clients. Securities brokerage firms also offer gold mutual funds to investors. Any investor seeking an investment in a gold mutual fund should refer to the mutual fund chapter of this book for additional details concerning all mutual funds.

Table 38-1 illustrates precious metal spot (current) quotations from a newspaper. Table 38-2 shows how futures contracts prices are given.

## HOW TO SELL

Generally, if the authenticity of a gold coin or of gold bullion can be determined, most coin dealers and gold and silver exchanges are prepared to purchase gold from the investor. Most securities brokerage firms also offer this service, but only after a fee has been charged for the assaying and authentication of the gold that is delivered for sale. Gold mutual funds and futures contracts involving precious metals are more easily liquidated simply by entering a sell order with a securities dealer, or by writing a mutual fund company for liquidation of the shares of the investor.

**Table 38-1.   Newspaper Format of Spot Prices for
Metals and Gold Coins**

**GOLD**

London morning fixing $330.45 off $0.80.
London afternoon fixing $326.15, off $3.10.
Paris afternoon $332.24, off $1.00.
Frankfurt fixing $331.04, off $0.60.
Zurich later afternoon bid $326.25, off $3.00. $328.75 asked.

**GOLD COINS**

| | | |
|---|---|---|
| Maple Leaf, 1 troy oz. | $343.75 | off $7.50 |
| Mex. 50 Peso, 1.2 troy oz. | $414.75 | off $6.50 |
| Aus. 100 crown, .9802 troy oz. | $326.25 | off $7.00 |
| Krugerrand, 1 troy oz. | $330.50 | off $5.00 |
| China Panda, 1 troy oz. | $349.00 | off $5.20 |

## TRANSACTION COSTS

Generally, a spread is offered between the buy and sell price of gold at
most gold and silver exchanges. This spread may range between 3 and 6
percent of the actual purchase price of gold bullion. This mark up will
change dramatically depending on the amount of gold bullion to be purchased. There can be a substantial quantity discount for larger purchases
of gold bullion.

The sales commission or markup charged to investors in gold collec-
tors coins (not Krugerands, Mapleleafs, and so on) is much more difficult
to determine over a short period of time. The numismatic value added to
gold coins can be very difficult to gage at any given point in time or at any
given geographic location. Investors should purchase these coins only
after studying comparative offers from more than one coin dealer.

**Table 38-2.   Newspaper Format for Gold Futures Contract Prices**

**GOLD (CMX)—100 troy oz.—dollars per troy oz.**
**Vol. Tue 50, 265, open Int. 125,765 − 825**

| | | | | | | | |
|---|---|---|---|---|---|---|---|
| 489.50 | 301.50 | Dec | 18,592 | 330.00 | 330.20 | 325.30 | 325.70–5.50 |
| | | Jan | | | | | 327.90–5.50 |
| 485.50 | 306.00 | Feb | 37,226 | 334.80 | 334.90 | 330.00 | 330.20–5.40 |

Additional transaction costs involved in gold investments include a state sales tax that is applied to purchases of gold bullion, safekeeping charges whether in the form of lock box at a local bank or through custodial services provided by a brokerage firm, and insurance expense any time bullion and gold coins are shipped.

For investors wishing to purchase small quantities of gold or precious metals, often these transactions charges can range as high as 15 to 20 percent of the total dollars invested in gold bullion and gold coins.

Typically, a sales charge on a gold mutual fund that contains a load is approximately 8 percent of the purchase price of the shares.

Transaction costs for commodities contracts vary considerably depending on the number of contract purchased and sold by an investor. It would not be uncommon to experience anywhere from 2 to 5 percent transaction costs in the commodities arena for a relatively small investor in gold futures contracts.

Traditionally transaction costs involved with the ownership of gold have been relatively high when compared with other securities.

## PORTFOLIO FIT

A rational investor will generally keep an extremely small percentage of his investment portfolio dedicated to gold and gold related investments as an inflation hedge. This percentage for small investors should start as low as 1 percent of assets dedicated to gold and precious metals.

As an investor builds a portfolio of traditional securities, the amount of the portfolio dedicated to gold can be increased. An investor that has achieved a very high cash flow from a substantial portfolio of investments can expand the commitment to gold and precious metals once his or her personal consumption and income needs have been met.

As a general rule, investors will scale their gold and precious metals investment percentage upward along with the growth in absolute size of their portfolio. Ultimately, an investor may wish to hold as much as 10 percent of a portfolio in gold.

## COMMENTS

Gold investments as a part of a portfolio are generally useful but often overdone by small investors.

Generally, it is inconvenient for smaller investors to hold gold as a portion of their investment portfolio. Small investors can overcome these inconveniences of storage, insurance, transportation, and high markups by purchasing shares of a gold mutual fund.

Larger investors may have the capital necessary to purchase gold bullion and/or coins in convenient increments.

As a rule of thumb, an investor should increase the percentage of gold and precious metals held in a personal portfolio as the overall size of the portfolio increases. This serves to provide a hedge against economic uncertainty and inflation for those assets that are held in more traditional securities investments.

## Exhibit 38-1.  High Risk: Gold & Metals

### INVESTMENT PROFILE

| INVESTMENT CHARACTERISTICS | Excellent | Good | Average | Poor | None |
|---|---|---|---|---|---|
| Liquidity | | | √ | | |
| Safety of Principal | | | | √ | |
| Price Stability | | | | √ | |
| Reinvestment Protection | √ | | | | |
| Growth of Capital | | | LT† | | |
| Cash Income | | | | | √ |
| Growth of Income | | | | | √ |
| Inflation Hedge | √* | | | | |
| Tax Advantaged | | | | | √ |

**Liquidity**—the ability to quickly realize cash from the sale at fair market value

**Safety of Principal**—the principal is safe from bankruptcy or default

**Price Stability**—the market value of the asset does not change in value

**Reinvestment Protection**—protection against reinvesting cash flow at lower rates as interest rates decline

**Growth of Capital**—the original investment increases over time to create capital gains

**Cash Income**—the cash income relative to treasury bills returns

**Growth of Income**—the ability of the cash income stream to increase over time

**Inflation Hedge**—the ability of total return (cash income plus capital gains) to keep pace with inflation over time

**Tax Advantaged**—the ability to reduce or defer current federal income taxes

*Gold has always been a commodity that people want to hold during periods of rising inflation. Therefore it does well in inflationary times.
†Gold held over long periods will keep up with average rates of growth.

# CHAPTER 39

# Oil Exploration Programs

## DESCRIPTION

Oil exploration programs provide capital needed for the exploration and development of oil and gas reserves. Typically oil exploration programs are organized as limited partnerships. These partnerships provide an individual investor with the opportunity to participate directly in the exploration for hydrocarbon reserves.

An individual investor typically participates as a "limited partner" in a partnership. The "general partner" is normally an established corporation that engages in the energy development industry on an ongoing basis.

As limited partners, individuals release control of all decisions concerning the business activities of the partnership to the general partner. The individuals supply the capital, the general partner supplies the industry expertise and they share jointly in the economic results. Investors are limited as to their liability in oil drilling ventures. Generally, an investor in a public oil drilling program is liable only for the amount of money invested.

It is important for investors to carefully read each section of this chapter to completely understand the entire structure of oil exploration programs.

## STRENGTHS

Oil exploration programs provide investors the opportunity to participate in an investment that offers potential for capital appreciation. Many oil

355

and gas wells have productive lives in excess of 10 years. Some wells pay back an investor's original capital several times over.

Unless changes are enacted in future tax legislation, several favorable tax treatments are offered as an incentive to oil exploration program investors. These tax incentives are detailed in the discussion of tax treatments later in the chapter and are an important strength of an investment in oil exploration programs. Table 39-1 contains composite information on the performance of drilling funds from 1970 to 1982.

Investors should note that the newest programs are still producing cash flow to the limited partners.

The total expected return ratio column in Table 39-1 is upwardly biased, because only the better-performing funds supply this data.


## WEAKNESSES

The major weakness of oil exploration programs is the very high degree of risk inherent in the drilling of any hydrocarbon exploratory well.

Most sponsors of oil exploration programs attempt to offer a diversified package of wells within a given program. If an oil exploration program fails to develop meaningful quantities of oil or natural gas, an investor can lose the entire investment!

A second, but far less important weakness, is the dilution typically suffered by an investor when entering an oil exploration program. The two principle sources of this dilution are fees charged by the general partner prior to undertaking partnership operations and the eventual division of partnership revenues between the limited partners and the general partner.

Table 39-2 illustrates the high risk of oil exploration programs. 41 percent of all programs formed from 1979 to 1982 have expected returns of less than 1 to 1 of investor's capital.


## UNIQUE FEATURES

Very few investments offer an individual the opportunity to achieve very high rates of return and substantial tax advantages in the same investment vehicle. Investors must always remember the high degree of risk associated with a hydrocarbon exploration investment.

A strength of oil exploration programs is that they offer an investor a diversified portfolio of oil and gas wells, spreading the risk among many

## Table 39-1.  Annual Drilling Fund Industry Performance

| Year of Program Formation | Cash Distributions | | | | Total Expected Return** | | |
|---|---|---|---|---|---|---|---|
| | Number of Programs | Investment (000's)* | Percent of Investment Returned In Cash | Average Annual Cash Distributions | Number of Programs | Investment (000's)* | Total Expected Return Ratio |
| 1970 | 19 | $  32,323 | 158% | 12% | 14 | $  14,405 | 5.5/1 |
| 1971 | 22 | 29,742 | 102% | 9% | 14 | 15,442 | 1.5/1 |
| 1972 | 28 | 38,329 | 132% | 12% | 18 | 17,808 | 2.6/1 |
| 1973 | 37 | 56,523 | 296% | 30% | 25 | 27,974 | 5.9/1 |
| 1974 | 35 | 92,928 | 127% | 14% | 22 | 43,542 | 3.6/1 |
| 1975 | 43 | 123,637 | 114% | 15% | 29 | 79,731 | 3.1/1 |
| 1976 | 65 | 168,146 | 66% | 10% | 40 | 102,435 | 2.1/1 |
| 1977 | 76 | 296,074 | 43% | 7% | 46 | 166,207 | 1.5/1 |
| 1978 | 82 | 347,188 | 52% | 11% | 46 | 214,995 | 1.5/1 |
| 1979 | 109 | 565,522 | 33% | 8% | 56 | 350,233 | 1.4/1 |
| 1980 | 143 | 882,912 | 18% | 6% | 70 | 532,267 | 1.6/1 |
| 1981 | 153 | 1,334,827 | 9% | 4% | 66 | 745,961 | 0.7/1 |
| 1982 | 125 | 756,281 | 7% | 7% | 45 | 407,788 | 1.3/1 |
| TOTALS/AVERAGES | 937 | $ 4,724,432 | 32% | 7% | 486 | $ 2,718,788 | 1.4/1 |

*Includes assessments.
**Based on programs of sponsors supplying complete balance sheet and reserve data.

*Source: Stanger's Oil and Gas Partnership Performance Yearbook.*

**Table 39-2.   Consistency of Drilling Fund Industry Performance**

| Total Expected Return Ratio | For Programs Formed 1970-1982* | | For Programs Formed 1979-1982* | |
|---|---|---|---|---|
| | Number of Programs | Percent of Total | Number of Programs | Percent of Total |
| 5.0/1 or over | 37 | 8% | 4 | 2% |
| 4.0/1 - 4.9/1 | 25 | 5% | 5 | 2% |
| 3.0/1 - 3.9/1 | 41 | 8% | 13 | 6% |
| 2.0/1 - 2.9/1 | 85 | 18% | 35 | 15% |
| 1.0/1 - 1.9/1 | 147 | 30% | 79 | 34% |
| Less than 1.0/1 | 151 | 31% | 96 | 41% |
| TOTALS | 486 | 100% | 232 | 100% |

*Based on programs of sponsors supplying complete balance sheet and reserve data.

*Source: Stanger's Oil and Gas Partnership Performance Yearbook.* Reprinted with permission.

wells. The investor does not need to make sophisticated geological decisions concerning technically complicated situations.

Most individual investors could not possibly undertake this type of investment without an oil exploration partnership.

## TAX CONSEQUENCES

Oil exploration programs generally provide very convenient tax reporting for the limited partners. Partnership returns are filed with the Internal Revenue Service by the general partner. The limited partners receive a detailed break out of their ownership interest in the partnership on a form called a *K-1*. Usually, these K-1 forms are prepared by the accounting firm that prepares the financial statements of the partnership. Well-managed partnerships are able to furnish these forms by the middle of March each year following a December fiscal year end.

Within the K-1 form the limited partner will be credited with the share of drilling expenses of the partnership, the depreciation expense for equipment purchased and owned by the partnership, any investment tax credits available to the partnership, and (hopefully) income produced by the partnership.

The actual revenues received by the limited partners may be partially sheltered from taxation by the depletion allowance available to hydrocarbon producers. The government permits the owners of a hydrocarbon well to receive a portion of the production on a tax free basis because the well is a depleting asset. Currently the depletion allowance is 17 percent of the total production of the well.

The costs associated with drilling the wells are considered an expense item by the government. Because most of the money invested by limited partners in oil exploration programs is immediately spent to drill the wells, the investor receives a large immediate writeoff the year the investment is purchased. It is not uncommon to receive a writeoff of 70 percent or more of the amount invested the first year.

Tax implications for the second and subsequent years of the partnership are not as predictable. If the partnership is very successful, taxable income may begin as early as the second calendar year of the investment. If the partnership meets with limited or no success, additional tax deductions will be available to the limited partners. Obviously, if the investor receives a 70 percent or larger deduction in the first year, he or she had better hope to be cashing some substantial checks by the end of the second year. If the checks are not forthcoming, the investor will yearn for the safety of an alternative investment.

In any event, a publicly offered limited partnership that does not use any borrowed capital should produce a 100 percent writeoff of the amount invested during the first two or three years. After the second or third year, most of the income produced by the partnership will be taxable income.

One last point needs to be made for oil exploration program partners. Under current tax law a unique tax advantage can be gained by gifting units of an oil exploration program to a minor child, or retired parent at the time the partnership begins to flow cash to the limited partner.

An investor simply transfers ownership of the limited partnership units to the minor child or retired parent. Many times the income from the partnership is taxed at a much lower rate than that of the original investor. Often the general partner will furnish the forms required to effect one of these transfers to the limited partner upon request.

The cost basis of the gift at the time the drilling is complete is very low. Most of the investor's capital has been expensed during drilling operations and the gift of the units is of little gift-tax consequence. Investors wishing to implement this idea should contact their investment adviser or the general partner for assistance.

## WHERE AND HOW TO BUY

An investor must sign a form called a *subscription document* to participate in the program. The investor's check is typically made payable to the program and is forwarded to the general partner with the subscription document.

The subscription document contains basic information about the investor: name, address, telephone, and tax identification number.

Oil exploration programs are structured by corporations in the ongoing business of developing hydrocarbon reserves. Typically a wholly owned subsidiary of the oil company serves as general partner of the oil exploration program. This entity, the "general partner" is responsible for all business decisions of the partnership. Limited partners have no control.

The general partner in conjunction with the oil company geological experts selects all the "prospects" that are included in the partnership. A prospect is one individual location selected for the drilling of an oil well. These locations are often solicited by the oil company by offering a cash payment to a land owner for the right to explore for hydrocarbons on that individuals land.

The general partner in conjunction with experts at the oil company arranges for the physical drilling of the wells. Generally it is preferable that all such work be done by unaffiliated third parties. It is difficult for an investor to justify permitting a wholly owned affiliate of the oil company to spend the oil exploration program's funds with the parent company. This would result in an obvious conflict of interest.

The general partner contracts for all legal services including lease documents, property title opinions, and division orders. The general partner also arranges for all accounting of the oil exploration program. The accounting statements are subject to the audit of an independent certified public accountant. Generally the legal and accounting work for the partnership are contracted to very prominent firms in each field. One benefit of the management of the general partner is a "turnkey" investment for an individual investor. Turnkey management means all of the partnerships business decisions are made by the general partner.

The individual is provided with annual accounting statements, regular reports on the activities of the partnership, and complete income tax information on a standard Internal Revenue Service form (Form K-1).

No discussion of suppliers of oil exploration programs would be complete without mentioning the reduction of program sponsors between the peak of oil industry activity in 1981 and the present. Many of the less experienced sponsors folded when investor demand declined in 1982 and 1983. Today, a select group of the oldest, most qualified oil exploration companies remain in the business of sponsoring public hydrocarbon exploration programs. Generally speaking, most of these companies have very good track records of finding hydrocarbons and providing investment benefits for the individuals that invest as limited partners.

Most sponsors of oil exploration programs employ securities brokerage firms to market these products to the investing public. Typically the brokerage firms receive a fee for providing these marketing services.

Security brokerage firms and the program sponsor are required by law to furnish an investor with a document called a *prospectus*. Typically these documents are comprehensive and full of difficult legal jargon. Investors should focus on the track record of the sponsor's previous oil exploration programs. Additional information of interest will be the exact terms of the offering including all expenses that are to be paid by the limited partners.

## HOW TO SELL

Oil exploration programs are *self-liquidating*. These investments begin to produce oil or gas soon after drilling is completed (1-1/2 to 2 years). As the production from the wells eventually declines the partnership income decreases. Typically the general partner will cause some type of asset liquidation after it becomes apparent that the costs of conducting business as a partnership do not merit continued operations. Often the remaining useful assets of the partnership including the mineral interests held by the partnership are sold to another oil and gas company for cash.

Recently a more popular method of liquidation of partnerships has been the *master partnership*. A master partnership is simply the combination of many previous oil exploration programs managed by the same general partner. In this case each oil exploration program is evaluated by independent hydrocarbon engineering firms. Each investor is given the option of maintaining his or her original partnership interests or trading those interests for units in the master partnership. The major advantage of these master partnerships is the ability to buy and sell the units in the same manner as a common stock. Often the units are listed on one of the major stock exchanges. These units then trade every day. An investor in what

**Table 39-3.   Master Limited Energy Exploration
Partnerships**

| *Name* | *Where Traded* |
|---|---|
| Apache Petroleum Partners | New York Stock Exchange |
| Belden and Blake Energy Partners | American Stock Exchange |
| May Energy Partners Ltd. | American Stock Exchange |
| OKC Limited Partnership | Pacific Stock Exchange |
| Snyder Oil Partners | New York Stock Exchange |
| TRANSCO Exploration Partners Ltd. | New York Stock Exchange |
| Petroleum Investments Ltd. | New York Stock Exchange |
| Dorchester Hugoton Ltd. | Over the Counter |
| Saxon Oil Development Partners | American Stock Exchange |
| Walker Energy Partners | American Stock Exchange |
| Con Vest Energy Partners | American Stock Exchange |

was originally a partnership with limited or no liquidity suddenly can liquidate a part or all of the remaining assets at will.

Income from the remaining oil and gas wells is distributed to owners of the master limited partnership units. The liquidity provided by a master partnership is very beneficial to an individual investor. Unfortunately, the general partner decides when and if one of these master partnerships will be formed.

Currently several master limited partnerships are in the formation stage. A list of existing master limited partnerships is included in Table 39-3.

One additional avenue has recently been created for liquidating limited partnership investments. A new exchange called the National Partnership Exchange, Inc. (NAPEX) has been formed to trade existing units of limited partnerships.

NAPEX sells memberships to members of the National Association of Securities Dealers. These NAPEX members can utilize computer terminals to list units of various partnerships for sale. An investor in an oil exploration program may wish to sell units of the partnership owned for several months or years. A member broker of NAPEX can offer these units to all other members of NAPEX electronically in just minutes!

If a buyer is found and the two parties agree on a price per unit NAPEX will execute the trade for a modest fee. This may well become the primary market for liquidation of oil exploration partnerships in the near future.

The added liquidity offered by both master limited partnerships and NAPEX may well increase the participation by investors in oil exploration partnerships in the future.

## TRANSACTION COSTS

Most oil exploration programs are sold by securities dealers. These dealers receive a sales charge for providing marketing services. In most, but not all, oil exploration programs these sales charges are paid at the beginning of the partnership and are charged directly to the limited partners (investors). The investor does not actually see a separate charge, the general partner simply spends a portion of the partnership capital for these services. Some of the best oil exploration programs have these fees paid by the general partner at corporate not partnership expense. This is generally a more favorable program structure for the limited partners.

It should be obvious to the limited partners that the more of the investment that "gets behind a drill bit" the more opportunity to find hydrocarbons. An investor should look for a minimum of transaction costs in an effort to maximize the return on investment. All organization and transaction costs are fully disclosed in the prospectus that must be furnished to investors prior to investment in the program. It does not necessarily follow that those partnerships having the lowest transaction cost are the most successful.

Typically, organizational costs including accounting and legal fees, (2 to 6 percent of capital) sales commissions (0 to 9 percent of capital) for the brokerage firm, and an initial management fee (2 to 8 percent of capital) for the general partner are borne by the limited partners.

It should be stressed that these fees vary considerably from one program to the next. Investors should not be bashful about discussing these fees prior to making the investment.

As a rule of thumb, any program with 90 percent or more of the limited partners money dedicated to the actual costs of searching for hydrocarbons is a fairly good program. This would be a less than 10 percent "front-end load." Front-end loads of greater than 15 percent should generally be avoided in public partnerships.

## PORTFOLIO FIT

An investor should use oil exploration programs to assist in tax reduction strategies consistent with the assumption of a very high degree of risk. Investors that achieve success in an oil exploration program receive the benefit of adding an inflation sensitive asset to their investment portfolio.

## SOURCES OF ADDITIONAL INFORMATION

Perhaps one of the best sources of information about investing in limited partnership of any kind is *The Stanger Report*. This publication is a guide to partnership investing.

The report is produced by the Robert A. Stanger Company and is generally considered to be the bible of partnership investing. Most stock-brokers, investment advisors, and tax experts are familiar with *The Stanger Report* if they work in the limited partnership area.

The Stanger Company rates each of the general partners in various industries (oil and gas, and real estate partnerships). A statistical recap of the actual results of previous partnerships is recorded. This is invaluable to limited partnership investors.

Other information is provided to investors. An excellent article concerning master limited partnerships appeared in the June 1985 edition of the *Stanger Report*.

The *Stanger Report* is available by contacting the Stanger Company at Post Office Box 7490, Shrewsbury, New Jersey 07701. Investors may call 201-389-3600 for subscription information.

## COMMENTS

Due to the high risk nature of oil exploration programs very few individual investors are suited for this investment. Only those individuals willing to lose the entire amount invested should consider this product.

If an investor has a large enough portfolio to permit a diversification into the oil and gas area a prudent limit would be 3 to 7 percent of portfolio assets.

In any event, investors should spend considerable time reviewing the track record of the general partner prior to investing in any oil exploration program.

### Exhibit 39-1.   High Risk: Oil Exploration Program

### INVESTMENT PROFILE

| INVESTMENT CHARACTERISTICS | Excellent | Good | Average | Poor | None |
|---|---|---|---|---|---|
| Liquidity | | | | √ | |
| Safety of Principal | | | | | √ |
| Price Stability | | | | | √ |
| Reinvestment Protection | | | | | N.A. |
| Growth of Capital | | | | * | |
| Cash Income | | | * | | |
| Growth of Income | | | | * | |
| Inflation Hedge | | * | | | |
| Tax Advantaged | * | | | | |

**Liquidity**—the ability to quickly realize cash from the sale at fair market value

**Safety of Principal**—the principal is safe from bankruptcy or default

**Price Stability**—the market value of the asset does not change in value

**Reinvestment Protection**—protection against reinvesting cash flow at lower rates as interest rates decline

**Growth of Capital**—the original investment increases over time to create capital gains

**Cash Income**—the cash income relative to treasury bills returns

**Growth of Income**—the ability of the cash income stream to increase over time

**Inflation Hedge**—the ability of total return (cash income plus capital gains) to keep pace with inflation over time

**Tax Advantaged**—the ability to reduce or defer current federal income taxes

*Note:* Most of the responses are a function of oil prices in the international marketplace. Until 1985 and 1986 many investors assumed that oil could only rise in price.
*The potential success of investments in oil exploration partnerships varies greatly. The investment characteristics are ranked according to the outcome most likely to occur based on prior performance.

# CHAPTER 40

# Movies, Equipment Leasing, and Other Exotic Partnerships

## DESCRIPTION

Many limited partnerships are formed for investment purposes. The most popular of these are real estate partnerships followed by oil exploration partnerships. A few more exotic investments are occasionally packaged for distribution to investors through the use of the limited partnership vehicle.

### Movie Partnerships

*Movie partnerships* most closely resemble oil exploration partnerships. Generally, movie partnership investors pool investment funds in one entity called a limited partnership. The limited partners hire a general partner who professionally manages the affairs of the partnership. The general partner is a company experienced in the production and distribution of motion pictures.

The limited partners in a movie partnership then share in the revenues of the movies produced. Very elaborate sharing arrangements are devised to allocate the expenses of producing the movies as well as revenues from the box office to the limited partners.

The general partner furnishes the management expertise, while the limited partners supply the investment capital. The portfolio of movies, owned by the partnership, will pay off expenses of production and distribution of the movies that can be deducted from taxable income by the limited partners. Often these writeoffs can be very substantial, varying from 30 percent to more than 200 percent of the initial investment of the limited partners. (The more debt used by the partnership, the larger the deductions.) Returns to the limited partners are less predictable. The revenues from any one movie may range from next to nothing to several millions of dollars. Depending on how well the portfolio of movies performs at the box office and on the sharing arrangements between the limited and general partner, the individual investor may or may not receive a substantial return on investment. In the worst case the limited partner can expect to lose 100 percent of the money.

### Equipment Leasing Partnerships

*Equipment leasing partnerships* can be designed to produce a stream of very predictable tax deductions or a cash flow to the individual limited partner. Once again a group of individual investors forms a partnership and hires an experienced general partner to manage the affairs of the partnership.

In the case of equipment leasing the general partner enters into leases on behalf of the partnership. The partnership will agree to purchase a piece of equipment (railroad cars, cargo containers, or computers) and lease the equipment to a company that will use the equipment. The cash flow from the equipment will be used to pay off debt incurred in the purchase of the equipment, and excess cash flow can be returned to the investors.

In the case of a highly leveraged partnership, virtually all of the cash flow is used to pay off the loan that provided most of the money to purchase the equipment. In some highly leveraged equipment leases, tax deductions in excess of 400 percent of the original investment are legally available to investors.

The primary risk in these highly leveraged partnerships is the estimated residual value of the equipment several years hence. Many investors worry that a default will occur on a highly leveraged lease. This is generally not a problem since many of the companies using the equipment are very substantial corporations with excellent payment records. However, if the equipment is worth less than the estimated residual value market value, the investor may receive a significantly lower return on investment than originally expected. The majority of return on investment to the limited partners is the money saved in federal income tax obligations. Actual investment returns on these highly leveraged Equipment Leasing Partnerships may range up to 20 percent for a 50 percent tax bracket investor.

Not all equipment leasing partnerships are highly leveraged and designed for tax deductions. Many of these investments are designed for high rates of cash flow to investors. Often this cash flow is tax sheltered in the early years by depreciation on the equipment.

These cash flow oriented equipment leasing partnerships use very little or no debt to purchase the equipment. They lease the equipment to very credit worthy companies and return the cash flow from the lease to the limited partners. The primary risk is the same as that mentioned before. At the end of the term of the lease, the equipment is to be sold for a value that is projected at the time the partnership is formed. If for any reason the equipment cannot be sold for the projected price, the investment returns will not be as substantial as originally projected. Income oriented investors often look for a total after tax return of 13 to 15 percent from equipment leasing programs.

While other types of partnerships exist, (including windmills, ski slopes, trash reclamation, cattle breeding operations, alternative energy sources, and research and development programs) movies and equipment leasing are the most likely to be considered by an average investor. Table 40-1 displays the dramatic growth of equipment leasing partnerships in recent years.

Table 40-2 shows the growth of exotic partnership investments from 1981 to 1985.

Exhibit 40-1 provides program sales by type of exotic partnership for 1983 and 1984.

## STRENGTHS

Each of the exotic partnerships offers specialized strengths. This is very evident in the highly leveraged equipment leasing partnership. The limited partnership is structured to reduce federal income taxes of the limited partners, not necessarily to make a profit.

In movies, the potential for high investment returns from an exceptionally popular movie lures many investors.

**Table 40-1.   Dollars Invested in Equipment
Leasing Partnerships**

| Year | 1981 | 1982 | 1983 | 1984 | 1985 |
|---|---|---|---|---|---|
| $ Millions | 200.0 | 240.9 | 386.5 | 478.0 | 600* |

*Estimated
*Source: Stanger's Partnership Sponsor Directory.* Reprinted with permission.

## WEAKNESS

Most of the exotic partnerships are high risk investments. The very high-risk nature of the ventures and potential for a complete loss of investor capital is well documented in the exotic partnership industry.

## UNIQUE FEATURES

Exotic partnerships offer so many unique features it is impossible to cover them in just a few pages.

Suffice it to say that generally the exotic partnerships offer either above average returns on investment, very substantial tax benefits to prospective investors or both. Typically the structure of the partnership is most difficult to analyze. Often the outcome is totally beyond the ability of a good investment adviser to predict.

## WHERE AND HOW TO BUY

Exotic partnerships are offered through securities dealers, financial planners, newspaper ads, and other media. Generally the partnerships offered

**Table 40-2.   Total Miscellaneous Partnerships
Dollars Invested, 1981 to 1985**

| Year | 1981 | 1982 | 1983 | 1984 | 1985 |
|---|---|---|---|---|---|
| $ Millions | 205.0 | 398.7 | 504.7 | 543.1 | 850* |

*Estimated
*Source: Stanger's Partnership Sponsor Directory.* Reprinted with permission.

**Exhibit 40-1. Publicly Registered Equipment Leasing and Miscellaneous Programs Sales**

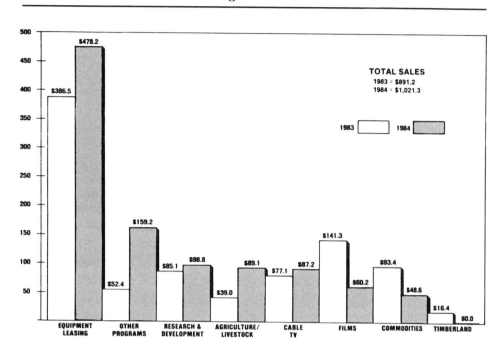

*Source: Stanger's Partnership Sponsor Directory.* Reprinted with permission.

by the established brokerage community are risky, but not illegal or fraudulent.

Typically investors are required to purchase in increments of $1,000 and meet minimum investments of $3,000 to $5,000.

An offering document called a *prospectus* must be furnished to an investor prior to purchase of the partnership. It is especially important for investors to review this prospectus prior to purchasing units of the partnership.

An investor must sign a form called a *subscription document* to participate in the program. The investor's check is typically made payable to the program and is forwarded to the general partner with the subscription document. This form contains basic information about the investor: name, address, telephone, and tax identification number.

Often the brokerage community offers special investment seminars to explain exotic partnerships to individual investors. These seminars are usually free and provide an expert in the particular product to make the presentations and answer questions from investors.

## HOW TO SELL

Most exotic partnerships are *self-liquidating*. Once the particular business purpose of the partnership is concluded, the partnership books and records are closed and a final tax form is filed.

Occasionally, a few final assets are sold by the general partner to a third party in an effort to close the partnership. For example, the remaining rights to a portfolio of movies that have been produced and shown in theaters are then sold for future syndication.

During the course of the partnership, the limited partners have received tax deductions, cash flow, and some returns of capital depending on the particular partnership.

## TRANSACTION COSTS

The two primary costs of exotic partnerships are selling commissions and the general partner management fees. A lesser cost is organizational costs of the partnership.

Transaction costs are usually loaded on the front end of the partnership. Selling commissions range from 8 percent to 10 percent in most exotic partnerships. Management fees (often labeled in several different ways) to the general partner may range as high as 20 percent of investor's capital. Management fees may be called acquisition fees, formulation expenses, finders fees, participation guarantee fees, loan guarantee fees, etc. The simple fact of the matter is that the general partner is not going to spend that portion of the money on the business of the partnership. Partnership organization costs are used to pay accountants, attorneys, and printers that put the partnership agreement into final form.

As a rule of thumb, exotic partnerships have higher fees than do real estate investment partnerships. Investors should generally avoid any partnership with a front-end load, for whatever reason, of over 20 percent of the amount invested.

## PORTFOLIO FIT

Most exotic partnerships are purchased by very high tax bracket investors that can afford to assume high levels of risk. The tax deductions associated with many of these investments subsidize the risk for high tax bracket individuals.

Most investors will not want to risk more than 1 to 2 percent of their investment assets in exotic partnerships.

## SOURCES OF ADDITIONAL INFORMATION

Generally information about exotic partnerships is available from the selling organizations. Many of these partnerships offer information to investors via newspaper advertisements of upcoming seminars.

## COMMENTS

Occasionally, exotic partnerships may provide the potential returns discussed at the time of sale to the investor. Generally only the partnerships formed without debt, and designed to provide a conventional business service, will frequently perform as predicted (nonleveraged equipment leasing for example).

It is extremely important for potential investors to examine the track record of the managing general partner before entering the investment. This track record cannot be discounted. Either the general partner has experience and a good track record of making money for the limited partners or he or she does not.

**Exhibit 40-2.   High Risk: Movies, Equipment Leasing, and Other Exotic Partnerships**

**INVESTMENT PROFILE**

| INVESTMENT CHARACTERISTICS | Excellent | Good | Average | Poor | None |
|---|---|---|---|---|---|
| Liquidity | | | | √ | |
| Safety of Principal | | | | | √ |
| Price Stability | | | | | √ |
| Reinvestment Protection | | | | | N.A. |
| Growth of Capital | | | * | | |
| Cash Income | | | * | | |
| Growth of Income | | | * | | |
| Inflation Hedge | | | | √ | |
| Tax Advantaged | √ | | | | |

**Liquidity**—the ability to quickly realize cash from the sale at fair market value

**Safety of Principal**—the principal is safe from bankruptcy or default

**Price Stability**—the market value of the asset does not change in value

**Reinvestment Protection**—protection against reinvesting cash flow at lower rates as interest rates decline

**Growth of Capital**—the original investment increases over time to create capital gains

**Cash Income**—the cash income relative to treasury bills returns

**Growth of Income**—the ability of the cash income stream to increase over time

**Inflation Hedge**—the ability of total return (cash income plus capital gains) to keep pace with inflation over time

**Tax Advantaged**—the ability to reduce or defer current federal income taxes

*Depends on success of the particular program. Could range from excellent to none.

# Index

*Moody's Bank and Finance Manual,* 110
Moody's bond ratings, 197
*Moody's Bond Record,* 227
*Moody's Bond Survey,* 204
Moody's Credit Reporting Service, 102
Moody's Investor's Service, 12, 212
Moody's Investor's Service
    *Over-the-Counter Industrial
    Manual,* 308
Mortgage real estate investment trust, 294
Movies, equipment leasing, and other
    partnerships, 367–75
Munibonds. *See* Short-term municipal
    securities
Municipal Bond Insurance Association
    (MBIA), 212
Municipal securities, 12
Mutual funds, 253–65
    for gold and precious metals, 347–48
    load versus no load, 254, 264
    for a two-career couple, 39–40
    types of, 253–54
    U.S. securities in, 11–12

**N**
NASDAQ Industrial Index, 147
National Association of Security Dealers
    (NASDAQ)
    NAPEX memberships sold to members
        of the, 274, 288
    over-the-counter stocks sold through
        member firms of the, 303, 306
National Partnership Exchange, Inc.
    (NAPEX), 274, 288, 362–63
Natural gas investments. *See* Oil and oil
    exploration programs
Needs of people a factor in investment
    selection, 4
Negotiable orders of withdrawal (NOWs),
    69
Net asset value of a mutual fund, 254, 259
New York Bond Exchange, 203, 224,
    225
New York Stock Exchange (NYSE)
    bond floor, 202
    real estate investment trusts offered
        through the, 295
New York Stock Exchange Composite
    Index, 326
Nonrecourse mortgages, 270

**O**
Oil and oil exploration programs, 355–65
    investments as an inflation hedge during
        the 1970s, 17
    as a real asset, 12
    risk level of, 21
    as a tax advantaged investment, 17
Options, 311–23
    for gold and precious metals, 347
    put and call, 311, 325
    risk level of, 21
Options Clearing Corporation, 317–19
*Over the Counter Journal, The,* 308

**P**
Pacific Stock Exchange, 322
Par value of a bond, 183, 207
Participating mortgages, 283
Partnerships as a tax advantaged
    investment, 17
*Penny Stock News,* 308
Personality of the investor, 19–20
Philadelphia Stock Exchange, 322
Portfolio fit, 6
    for annuity contracts, 124–25
    for blue chip stocks, 141
    for certificates of deposit, 79
    for convertible securities, 226–27
    for corporate bonds, 204
    for futures contracts, 344
    for Ginnie Maes, 242
    for gold and precious metals, 351
    for growth stocks, 151
    for long-term municipal bonds, 215–16
    for money market accounts, 71
    for money market funds, 65–66
    for movies, equipment leasing, and
        other partnerships, 373
    for mutual funds, 264
    for new issue stocks, 171
    for oil exploration programs, 364
    for options, 319–22
    for over-the-counter stocks, 307–8
    for public utility common stocks,
        159–60, 161–64
    for real estate growth partnerships,
        275–76
    for real estate income partnerships, 289
    for real estate investment trusts, 298
    for short-term municipal securities, 102

# Probus Publishing Company Presents

## Titles in Investment/Personal Finance

**The Investor's Equation: Creating Wealth Through Undervalued Stocks,** by William M. Bowen IV and Frank P. Ganucheau III. ISBN 0–917253–00–0.

**Stock Index Options: Powerful New Tools for Investing, Hedging, and Speculating,** by Donald T. Mesler. ISBN 0–917253–02–7.

**Winning the Interest Rate Game: A Guide to Debt Options,** by Frank J. Fabozzi. ISBN 0–917253–01–9.

**Low Risk Strategies for the High Performance Investor,** by Thomas C. Noddings. ISBN 0–917253–09–4.

**Maximize Your Gains: Tax Strategies for Today's Investor,** by Robert W. Richards. ISBN 0–917253–10–8.

**Increasing Your Wealth in Good Times and Bad,** by Eugene M. Lerner and Richard M. Koff. ISBN 0–917253–06–X.

**The Insider's Edge: Maximizing Investment Profits Through Managed Futures Accounts,** by Bertram Schuster and Howard Abell. ISBN 0– 917253–12–4.

**Personal Economics: A Guide to Financial Health and Well-Being,** by Robert A. Kennedy and Timothy J. Watts. ISBN 0–917253–08–6.

**The New Mutual Fund Investment Advisor,** by Richard C. Dorf. ISBN 0–917253–13–2.

**Floating Rate Instruments: Characteristics, Valuation and Portfolio Strategies,** by Frank J. Fabozzi. ISBN 0–917253–15–9.

**Smarter Money: An Investment Game Plan for Those Who Made It and Want to Keep It,** by Frank J. Fabozzi and Stephen Feldman. ISBN 0– 917253–16–7.

**Warrants: Analysis and Investment Strategy,** by Donald T. Mesler. ISBN 0–917253–25–6.

**Mastering Your Money: The Complete Guide to Computerwise Personal Financial Management,** by Colin K. Mick and Kerry Mason. ISBN 0– 917253–20–5.

**Superhedging,** by Thomas C. Noddings. ISBN 0–917253–21–3.

**High Performance Futures Trading: Computerbased Strategies and Techniques,** by William T. Taylor. ISBN 0–917253–22–1.

**Executive Economics,** by Timothy J. Watts. ISBN 0–917253–23–X.

**Self-Directed IRAs for the Active Investor: Taking Charge of Building Your Nest Egg,** by Peter D. Heerwagen. ISBN 0–917253–32–9.

**The Investor's Desktop Portfolio Planner,** by Geoffrey Hirt, Stanley Block, and Fred Jury. ISBN 0–917253–33–7.

**The New Guide to Tax Sheltered Investments: How To Evaluate and Buy Tax-Favored Investments That Perform,** by G. Timothy Haight and John C. Chanoski. ISBN 0–917253–30–2.

**The Stock Index Futures Market: A Trader's Insights and Strategies,** by B. Thomas Byrne, Jr. ISBN 0–917253–28–0.

**The Trader's and Investor's Guide to Commodity Trading Systems, Software and Data Bases,** by William T. Taylor. ISBN 0–917253–41–8.

**Timing the Market: How to Profit in Bull and Bear Markets with Technical Analysis,** by Weiss Research. ISBN 0–917253–37–X.

**The Handbook of Mortgage-Backed Securities,** by Frank J. Fabozzi. ISBN 0-917253-04-3.

## Titles in Business

**Revitalizing Your Business: Five Steps to Successfully Turning Around Your Company,** by Edmund P. Freiermuth. ISBN 0–917253–05–1.

**Compensating Yourself: Personal Income, Benefits and Tax Strategies for Business Owners,** by Gerald I. Kalish. ISBN 0– 917253–07–8.

**Using Consultants: A Consumer's Guide for Managers,** by Thomas A. Easton and Ralph Conant. ISBN 0–917253–03–5.

**Cutting Loose: Making the Transition From Employee to Entrepreneur,** by Thomas A. Easton and Ralph W. Conant. ISBN 0– 917253–14–0.

**What's What in American Business: Facts and Figures on the Biggest and the Best,** by George Kurian. ISBN 0–917253–17–5.

**Competing for Clients: The Complete Guide to Marketing and Promoting Professional Services,** by Bruce Marcus. ISBN 0–917253– 26–4.

**Compensating Your Sales Force: The Sales Executive's Book of Compensation Programs and Strategies,** by W. G. Ryckman. ISBN 0–917253–38–8.

**Leasing Industrial and Business Equipment: Strategies and Techniques for Lessors and Lessees,** by Lloyd A. Haynes, Jr. ISBN 0–917253–31–0.

**Not Heard on the Street: An Irreverent Dictionary of Wall Street,** by Maurice Joy. ISBN 0–917253–40–x.

**Public Relations for the Entrepreneur and the Growing Business: How to Use Public Relations to Increase Visibility and Create Opportunities For You and Your Company,** by Norman R. Soderberg. ISBN 0–917253–35–3.

**The Executive's Guide to Business and Economic Forecasting,** by Charles E. Webster. ISBN 0–917253–36–1.

**The Entrepreneur's Guide to Capital: More Than 40 Techniques for Capitalizing and Refinancing New and Growing Businesses,** by Jennifer Lindsey. ISBN 0–917253–34–5.

**The 101 Best Performing Companies in America,** by Ronald N. Paul and James W. Taylor. ISBN 0–917253–39–6.

**The Operating Executive's Handbook of Profit Planning Tools and Techniques,** by Charles J. Woelfel and Charles D. Mecimore. ISBN 0–917253–24–8.

**The Valuation of Privately-Held Businesses: State-of-the-Art Techniques for Buyers, Sellers and Their Advisors,** by Irving L. Blackman. ISBN 0–917253–27–2.